WORLD WAR ONE
AIRCRAFT
CARRIER PIONEER

WORLD WAR ONE AIRCRAFT CARRIER PIONEER

*The Story and Diaries of Captain
J M McCleery RNAS/RAF*

by

Guy Warner

Pen & Sword
AVIATION

First published in Great Britain in 2011 by
Pen & Sword Aviation
an imprint of
Pen & Sword Books Ltd
47 Church Street
Barnsley
South Yorkshire
S70 2AS

Copyright © Guy Warner, 2011

ISBN 978 1 84884 255 7

Typeset in Sabon by
Phoenix Typesetting, Auldgirth, Dumfriesshire

Printed and bound in Great Britain
by the MPG Books Group

Pen & Sword Books Ltd incorporates the Imprints of Pen & Sword Aviation,
Pen & Sword Maritime, Pen & Sword Military, Wharncliffe Local History, Pen
& Sword Select, Pen & Sword Military Classics and Leo Cooper.

For a complete list of Pen & Sword titles please contact
PEN & SWORD BOOKS LIMITED
47 Church Street, Barnsley, South Yorkshire, S70 2AS, England
E-mail: enquiries@pen-and-sword.co.uk
Website: www.pen-and-sword.co.uk

Contents

Foreword by Commander David Hobbs MBE   vii

Introduction   1

1. Childhood   3
2. The Admiralty and Crystal Palace   6
3. Eastchurch   15
4. From Cranwell to Freiston   40
5. Calshot and the Isle of Grain   62
6. The Development of Naval Aviation before HMS *Furious*   77
7. HMS *Furious* – the 1917 Conversion and Operations from Rosyth   89
8. Flying from East Fortune and Grain   144
9. HMS *Furious* – Reborn and Very Active   168
10. From the Tondern Raid to the Armistice   212
11. The Surrender of the High Seas Fleet   243
12. Jack's Last Weeks in the Service   252
13. What Happened Afterwards   263

Appendix 1 The Rank Structure of the RN Air
    Branch/RNAS   267

Appendix 2 Royal Navy Seaplane and Aircraft
    Carriers of World War One   269

Appendix 3 Instructions Regarding Precautions
    to be Taken in the Event of Falling into
    the Hands of the Enemy   272

Appendix 4 Extract from 'Mitteilungen aus dem
    Gabiete des Luftkrieges Nr 38, 29-6-18'   278

Appendix 5 Hints for Flight Sub-Lieutenants   281

Bibliography   285
Index   288

Foreword

The Royal Naval Air Service was a dynamic force which, in its short existence, became the first to create the technologies and techniques that enabled aircraft to operate from ships at sea on a regular basis. While the British Army had found it relatively easy to operate aircraft from fields near the troops when the Royal Flying Corps was established in 1913, the Royal Navy had no such capability. Its air service had to start from scratch to work out how to launch aircraft from ships in the open ocean in all but the most severe weather; how to arm and equip them to play an effective part in fleet operations; and, most difficult of all, how to land safely back onto a moving, pitching and rolling ship at the end of a sortie. HMS *Furious*, which commissioned for service in the Grand Fleet in July 1917, represented one of the most significant advances.

In this fascinating book, Guy Warner brings the experience of Flight Sub Lieutenant Jack McCleery RNAS, the son of a Belfast flax mill owner who served in HMS *Furious*, vividly to life. His sources were Jack's wartime diaries, hundreds of letters home made available by his son and three albums of unique photographs taken by Jack and his friends. After volunteering for the RNAS in 1916 Jack proved to be an exceptional pilot and was hand-picked for *Furious* by its first senior pilot, Squadron Commander Dunning. He stayed with her until after the Armistice in November 1918 and saw or participated in many historic events; among them Dunning's epoch-making first deck landing in August 1917 and the later trials with the landing deck fitted aft. He flew reconnaissance missions in wireless telegraphy-fitted Short 184 and Sopwith 1½ Strutters from the ship into the German Bight, having to 'ditch' into the sea after them to be rescued by sea-boats from destroyers. The very word 'ditching', when an aircraft comes down in the sea, stems from the RNAS of this period when aircraft that went into the water were said to 'fall into the ditch' or simply to 'ditch'. His colleagues flew seven Sopwith 2F1 Camels from the ship in July 1918 to carry out the first successful carrier air strike in history, destroying the Zeppelins L 54 and L 60 at Tondern and he served with some of the great RNAS personalities, including Wing Commander Bell Davies VC and Squadron Commander Rutland, of Jutland fame. Jack witnessed and subsequently wrote about the first air battles ever fought over the sea.

Flying from the first aircraft carriers was a huge technical achievement, not followed by any other nation on a regular basis until some years after the British but it has received scant attention, much greater emphasis having been given to the more easily seen and photographed land-based operations of the RFC and then the RAF in France. Guy's book redresses this shortcoming and gives an important insight into the embarked flying by RNAS aircraft using Jack's own words from the diaries and letters interspersed with well-thought-out comments and historical explanations. Jack was deeply moved by the sight of the German fleet arriving off the Firth of Forth to surrender and the quality of his writing is emphasised by the fact that the impression of the event he sent to his father was subsequently published in the *Belfast Telegraph*. Guy ends this book with several interesting appendices which add to an understanding of the RNAS in its final year.

Having sat down to have a glance at the book when I received it, I found myself totally absorbed, unable to put it down until I had finished. The large collection of previously unpublished photographs complements a work of major significance and Guy Warner is to be congratulated on producing an excellent book which tells the story of a young Ulsterman at war who played no small part within the RNAS in operations which changed the face of naval warfare for ever. I am sure that the book will attract considerable interest and that many others will enjoy it as much as I did.

David Hobbs MBE
Commander Royal Navy (Retired)
Former Curator and Deputy Director
of the Fleet Air Arm Museum
Twyford
September 2009

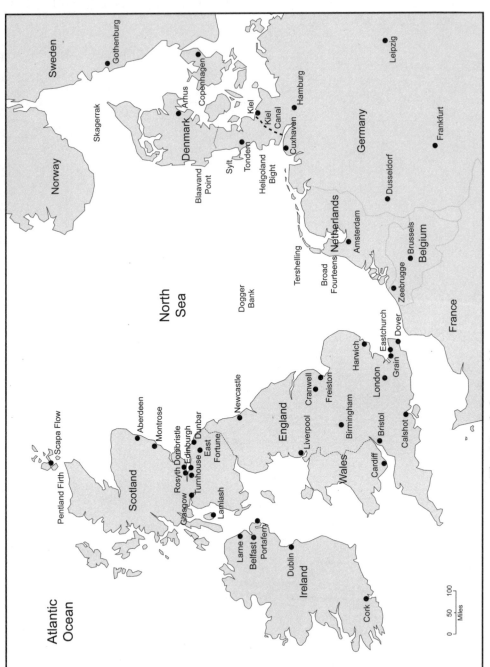

The North Sea and home waters 1914–18

Introduction

Jack McCleery was one of the world's first carrier pilots. Between 1917 and 1919 he served in and flew from the Royal Navy's 'hush-hush' ship, the aircraft carrier HMS *Furious*, the most technologically innovative and advanced naval aviation platform of its day. Much of the following account is in Jack's own words; he kept a diary throughout his naval service and also wrote more than 150 letters home to his parents in Belfast. For the most part his original spelling, syntax and punctuation have been retained. To this have been added linking passages, notes and remarks explaining the importance of key events, people, places, aircraft and ships, setting the story within its historical context.

It was truly a happy chance that I was first given access to the McCleery family archive in the spring of 2009, the hundredth anniversary year of British naval aviation, celebrated by the RN's Fleet Air Arm as 'FlyNavy 100'. This book is therefore dedicated to the gallant naval airmen (and women) of the Royal Naval Air Service, Royal Air Force and Fleet Air Arm. The photographs and drawings which illustrate the text have all been supplied from albums kept by the family since Jack compiled them in 1919. Grateful thanks are due to the family, and in particular Jack's son, John, for his invaluable help and encouragement. I would also like to express my appreciation to Commander David Hobbs for his Foreword; I hope that my text does justice to his very kind words. Thanks also to several friends and fellow members of the Ulster Aviation Society: Ernie Cromie for proof reading; to Graham Mehaffy for his map making expertise; and to Michael Clarke. Thanks also to the archival staff at the Fleet Air Arm Museum, David Wragg, Angela Campbell and her very helpful staff at Greenisland Library and, as always, my wife, Lynda. It would also be very remiss of me not to thank Peter Coles and all the helpful team at Pen & Sword for their hard work, advice and expertise.

In a remarkably prophetic letter John McCleery wrote to his fourteen-year-old son Jack at boarding school on 11 July 1912.

> My dear old Jack,
>
> I was greatly interested in your nice long letter which I got yesterday. It was very well put together and your bicycle tour was very well described. If you take care, and give some thought to it, you ought to turn out a very good letter writer indeed, and believe me that is something worth striving for, for there are not many can write a really interesting description or narrative. Perhaps you might be able afterwards to write something more enduring, who knows? Have you ever yet had a wish to do something for your country?... Now good bye for the present, dear boy. God take care of you. Your loving father
> JO McCleery.

As we will see, Jack did indeed serve his country in two World Wars and it is my hope that this volume will meet the wishes expressed by John Orr McCleery more than ninety years ago.

CHAPTER ONE

Childhood

Jack was born in Belfast on 15 March 1898, the eldest of five children, with two brothers, Tony and Kenneth, and two sisters, Peggy and Kitty. Tony was two years younger than Jack, while Kenneth was two years younger again. Peggy was born in 1908 and Kitty in 1911. His father John, Uncle Hamilton and grandfather Hamilton earned their living in the linen trade as flax spinners; whereas his mother Fanny's father, John Milligan, was a prosperous, self-made cotton yarn agent in Liverpool. The McCleery family's experience in flax spinning dated back to the 1850s when Hamilton senior left Portaferry in Co Down on the shores of Strangford Lough (where there had been McCleerys living since the 1600s) to serve his apprentice-ship in Belfast; he and his sons worked in or managed ten different spinning mills prior to 1898, when the brothers John and Hamilton purchased William Ross & Co., Flax Spinners, which was located on the Falls Road in Belfast, with Robert Anderson, later Sir Robert and thrice Lord Mayor of Belfast, as a third (non-executive) shareholder.

Jack first set foot in a boat at the age of five months, in the narrows, from the shore at Portaferry. One of his earliest public appearances was on 2 February 1901 when he attended St Enoch's Church for the first time, for a memorial service in memory of Queen Victoria, who had died on 22 January. It was claimed to be the largest Presbyterian church in Ireland and dominated one side of Carlisle Circus at the junction of the Crumlin and Antrim Roads, in North Belfast not far from the family home on the Old Cavehill Road. 'He conducted himself very well indeed', wrote his proud father. In 1903, his father wrote that at Duncairn Infant School, 'the children played Blind Man's Bluff, and Musical Chairs – but Jack wouldn't join in. However he did enjoy the lantern views of China shown afterwards, immensely.' Holidays were often spent in Portaferry and the village always acted as a magnet for the family when the opportunity presented itself. They were always welcome to stay with Aunt Eliza and Jane [Orr], in their High Street house for holidays or weekends; days there were filled with boating, fishing, swimming, walking, tennis and picnics.

Jack and his brothers attended Belfast Royal Academy, and Merchiston Castle School, Edinburgh. When the Great War began in August 1914 many Irish citizens from all parts of the country volunteered for service. The mood of the country was well summarised in the *Belfast Telegraph*.

> We go to war to save honour, reputation, good name and respect. This War is due to German aggressiveness. We must teach the Kaiser a lesson. We did not want this war and stayed out of it for as long as we decently could. Through no wish or part of our own we find ourselves engaged in the greatest struggle the world has ever known.

John McCleery joined the Irish Home Defence Corps in May 1915, drilling at Belfast's St George's Market. In September 1915 he commenced regular patrolling in the docks, after his day's work at the Mill, often from 8 pm until midnight or sometimes as late as 3 am, as a member of the Belfast Volunteer Defence Corps.

Jack went straight from school into the family business in September 1915. During his apprenticeship, he was required to climb to the top of the mill chimney, well over 100 feet high, watched by many of the workers. This initiation did not cure his vertigo or prevent him applying for service in the Royal Flying Corps in February 1916. He was unsuccessful in this, receiving a letter from the War Office stating that no further direct commissions in the RFC were being given and that he should apply for service in an Officers' Cadet Battalion prior to selection for training at one of the RFC Schools of Instruction at either Reading or Oxford. He next applied to the Royal Naval Air Service and was supported in this by a letter to the Admiralty from the Lord Mayor of Belfast, Crawford McCullagh, which stated:

It gives me much pleasure to recommend him. He is well-educated and most exemplary in every respect and is the son of Mr JO McCleery, one of our well known citizens, for whom the highest respect is entertained.

CHAPTER TWO

The Admiralty and Crystal Palace

Jack attended the Admiralty in London for interview on 18 October 1916; he was just over eighteen and a half years old. That evening he sent a postcard to his mother, who was on holiday at the Strathearn Hydro at Crieff in Perthshire, perhaps enjoying the waters while his father played golf. This was the first of the missives he wrote to his mother and father between 1916 and 1919. In this he stated:

> I had a lovely crossing on Monday night…..Yesterday it poured all day, went to Zoo. Today fine – did some sightseeing. Went to Admiralty and they are to communicate results to me. Am certain I'm through. Tell you all later. Saw a balloon when coming down here. Lovely searchlights tonight……Excuse scribble. Jack

This first communication is untypical in its brevity and in its closing salutation. All the rest of his letters, apart from two, he concluded with, 'I remain, Your loving son, Jack'.

According to contemporary reports the Admiralty interview would have covered such topics as the candidate's ability to ride a horse or sail a boat or ride a motorcycle. Random questions were barked out by senior officers with fierce eyebrows and much gold braid. A public school education was a decided advantage. The interview must have gone well, as no sooner had he reached his uncle and aunt in Birkenhead, breaking off his journey home, that a telegram arrived summoning him back to London that evening,

> Uncle Willie and the other two aunts saw me off to London again by the 10 pm train. As there was talk of a troop train, I travelled 1st Class by their advice. Had to change at Chester and Crewe. From Crewe the troop train business started and soldiers filled every carriage. They were lying on the floors – everywhere. There were six in my *first* class carriage! So I got no sleep! We arrived at Euston at 4.30 am. About ¾ hour late. Then the tube did not start till 5.30 and there were no taxis! Well, at any rate I got here [Finchley] by tube, train and legs at about 6.30! Uncle Arthur let me in and had some grub ready for me, also a hot water bottle in my bed – I was glad of it as I was nearly frozen. As the soldiers had all smoked hard I woke up with a most awful headache and my eyes seemed all sore. My throat was like coarse sandpaper. Well I *passed* my exam and I am now a Probationary Flight Officer! They will probably call me up in a fortnight or three weeks they said. The Admiralty said that if I was stopped to refer the other person to the – Admiralty! They say that I'm really an officer in the Navy now and no one has the right to interfere with me outside the RN! – even though I haven't got my togs [uniform] yet. When I am called up they say I get a 1st Class pass anywhere. We aren't allowed on buses but I can go on other vehicles I believe. I go to Crystal Palace for a month or two and then to an aerodrome and later possibly to Winder-mere [civilian and then RNAS flying training on the lake at Hill of Oaks had been ongoing there since early 1915] for instruction in seaplane work. I was the only prospective pilot to get through the medical exam! I was the only one in for it!! They are awfully strict though. I remain, Your loving son, Probationary Flight Officer JM McCleery RN!

The medical examination included such items as climbing a rope in the nude, hopping around the room on one foot and a colour blindness test, which involved sorting beads. Back home, having crossed from Liverpool to Belfast in the SS *Graphic* of the Belfast Steamship Company; as his parents were still away, he stayed with his Uncle Hamilton,

> I was out at Dunmurry at about 4 o'clock. I said I would lie down. I just lay on the bed and pulled the eiderdown over me. *And* fell asleep. I woke up in darkness. I looked or rather groped all round for matches to light the gas. I could not feel any. Then I remembered they used candles so I tried to find a candlestick but could not. So I went to the door to see my watch and it was 10.30 pm! I got on my slippers and went to the drawing room. They *were* surprised! Uncle H had gone into my room at teatime and said 'Jack' and as I did not answer, he concluded I was in for the night. So I had some supper, read your letter and went off again, after having been told they used electric light!

Jack's mother must have enquired about the clothes he would need when he went away:

> They will send me a list of the kit I will require when they send for me. I don't know whether a muffler would be any use, thank you, but even if it wasn't I would be glad of it on the bike. [Jack was a motorbike enthusiast.] I'm sure the mittens would be useful. But if you really do make them, please make them a tight fit, as my last pair was too loose. Thank you for offering to make them.... You must not address your letters to Prob. — — RN, really. I'm still 'Mr' when at home without a uniform, what I said in my letter was more or less a joke. Of course, it doesn't matter and you can if you like.

There wasn't much time to prepare Jack for his naval service but no doubt the experience of sending him away to boarding school in Edinburgh helped with deciding what to pack. By the first week of November he was back in London.

> We went straight to Gamages [department store] to ask about my badges and had to get another for my cap. I'm just in from Church as I had not time to wait for the

sermon..... I will write as soon as possible when I get there....Thanks for the sweets.

The Crystal Palace at Sydenham in South London had been taken over by the Royal Navy in early September 1914 to be the RN Divisional Depot, where large numbers passed through its training battalions. More importantly, it was the initial training establishment for all Royal Navy Volunteer Reserve (RNVR) personnel and also for officers destined for the Royal Navy Division (RND). Later, other categories of naval personnel, including the Royal Naval Air Service (RNAS), also got their initial training there – from 1 April 1916 all newly entered RNAS officers went first to Crystal Palace for basic disciplinary and technical training. Its official name as a RN shore station was HMS *Victory VI*. Jack was one of over 125,000 men serving in the RNAS, RND and RNVR who were trained for war service there.

On 12 November 1916, Jack wrote:

Here I am at the Crystal Palace. There seems to be no end to it so far! I sleep in a house called Ashurst in a room with three other chaps. I paid 5/- for servants' wages in the house. I am writing this at the club which is situated in the CP itself and is very nice and comfy. I think the distance record for not having to salute must be 4½ feet here! We were told we would be here for five weeks and would then be sent to our air station, presumably to learn to fly. I have to get my buttons changed to RNAS ones. [The emblem of the RNAS was an eagle with outstretched wings which replaced the RN's fouled anchor on buttons and cap badges.] They seem to be a fairly decent lot of chaps here. Well I'll close now as it's nearly dinner time – quite good grub on the whole!

Over the next week or two a regular flow of letters described aspects of Jack's experiences at Royal Navy Depot, Crystal Palace. He wrote on 14 November:

Just a few lines to keep the home fires burning. Life is very strenuous here if one really wants to get on, there is little time for letters. I am not allowed to give any particulars of this place or as to numbers of men. We get our first drill at 7.15 am and it's work from that till 7.30 pm (dinner). After dinner we are free and I come up here to swot. It's more secluded than the club. We do only three weeks' drill here and then two weeks' of lectures. Then if we pass our exams we go to some aerodrome. I forgot to say that we get our pay by the month and can deposit it with the Paymaster if we wish. But the State takes no liability if it's lost, so I'm going to put mine in my cash box in my locked trunk. We had to apply for our £15 kit allowance. I haven't got it yet but will send it on to you when I do. We can live here on our income all right I think. Things are very cheap at the stores here – boots etc.

In his next letter he advised that officers were not allowed to go to YMCA services but that he was going to take men to the Presbyterian Church on Sunday morning and that Mr and Mrs Norton of the YMCA had befriended him. He had also discovered that his room-mate had served in France from 1914 but had been invalided out of the Army with shell shock and broken nerves, from which it must be hoped that he had fully recovered as he was now learning to fly. On a more martial note Jack added:

I'm getting on quite well here, have been drilling a squad, learning musketry and revolvers and later the Lewis Gun. At present it is nearly all military drill except for a class in seamanship – tying knots. Also physical drill – Swedish.

The drill was conducted on the cycle track by Royal Marine Light Infantry Drill Sergeants. Some more domestic details were revealed in Jack's letter of November 19:

We get up about an hour later than I did at home. Breakfast at the same time (about) as you: this consists of good porridge, toast and bacon or fish (or both) and then tea or coffee. That's all right!! Lunch is about an hour and a quarter earlier than official time at my last station in Belfast [home]. It is soup, meat or pie or fish, potatoes, vegetables

and usually stewed fruit or tart after. Cheese and if one
wishes, coffee can be got in the club (you can get stronger
things too). Tea at 4.45 – bread butter, tea or coffee, jam,
marmalade or honey. Dinner is three quarters of an hour
later than yours and reminds one of Crieff. Entrée (all sorts
of weird things), soup, meat of some sort, good rolls,
potatoes and vegetables and tea or coffee and the King's
health in water! So the food's all right. Of course, we wear
full uniform for dinner.

The mention of drinking His Majesty's health in water would
have been important to Jack's father, as he was a dedicated
member of the Irish Temperance League from 1890 to 1927,
becoming president in 1911. Jack also noted in his letter that he
had sent a booklet to his best friend, George Herriot, who was
also hoping to join the RNAS. This is a little hardback about the
size of a small pocket diary and was titled *Hints for Flight Sub-
Lieutenants Royal Naval Air Service by 'Flight Lieutenant'* (some
extracts from which have been included at Appendix 5). Jack
concluded his letter with a few thoughts concerning the family
pet, Jock:

I think a coat of tar would do the barrel good [Jock's
kennel]. Also a couple of boards hammered on the front
like this [here he added a drawing of the barrel, with dog
and boards in position] to keep Jock warmer.

His last letter of the month was written while on weekend leave
in the house of a Mr Bowden and his sister, YMCA colleagues of
Mr Norton.

They are very nice people indeed. Yesterday afternoon, Mr
Norton, his wife and I went into town and into St Paul's. It
is fine inside. We stayed for about 15 minutes during the
service and then came away. We then went to the central
YMCA in Tottenham Court Road and it really is a splendid
place, I believe Mr N said they pay £5000 a year ground rent.
There's a rifle range, a really beautiful swimming bath,
about the finest I've seen and a very fine gym. About 600
men sleep there every night. Fine lounges and two very

nice-looking restaurants. Then we had tea at an ABC, after which it was very dark so we went to a picture house. This morning I went to a congregational church with Mr N – these people are C of E. It was a good service only they sang twice as quick as at home. I'm just down after having a bath. You have to take things when you can here. I don't think I was ever as 'done' as this weekend. I nearly fell asleep last night at supper and also today during the sermon – not that I wasn't listening! On Friday night I went to a Mrs Pilkington's (another YMCA lady) for supper. We played music for a while. I played a beautiful mandoline and then had a shot at a banjo and was just getting 'Swannee River' when I had to go. There is also a boy and a girl in the family – two girls to be exact, one between Peggy and Kitty's age and the other – well I didn't like to ask her, but she's about my age. I'm probably going again next Friday.

He then went on to outline what was in store at Crystal Palace and further progress with weapons training,

Next week, or rather this one is our hardest. We have squad drill all day and they start to examine us on Thursday. I hope I get through. I believe it's a great help to yell at your men for the least little thing, or if there isn't anything wrong to pretend there is! They understand being for the most part brother officers. So I intend to try. We did revolver shooting last week – a huge, long Mark VI Webley. I did all right and pretty well in the miniature rifle shooting. I passed my test in the Lewis gun all OK and was being instructed in the Webley Scott automatic pistol yesterday. You can strip them in under six seconds! I did it in 12 which was the best of our squad. We are having lectures on 'Aero Engines' and 'Theory of Flight' in the evenings. It's very interesting but there are a lot of notes! I'm really very well, though tired and I'm sure I'm growing! You could tell the manager [at the Mill] and any of the foremen you come across that I was asking about them please, Father.

At the beginning of December, Jack was able to meet with his friends George and Hunter Herriot for a weekend and reported not only that he had had a good time with them but also had passed his exam with flying colours. George was the same age as Jack, while Hunter was four years older. The following weekend he spent with his new friends, the Pilkingtons. He had now reached a decision about the future direction of his training,

> I'm off Windermere now. If I learn there, I'll never be able to learn [to fly] land machines, so I'm going to some land aerodrome and when I can manage a land bus [aeroplane] I'll volunteer for the others. Then I'll know both. You can't learn both if you start with seaplanes as once they've got you they'll not let you go. They are always only too pleased to get seaplane pilots. [The first (relatively) successful ascent from water by a British seaplane was on 18 November 1911 by Commander Oliver Schwann RN flying an Avro Type D biplane at Barrow-in-Furness.] Oh, while I remember, my collars are 15s and I would like *soft* cuffs. Also another pair of shirts. It's cold and miserable here today. This is as unpleasant a morning as we've had yet and my fingers are nearly – not quite though, numb. I'm wearing a waistcoat under my sweater now. Would you please let me know how much the jackets are, and if you'll get Paine to make me another, I'll send you the money for it. A gold eagle on the <u>left</u> arm, six inches up the cuff, and eagle buttons. Also strong pockets and if he'd make it a little freer under the arms and round the chest. The sleeves and length are right.

Some trainees from the depot were being sent to France and at one stage Jack thought he might be one of them, where at Vendôme, west of Orleans, a training unit for the RNAS had just been opened in November 1916. It owed its existence to the bad weather of the winter of 1915–16, which had seriously interfered with flying training in the United Kingdom; consequently a new site for a training aerodrome was sought in an area where good flying weather might reasonably be expected. In the event he was not chosen and was able to reflect in his letter, his pleasure at being in an aeroplane for the first time. Several instructional airframes were supplied to Crystal Palace for non-flying duties. These were outmoded Short S.38 Pusher Biplanes.

I was in an aeroplane today, a proper one, but it was only adjusting some of the control wires. I also started up an aero engine by 'swinging the prop'. It takes a lot of doing and makes a fine row. So I've enjoyed my morning's work. When the engine is started it takes about 6 or 8 chaps holding on to the tail of the machine to keep it from running forward. I can send messages by Semaphore all OK now and can read slowly. I'm not very far on with Morse yet.

A little six-page booklet, printed on heavy card, has been preserved. It is titled *Signal Card 1908 (Reprint 1915)* and bears the inscription 'Flight Officer JM McCleery Dec. 12. 1916'. It contains full colour illustrations of the 'Flags and Pendants used in Naval Signalling', 'Semaphore Signs and Significations' and 'Signs used within the Morse Code'. No doubt it was three pence well spent.

CHAPTER THREE

Eastchurch

Jack's time at Crystal Palace had been completed successfully and his next letter, which was dated 15 December, comes from RNAS Station, Eastchurch, Kent.

Eastchurch, on the Isle of Sheppey, was the first Royal Naval Air Station. Originally, it was the home of the Royal Aero Club flying field, which was, by 1910, rapidly developing as a centre for civilian flying. The Short brothers, Horace, Eustace and Oswald, who were well known for manufacturing balloons, set up a factory at Eastchurch when they branched out into aircraft manufacture. The first Royal Navy officer to learn to fly was Lieutenant GC Colmore, who did so at his own expense, gaining his Royal Aero Club Aviator's Certificate (No. 15) at Eastchurch on 21 June 1910, flying a Short biplane. Francis McClean, a pioneer aviator (who himself qualified for his Royal Aero Club 'ticket' No. 21 in September 1910) and philanthropist, owned much of the land at Eastchurch, and leased it to the Royal Aero Club for a 'peppercorn' rent. In February 1911, he offered the Admiralty the use of two of his Shorts aircraft, so that naval officers could learn to fly. Cecil Grace, another pioneer aviator (Certificate No. 4) with a hangar at Eastchurch, offered to provide free flying instruction for the four men selected by the Navy. Unfortunately, Grace was killed before training could commence, but his offer was picked up by another pioneer, George Cockburn, who held Certificate No. 5. The only fees paid by the Admiralty were £20 per officer paid to Short Brothers for six months' technical instruction plus running costs and any repair bills. The four officers were Lieutenants CR Samson, AM Longmore, R Gregory (all RN) and EL Gerrard (Royal Marine Light Infantry). They were awarded Certificates 71 and 72 (on 25 April), 75 and 76 (on 2 May).

In December 1911, McClean acquired a further ten acres of land next to the club field, and in an act of further generosity and patriotism, gave this to the Navy for the establishment of their own flying field. Eastchurch thus became the first Royal Naval Air Station, and soon became known as the Eastchurch Naval Flying School.

In 1912, military and naval aviation was combined into a single service, the Royal Flying Corps, with a Military Wing, and a Naval Wing. It was intended that the RFC would employ unified training at a Central Flying School, a single source of aircraft supply from the Royal Aircraft Factory at Farnborough, and a unified Reserve. This was an uneasy relationship at best. The Admiralty naturally enough jealous of its position as the 'Senior Service', had no intention of being subservient to the Army, and kept Eastchurch as a flying school, rather than defer to the Central Flying School. It did not take long before the name Naval Wing was dropped, and the unofficial name Royal Naval Air Service came into general use. June 1914 brought the final breach between the two wings of the RFC when the Admiralty issued a series of regulations governing the organisation of the Royal Naval Air Service, which thereby became a distinct branch of the Royal Navy in much the same fashion as the Royal Marines. Remarkably the Admiralty was able to make this move without either being questioned or contradicted by either Parliament or the press. It was very much a unilateral declaration of independence.

The first operational unit to be prepared for overseas service with the naval element of the British Expeditionary Force was set up at Eastchurch on 8 August 1914 and was known as the Eastchurch (Mobile) Squadron. This title soon lapsed and on 1 September 1914, when stationed at St Pol, it became No. 3 Squadron, being commanded by Longmore and then Samson. As well as the Naval Flying School, Eastchurch was the home of various RNAS squadrons, wings and units from 1914 onwards, including, No. 2 Squadron, the Gunnery Schools Flight, the

Observers' School Flight, D Test Flight, the Spotting Flight and the Eastchurch War Flight.

The Commanding Officer at Eastchurch in December 1916 was Wing Commander Arthur Longmore, who had returned to the station where he had learned to fly following active service in France, Belgium and at the Battle of Jutland. He noted:

It had grown considerably since I had last seen it, and the aerodrome had been extended to the north-east with new hangars. Total strength 90 officers and 900 men. Eastchurch was never a very lively spot and it was even less so in war time, particularly in the middle of winter. A pack of beagles hunted the strong marsh hare, and provided good sport. There were cross country runs for the officers and men, and bleak walks on which my dog [also called] Jock used to accompany me.

Jack's first impressions were as follows:

We were told by our 'loot' [lieutenant] in charge yesterday morning that we were to be at the CP over Xmas. Then about an hour later our names were up on draft and here I am. If the weather is good we have to fly on Sundays as this is a war station. It's about the biggest aerodrome in the country, miles from anywhere decent. This place is a sea of mud literally. No drinking water as the huts are new and it's not all laid out yet. So *I* drink lime juice and soda and most of the others, things more manly! You will probably get a note from Gieves, tailors, saying I have opened an account. The reason is that we were advised to when we left CP as this place is so far away. Accounts are then furnished monthly to me. I bought a regulation tin box – a long 42" affair for a trunk and helmet (black and fur-lined) 37/-, goggles (Triplex unbreakable glass, fur-lined) 16/6, gloves (tanned leather gauntlets, rabbit fur inside) 18/6 and 9/6 for cash, as I was short. I would like a good *thick* cardigan *and* a blue knitted muffler, both worn for flying. Any mittens will be very useful. On account of the mud I would also like a pair of plain black rubber (leather heeled) knee boots. There are what is usually called gum boots *but* not thigh boots. At the Palace one could always pay for anything one wanted, but here you have to *sign* a 'chit' or docket, which comes back as an account each month. *Money* seems to be no use here except about once a month. If you're sending a parcel, would you mind putting in some Oxo or Bovril *cubes* as we are going to cook in our room in the mornings before early parade? I'm afraid this letter is nothing but please send me — etc, so far. Oh and I'd like two pieces of Pears soap and two 1/- tubes of toothpaste! We were told today to get flying kit that we hadn't got yet – boots and coat, so if father would send me £11.11.0 I would buy them here. The boots are black knee boots lined with fur and the coat is black chrome leather with fleece lining. I will have to get them sometime and they last for nearly ever, I might as well get them now. That does away with the other boots altogether. I hope, if the weather's good, to be up tomorrow flying with dual controls.

His next letter was to his best friend, George Herriot, one of very few of these, signed 'Your old Chum', which has survived. His frustration is evident:

I *was* sold today. We all went to the hangars this morning and I was to go up with the instructor for a 'joy flip'. There were about 15 machines all drawn up and I got in behind the loot. After I had expended about 1000 lbs of kinetic energy, or something equally as hard, I managed to get my belt fastened around me. The engine was warmed up – they tick over very nicely with pilot jets, then accelerated and with a roar we bounded forwards – ah that 'spreme moment – then there was a yell and one of the mechanics pointed to something at the engine (behind). Some stud was gone, so we had to get out and I didn't go. What I said remains to be ….not seen, but wafted over to Belfast like a thick blue mist. I was the only one in our lot *not* to go up.

However, there were still sights and sounds to savour:

Those Bristol Scouts or Bullets and the Sopwith Pups are worth seeing and dreaming about. They rise [drawing inserted showing ascent] like this at a most weird angle, it just about takes your breath away to watch them. And when they start to loop, tail slide and side slip, with the greatest ease and a *lovely drone*. Well it leaves you with just about *no* breath! Of course they are from the War Flight not the School Flight. There were about 10 buses up at once this morning. Two crashes. One chap, when starting off solo in a Curtiss – big all enclosed sort of machines, first of all broke a wheel (the ground was frozen hard) which caused him to bust a bit of his prop and then hit the ground with his left wing. Then he oozed up about 50–100 feet and came down again and ran along the ground until he came to a ditch whereupon the bus stood on its nose and smashed his landing chassis and his prop. It was quite amusing. He was all right of course, except for getting 'strafed' for it. So in spite of not getting up it was quite cheery. It's great to hear about 10 or 15 buses, all lined up, warming up their engines.

Jack also spotted some very unusual types:

They've several fine triplanes and a quad experimental. Also PBs with dihedral planes [wings]. Weird looking buses but quite fine machines.

These aircraft were the Blackburn Triplane, N502, and the Sopwith Triplane, N509, which were being test flown by Squadron Commander Harry Busteed of the Design Flight; the Supermarine PB31E Night Hawk, 1388, a very strange-looking, twin-engine machine with a raised, fully enclosed, glazed cockpit and the Pemberton-Billing PB 25s 9002 – 9003.

No doubt hardly able to contain his excitement enough to put pen to paper, Jack wrote to his parents and to George on the following day.

I've some great news to tell you and you can easily guess what it is. Yes I've been up! Absolutely grand, ripping, gorgeous etc, etc. I was up for about 10 minutes this morning in a Maurice [Farman S.7 Longhorn] and up to about 1200 feet. I could have yelled for joy. First of all you are strapped in, then you hare along the ground at about 50 and then almost without any warning you find you're up in the air. People and sheds get smaller and smaller as you go up and you gradually lose all sense of speed as you rise till you nearly crawl, even though you're doing 55–70 mph. Then she turns and you feel the wind. Banking is great fun; you look almost sheer over the side, right down clear to the ground. You see roads and trees. Then we spiralled down a bit to get out of the mist at 1000 feet as we couldn't see the ground and that was better still, almost nose diving only turning around in a small circle. You hardly hear the row but there's *some* breeze if you lean over to look down! You simply couldn't feel dizzy. I *tried* to and *couldn't manage it*. As you come down the pace seems to get quicker as you near the ground. You don't feel her land at all if well done – I didn't and then we taxied back. It's simply fine. I'll dream about it tonight!

He was aware though that all days in the air (or indeed on the ground as he spent his first Christmas away from home) wouldn't be as glorious as his first experience.

I hope to be up again tomorrow if the weather is good. Some days which seem lovely for flying you dare hardly go up on account of 'bumps' which are like *very*, *very* bad bumps on the road, and also on account of air pockets, when you simply drop sheer until she steadies up. I'm on duty on Xmas Eve from 8 am until 8 am Xmas morning. That's 24 hours and up all night doing rounds etc. So I'll not get any leave nor will any other junior officers I think. I am enclosing with this letter a small parcel which contains something for both of you. You needn't open them till Xmas morning. I am enclosing 10/-. Please keep 5/- for Tony and Kenneth and give them some to buy Kitty and Peggy something 'from me' and something for Aunt Eliza, if it will spin out. I don't really know of anything special I would like for Xmas from father, thank you, as I've been getting such a lot of things the last few weeks. So please don't worry about me, thank you all the same.

This time he signed off: 'I remain, Your flighty son, Jack.'

However, he was not to be overlooked in the matter of Christmas presents, as his next letter thanks his family for gold cuff links and £12 from his mother and father, ink from Kenneth, stamps from Aunt Eliza, a warm cardigan from Uncle Hamilton and Aunt Amy, a book on Kitchener from Uncle Willie and a parcel with 'grub' – including cocoa, Oxo and Edinburgh Rock. Christmas at Eastchurch hadn't turned out too badly after all:

> I had quite a decent sort of Xmas but after being up most of Sunday night and when *not* outside sleeping in my clothes on a couch in a bitterly cold room, you may be sure I was pretty tired and sleepy. We had quite a decent plum pudding and very good turkey indeed. Then there was an impromptu pantomime got up by the officers and ratings. It was held in one of the big sheds [aircraft hangars] and was a huge success all round. Kids were invited from Sheerness – poor kids, and they had lots to eat and drink and were then pelted with crackers by clowns from the stage.

He finished his letter with two final thoughts, the first of which would have gladdened any mother's heart and the second of historical interest:

> I'll very probably send you a pair of socks which need mending. I'm glad we are going to make yarns for aeroplane fabric [at the Mill in Belfast]. Perhaps I will use some of it some day!

Before the end of the year there was more excitement:

> Just a small letter to let you know how I'm getting on. I took control of a machine yesterday [28 December] for the first time. I took the bus up from about 1500 to 2100 feet and practised turning, and ordinary flying up and down. Then I brought her down to about 600 feet and the instructor finished. He sits behind, there's dual control of course, and he puts his hands out at either side of me, so as to let me know I was flying her. When I came down he said I'd a very

good idea of it. So I was quite pleased. There were 11 instructional machines up at one time yesterday. I hope to have leave tomorrow and if so will go to the Pilkingtons [which he did, also seeing the kindly Mr and Mrs Norton].

The Farman Longhorn, in which Jack took his initial flying training, was a 'pusher' biplane with a 70 hp Renault engine at the rear of the pilot's nacelle. When running slowly the engine made a noise 'like a pair of alarm clocks ticking upon a marble mantelpiece.' It could be readily distinguished from the Shorthorn version by the presence of the forward elevator mounted on outriggers at the front, which was very useful for ensuring that the pilot was lined up correctly with the horizon. The tail was suspended from twin booms trailing back from the wings. Captain WE Johns, the creator of James Bigglesworth, wrote of the Longhorn:

> Some people call it a Rumpety. Others call it a bird-cage, because of the number of wires it has got. The easiest way to find if all the wires are in their places is to put a canary between the wings; if the bird gets out you know there is a wire missing somewhere.

The fictional Biggles learned to fly in a Rumpety at about the same time as Jack. In most respects the Longhorn was delightful to fly, floating through the air, with an excellent forward view. The control column was in the fashion of a handlebar shaped like a pair of old-fashioned spectacles and the rudder was operated by pedals like those on a harmonium.

One of the presents received by Jack for Christmas was a black, leather-bound pocket diary, which he was to keep regularly for the whole year, missing only a few days here and there. It will now be possible therefore to intersperse extracts from his letters between the diary entries.

MONDAY, 1 JANUARY 1917, EASTCHURCH

Decent enough day. Went down to sheds after divisions at 8.15 and waited for air to be tested. Bowater and Wallis went up in two of the Maurices, but had to come down as it was far too windy and the bumps were very bad indeed. So there was no flying for us at all. Got a parcel from home with letter from Mother, blue muffler from Aunt Eliza and Oxo cubes from Tony. Also three apples. Tried to write a letter home but was too tired. [Captain AW Bowater later served in France and was shot down while flying a DH4 in 1918 and made a prisoner of war.]

The phenomenon of 'the bumps' as experienced by Jack is well explained in a little book, *Flying Simply Explained*, which was purchased by the author's father in the 1940s, when he was a youth:

Bumpiness. The novice pilot on his early flights is often surprised to find that the air is not as smooth as he imagined. At times it can throw the machine about, bouncing it up and down like a cork on choppy water. On such occasions the air is referred to as being bumpy. One sometimes hears people talking about air pockets. It is quite commonly supposed that pockets or vacuums exist in the atmosphere and that these cause the sudden losses of height to which an aircraft may be subject over certain areas and in certain weather conditions. Pockets or vacuums in the air do not exist. The conditions which have given rise to the belief are caused in the following manner. One is accustomed to thinking of wind as a current of air flowing horizontally over the ground. However, the flow of air over the earth's surface is not always horizontal. There are various causes present which tend to produce vertical currents as well. These, and minor disturbances due to gusts and squalls, tend to prevent steady flying and produce the conditions known as bumpiness. If an aircraft is flying in a steady horizontal wind flow and enters a region where there is an up current, it is subjected to a sudden lift which is called a bump. Similarly, if it enters a region of descending air, it experiences a decrease in lift. This is sometimes referred to as an air pocket. Other reasons for disturbed air arise from what are called temperature thermals – columns of air which are warmer than the surrounding air, and thus rise. Many of us are familiar with the expression hot air rises. It is the exaggerated condition of these rising columns which may produce clouds and sometimes thunderstorms with violent air eddies. A pilot frequently finds that bumps occur when flying low, especially over hilly country or the roofs of a town. This is because these obstructions in the path of the wind tend to divert it from its horizontal course and send it shooting upward. When an aeroplane is flying through a bumpy region, it is often thrown out of its level attitude. At times it may be necessary to correct these changes by a movement of the controls. In the most severe cases the aeroplane will tend to right itself when the disturbance has passed. It does this because of its stability, and this characteristic we have already discussed.

It appears that Jack was fairly untroubled by the bumps and in due course, as we will see, began to rather relish them, particularly if he was taking a passenger for a ride.

TUESDAY, 2 JANUARY
Another windy day and so we had lectures all day. Had two letters. Ordered a walking stick, flying boots again and six butterfly collars from Gieves. Some wonderful stunt flying by a Spad.

WEDNESDAY, 3 JANUARY
No flying again today owing to the wind. The best pilot on the station, called Johnston, went up in a Hispano Suiza-engined Sopwith Triplane to try for an altitude record at 40,000 feet, equipped with oxygen etc. Went up at 10 am and no more word of him late at night. He had only 2½ hours fuel as she climbs 10,000 feet in 8 minutes. Presumed blown to the North Sea as SE wind was blowing and big clouds about. Father sent me dividends from Levers, 9/-. First letter from George at Crystal Palace. Got a few lines wrote back.

THURSDAY, 4 JANUARY
Another nice but windy day; no flying for us. Engine lectures in sheds. Went into Eastchurch with Penny and

England after Morse, watched BEs pancaking down [landing] on the way back. Also an 'Old Man Short' up; big bus and just like a huge dragonfly when high up. Johnston picked up in channel by French warship; bus went down. Wrote to kids and T & K this evening. Very tired.

Flight Lieutenant PA Johnston of the Eastchurch Design Flight, following his forced landing in the sea off Dieppe in the Sopwith Triplane N5423, was picked up by a French trawler, which may have been fishing or perhaps had been requisitioned for patrol duties. The 'Old Man Short' was the large and impressive Short Bomber.

FRIDAY, 5 JANUARY

Just as the last few days, only less wind, so there was a good deal of flying done. I had my usual luck and watched the others go up, but didn't get up myself. We had a weird show of buses out: I counted at least 35: Dyotts, Vickers Gunbus, triplanes etc. One crash: a Sopwith undercarriage breaking when taxiing. Lectures in the evening as the wind rose too much, and a mist came up which forced 2 or 3 'Old Man Shorts' to come back, who were on their way to Dunkerque [to join 3 Wing RNAS for operations].

SATURDAY, 6 JANUARY

A very nice day but of course the usual Saturday exams did not permit us to fly. Had a good fire at night and was quite comfy. Lovely night. Got my gum boots and oiled socks today. Several chaps left for Cranwell today. Port watch for leave, I hope to get it next week. Wrote to George, Miss Craig, Mrs Herriot and Bunty. [Mabel Hunter, about whom Kitty and Peggy would tease Jack for being his 'best girl'.] Got letter from George and then started a second to him.

SUNDAY, 7 JANUARY

A glorious frosty day. Went up in the morning for 5 minutes with Flight Lieutenant Scott. He dropped me in some fields and took up several friends; told me to walk back slowly, which I did. Came back in an hour and swore at me for returning to station. Went up again in afternoon; 18 minutes about, and fearfully cold. Scott not a very decent instructor. Watched a Spad doing corkscrew nose dives, very difficult to do and thrilling to watch, a BE2c looping and some others coming down, engines off, so slowly you could hardly see them move. One of our chaps smashed three machines when taxiing into the sheds. He failed to close his throttle, as it jammed. Some mess! He's had his leave stopped till they're fixed again. Wrote to Barbara [the elder Pilkington girl] and home and George. Got letter from home.

This letter may well have been the one which follows. It is from an old lady, who may have been Jack's nurse, living in the little seaside village of Millisle in Co Down, not far from Donaghadee. Jack had fond memories of her potato bread, a traditional Ulster delicacy. It is very touching in its sincerity and simplicity:

Millisle 4 January 1917

My Dear Friend Master Jack
    I was taken in when I got your likens [photograph] from your Father & Mother. I am sure it vexed them to part with you for the armey but you will have there ernest prayer for God to take care of you & bless you for your job is a very dangris one & I do pray our dear heavenly father will guide & take care of you for Christ our dear savours sake & may he rest & be with you every day you rise is my prayer for you. Do you not feel disey when you are up so high in the air? I am sure it keeps a great noice for I herd the noice of one that flue over here in summer last summer. I trust we will be spared to meet aguin & that this cruel war will soon be over & may God bless all your dear friends at home & comfort them knowing that God is able to watch over you & bless you & guide you & I hope dear Jack you pray to God for his guiding care over you.
    So good By & my blessing & Gods blessing rest & abide with you is the prayer of your old friend
    Ellen Major. Good By My dear big son.

I had a dear sister died in Scotland 3 weeks ago. She come over every summer in July to see. She died very sudently of heart trouble. Excuse this scrible as I am in great trouble about my dear sister. Burn this poor scrible & God take care of you again.

MONDAY, 8 JANUARY

Too windy and generally unsettled for flying; only saw a BE2c and a Curtiss up. Started lectures on Aero Construction. Much colder today and it has started to rain as I write at 4.30, just after tea. Wrote a fairly long letter home; want to send some sugar to Barbara as a joke but have no paper. Enclosed my Crystal Palace report and appointment in my letter home. Have to go to lectures again at 5 till 6.30 pm in sheds. Was put into a slightly quicker Morse class (five or six words per minute).

With his letter home Jack enclosed an ignition key and gave permission for his younger brother, Tony, to use his motorbike. Somewhat optimistically he also predicted that the war would be nearly over in six or eight months. He had also discovered that it was possible to get permission to use cameras on site, so requested that his be sent over to him, along with some films. The only problem he noted was that the camp laundry made a habit of returning his socks and underwear in a shrunken condition.

TUESDAY, 9 JANUARY

Damp sort of day. Very windy indeed, so no flying except two Curtiss and a BE.

Lectures all day. No letters. Played hockey in lower hockey field; about six aside; very good sport and quite humorous. Played in gum boots, riding pants and sweater. Came a cropper, and did same for someone else.

WEDNESDAY, 10 JANUARY

Nice day but too windy for our flying. Lectures as usual; Morse after dinner. Went to drome in afternoon but it was too bumpy; they tried to get the Quad up, but didn't succeed. Got letter from Mrs Herriot.

THURSDAY, 11 JANUARY

No flying again today, worse luck; there was snow on the ground in the morning and it was a beastly day. Got letters from Barbara, George and Bunty, then a business one from Gieves, and then again one from father: five in one day, not so bad. Wrote a short letter home.

A brief but thoughtful letter home informed his parents about some changed arrangements:

I want to let you know about our letters. They're all to be censored here and then kept two days before being sent on. I don't know why it is but I'm just writing now to let you know my letters will be later in future. I've bent the nib of my pen so it's horribly scrappy to write with.

FRIDAY, 12 JANUARY

Rotten day again. Some mud too! Got a letter from Gèorge this evening asking if I would be going to Woodford with him. I've arranged to go to Mrs P's and so had to telephone to Crystal Palace; got through in 1½ hours and left a message for him not to leave CP till 1.30. I'm going to try to sneak off and get the 10.30 from Queensborough. Censoring of letters starts today.

SATURDAY, 13 JANUARY

Dirty sort of morning. Did exam in about 20 minutes and went to catch taxi with 3 others. Taxi not ordered! Got duty car and tore into Queenborough for 10.30 train; two minutes to spare. Couldn't find ½ fare voucher in time so paid full. Terrific double skid in car at 40 mph, road awfully greasy, we were between 35 – 40 all the way. There was a stream of slush went over some chap and simply caked him with mud. Met George and Hunter at low level Victoria. Hunter looked very well but George looked as if it was rather harder work than he is used to. Had some lunch and paid 6/11 for it! War on, or something. Took taxi to Liverpool Street and thence to Mrs Johnson's at Woodford. Met Charlie Johnson just home from front. We three slept in one bed! Some crush.

SUNDAY, 14 JANUARY

Stayed in during the morning. Went [for a] short walk in the afternoon. Took 6.30 train to Liverpool Street and 7.40 from Victoria; arrived Eastchurch at 10.30 in thick snow. Three letters waiting.

The 'highlights' of Jack's next letter to his parents were all of a domestic nature:

I don't think Mother need send me the jerseys, thank you, but I could do with some more socks. I intend sending mine home to be mended and some collars to be washed. I'd my first decent bath here last night and the water was nearly clear from the taps. Our drinking water is brought up in the mornings from somewhere or other. The chap in my room is quite a decent chap; he comes from Coventry or some such weird, unearthly place.

MONDAY, 15 JANUARY

Lovely day: no wind, snow on ground. Some fine fights! Did lectures all morning. Flying in afternoon, but had my usual luck – along with two others. Sent £16 home. Went into Eastchurch and registered it. Bought biscuits and condensed milk.

TUESDAY, 16 JANUARY

No flying as it was too dirty a day, rain and sleet all day; ground in a horrible mess. Ordered a pair of flying boots from Robinson & Cleaver and a leather waistcoat. Sent two pair of socks home to be mended. Had a glorious fire in my cabin this evening; also a ripping bath in clean water. Lectures till 4 pm.

WEDNESDAY, 17 JANUARY

Dry but very windy day. I am Flying School Duty Officer and so had to put up flags. No flying as it was so bumpy and windy. Lectures just as usual all day till 4 pm. Got a letter card from Tony at Merchi [his old school], says he has a cubicle, lucky chap. I wrote back to both of them [his two brothers]. Has offered to send on to me weekly papers like *Motor Cycle* and *Flight*, which would be good.

THURSDAY, 18 JANUARY

Too windy for flying, so did usual lectures morning and afternoon. Got four photos of self from home. Sent my coat to Gieves in Sheerness to have some alterations made. Heavy gunfire this evening, and could hear the shells whistling through the air; some chaps saw them bursting. It was anti-aircraft shrapnel I think. Quadruplane tried to get up today, but failed.

FRIDAY, 19 JANUARY

Rotten day, so no flying. Got letters from Father, Bunty and Mr Hayward. Received my camera from home and six films, so must try to get some photos. Wrote to Tom McCleane, Manager [at the Mill], Father, Mother and Bunty. The mud was specially bad today. The Quad tried to rise again today but couldn't. Watched shrapnel and star shells this evening: some lovely effects.

When the weather was too bad for flying there were always lessons and lectures on navigation, meteorology or the theory of flight to attend. A substantial hardbound book has survived in which Jack made copious careful, neatly written notes on such subjects as: the Renault engine's construction, component parts, dismantling and reassembling it, adjusting the timing and clearances; similar details of the Gnome engine, including how to recognise, diagnose and deal with engine faults; the BE2c's construction (spruce, ash, steel tube and piano wire), its controls (ailerons, rudder and elevator); and similar details of the Maurice Farman. The book is illustrated with very well executed technical drawings in pen and pencil, as well as more informal illustrations cut out from *Flight* or *Aeroplane* and pasted in. At the back of the book are some pages extracted from *Motor Cycling – The Light Car and Cyclist* with articles on 'Getting the Best Out of a Car', 'The Proper Use of the Clutch', 'Sparking Plug Notes' to list but a few. Jack was able to give his parents a flavour of one of the lessons but still thought about home, an acquaintance in training and Jock:

Spent all day today trying to 'catch' Zepps on charts, taking into account wind veering, height, compass deviation and variations and a lot of other rot. It's quite interesting though. I would like to be able to be at the Mill to see the new extensions but I'm afraid I can't be just at present. I hope you'll not have trouble getting a new machine master but I remember it was difficult last time. I see from today's paper that one of the chaps I was most friendly with at CP is 'slightly injured'. He's called CP Lee. He went to an aerodrome in the North of Yorkshire [probably Redcar] at the same time as I came here. Have you tried Jock with dog biscuits? If not, Pratts are the best, not Molassine. Could you please send me about 3/- or 4/- of stamps please, as we get them by the book and the halfpenny ones are only a nuisance. I *do* run through a lot of stamps here.

SATURDAY, 20 JANUARY

It was drizzling sleet all day today. Had navigation exam in morning. There has been a very bad explosion in London in some munitions factory; said to be 1500 killed. Somewhere near Woolwich, but we didn't hear it. Saw some more very fine star shells and shrapnel this evening; could hear the shells whistling quite plainly. Penny showed me some of his Egypt & Peninsular photos of the armoured car division. Some jolly good ones. Slept most of the afternoon!

That Friday evening a small community in the East End of London was ripped apart by an enormous explosion – the biggest the city had seen before or has since – when Silvertown's munitions factory blew up. Working flat out to meet a chronic shortage of shells for the war effort, the Brunner Mond works exploded, killing seventy-three people and laying waste a huge expanse, destroying whole streets and leaving hundreds injured. At 6.52 pm the streets were busy, with workers going on and off shift. A fire in the melting-pot room of the factory caused 50 tons of TNT to explode. The works became a bomb, showering large, red hot lumps of metal for miles around. Electric lights all over London flickered and the blast was heard as far away as Cambridge and Guildford.

SUNDAY, 21 JANUARY

Quite a decent day, only a good deal of wind. Slacked most of the day in front of a roaring fire.

MONDAY, 22 JANUARY

A lovely day, only slightly misty; flying all day. I did 25 minutes both morning and afternoon, doing front seat work. It was very cold. We all had to help to shove the machines back and it was some job in the mud. Wrote home to Mother. I think the terrible munition explosion occurred on Friday; we didn't feel it here, (but) one chap only said it shook his window.

TUESDAY, 23 JANUARY

Too windy for flying. Did second week engine lectures; Gnome engine this week, am glad I know most of it. Got letters and a box of nice fruit cake and some cocoa tablets from Mrs P——, with letter from Barbara. Reminded Robinson & Cleaver's man that I ordered boots a week ago. Wrote to George.

WEDNESDAY, 24 JANUARY

Beautiful bright day and hard frost; too windy for our flying. Lectures as usual. Letters from Miss Craig, George and someone else – I forget who. Boxing tournament in evening, but a rotten show. Have a rotten cold. Fight in Channel with TBDs [Torpedo Boat Destroyers]. Huns got the worst of it and had to bolt, their flagship ran into Holland.

The first Royal Navy ships to bear the formal designation 'Torpedo Boat Destroyer' (TBD) were the *Havock* class of 1893. *Havock* had a 240 tons displacement, a speed of 27 knots and was armed with a single 3-inch gun, three 6-pounders and three torpedo tubes. She had the range and speed to effectively travel with a battle fleet and offer protection against small and nimble torpedo boats. Many classes of TBD were produced over the next twenty years or so and were refined and improved. Some eighty British destroyers, as they came to be more commonly known, took part in the Battle of Jutland. During the war, service in a destroyer was a virtual guarantee of action either guarding heavy units of the Fleet, raiding the enemy coast, skirmishing with the enemy's light forces, mounting anti-U-boat patrols or protecting convoys – to name just a few of their duties.

Thursday, 25 January

Too windy for flying; hard frost all day. Letters from George and Mr Norton. CP in quarantine. Wrote to Barbara, George and Mr Norton. Cold a little better. Went through our power house tonight, quite a decent one. Hun machine reported from Dunkerque heading here – Scout went up, but heard no more about it. Report genuine enough. Letter from Mother and Kenneth at school. Put Gnome engine together and stripped in 1½ hours with Penny.

Friday, 26 January

Slight bombardment of Suffolk coast today; nothing much though. [Warships of the Imperial German Navy would from time to time undertake hit and run raids on English coastal towns.] Wrote home and had letter from Kathleen. [Kathleen Hamilton appears in pre-war photographs, making a jolly, laughing foursome with Jack, Tony and Bunty.] No flying as too windy; the coldest day we've had this Winter: it was the limit. Lectures as usual. War as usual. Soccer this afternoon officers v ratings, they won 4–0.

Saturday, 27 January

A lovely day but fearfully cold wind. Caught 12.10 train and arrived at Dulwich about 4 o'clock. Exam in morning on aero engines. I was top with 98%; quite pleased with myself. Barbara and all well. Letter from Tom McCleane. Got out at SE Dulwich and had to take two buses. Should have got out at W Dulwich. Tram fare up from 1/6 to 2/3. Our fare from Eastchurch still 7/6.

Sunday, 28 January

Dry but very cold day. Brekker at 10. Went to see Mr and Mrs Norton but only Mrs Norton was there; Barbara came with me. Had to catch 7.40 train as usual. Big crush and train very cold. Arrived after bitterly cold drive in duty car at 10.30 pm, nearly frozen. Letter from Bunty waiting for me.

MONDAY, 29 JANUARY

Too windy for flying, so had navigation lectures. Looks like snow. Nothing special today. No letters.

TUESDAY, 30 JANUARY

Snowing slightly and wind too high for flying, so did lectures as usual. No letters. Farewell dinner to Wing Commander Longmore who is going East. He was one of the first 4 RN men chosen to fly. Gave us a short history of Eastchurch as home of RNAS. Several speeches: – Johnston, our finest pilot, was asked to give a speech on 'Elementary flying, or How he spun the Spad'. But he was too shy and couldn't say anything.

WEDNESDAY, 31 JANUARY

Snowing in morning and did lectures, but cleared up by dinner and there was flying. I didn't get up, as our engines weren't firing right. Fine snow fight with the mechanics before divisions. The snowballs came in on us officers like hail! There was tobogganing but I'd rather break my leg in an aeroplane. Rudd knocked his ankle out and got water on the knee; two others ditto.

THURSDAY, 1 FEBRUARY

No flying in morning. Got a letter from Mother and also George to say he hopes to be here this weekend. Flight Lieutenant Wallace broke his leg tobogganing today. Rudd has gone to Sheerness hospital. I was up 36 minutes this afternoon and did landings and take-offs. It was snowing gently and the ground was white. Would have gone up solo only no time. Am going to next time. Fearfully cold up and I was quite glad to come down! It's quite difficult to judge a landing in the snow and the glare off the ground is rather unpleasant. I am very bucked with myself after only 2¼ hours to go up solo. We chased some hares in a field. An Avro and a Voisin crashed this afternoon.

FRIDAY, 2 FEBRUARY

Main Station Duty Officer. CO's rounds, so was busy most of the morning. 700 liberty tickets to sign this afternoon. A lovely day, no wind and pretty clear. Had a pretty busy night and a cold one too. Wrote to Mother and Barbara. Letter from George saying he won't be here this week but may next. Bought a ripping pair of fur gloves from Gieves.

SATURDAY, 3 FEBRUARY

Glorious day though a bit misty. Went up for some landings with Scott and was up 26 minutes; lovely up. After dinner, went up for first solo and stayed up an hour. Got the wind up once on a bank, I got into a crowd of bumps. Scott seemed pleased with me. One crash – a Curtiss on her nose. Took three photos – two of myself by another chap. Got on quite decently and made what must have been a jolly good turn out of aerodrome, from what Scott said.

SUNDAY, 4 FEBRUARY

Lovely day, though a bit of a mist on. Flew solo for one hour 11 minutes in morning, and two hours 10 minutes in afternoon making three hours 21 minutes altogether. Got on rippingly in afternoon, doing quite good right hand spirals and good turnings. Burst a tyre as the snow caused the machine to swerve as it touched the ground. Got slightly strafed, but Maude, Scott and Bowater seemed quite impressed with my doings and later said I'd go on Curtiss as soon as there is a vacancy. Jolly pleased with myself altogether, but my ears are humming now at 8.30 pm. Quite warm really. Lost my bearings for some time. Letter from Father which I am going to answer tonight.

He sought to reassure his mother that he wasn't taking any unnecessary risks now that he was flying solo:

I managed OK, but wasn't too confident of course, my first time. It was very fine up and not at all cold. Mother needn't be anxious about me at all, as I'm as safe here as on my bike, only I use up more petrol in an hour here than I'd use in 10 days on the bike, seven or eight gallons per hour!

MONDAY, 5 FEBRUARY

No flying as it was snowing very heavily all morning and most of the afternoon. Did construction lectures. Had some very fine fights in the snow, which was in some places up to our knees. Some of the senior officers were skiing down the hill. Wrote home, and to George.

TUESDAY, 6 FEBRUARY

Lovely day but wind almost force four. Flight Lieutenant Scott tried the air and it seemed very bumpy; sent me up for the experience: I never had such an exciting five minutes as when taking off! Bumped all over the place; then went up to about 2000 feet and did both hand spirals and S turns. No bumps over 1000 feet or very few. Did a good many landings; all of them good ones. Did them so as to know how to if bumps are bad; crabbed a lot. First two or three turns I side slipped a bit, got on all OK after. Letter from Tony. See Spencer-Smith died of scurvy 8th March 1916 in the Barrier. Poor old Spencer.

The Reverend Arnold Spencer-Smith was the first ordained clergyman to set foot on the Antarctic continent. A 'muscular Christian', he had gone on Ernest Shackleton's expedition in search of suffering to purify his soul and resolve any theological doubts that he might have harboured. He acted as the expedition's photographer. Before the war he had taught at Merchiston. Sadly, he contracted scurvy and became the first ordained clergyman to die in the icy wastes, aged thirty-two.

WEDNESDAY, 7 FEBRUARY

Nice but windy day. Tried four Maurice Farmans but all konked out. Scott had told me to see how high I could go. Got 52 minutes on my old MF 8835 however and had quite a decent time spiralling etc. Went on Curtiss in afternoon as passenger for 50 minutes; nice bus. Then went up solo for 20 minutes and took her up to about 3000 feet and spiralled down; they're rather nose heavy busses. Had to come down as it was getting rather dark and I couldn't see my instruments (altimeter, rev. counter, air speed indicator and levels). I've got on very fast; being first of all our lot now

even in time! Letters from Barbara, Kitty and George. Got
my leather waistcoat. Felt very done in evening.

The Curtiss JN.4, built by the Curtiss Aeroplane Company of
Hammondsport, New York, was familiarly known as the
'Jenny'. It was a rather more modern-looking two-seat biplane
than the old Longhorn and was a tractor with the engine in front
of the pilot, rather than a pusher with the engine to the rear –
which is why Jack would have thought it nose heavy until he got
used to it. More than 8000 were built and it has a strong claim to
be recognised as the most useful and effective American aircraft
of the Great War – with an honourable mention for the Curtiss
H series 'Small America' and 'Large America' flying-boats.

THURSDAY, 8 FEBRUARY

Just like yesterday, fine but very windy. Took a Curtiss up
to about 5000 feet (Some View!) and spiralled down. Stayed
up 80 minutes and had a ripping time. Drifted several miles
coming down. When I landed instructor said, 'You seem to
know all about them now, so I'll put you on to Avros.'!!
Am keeping very well. Letter from Mother. All seem to be
keeping well. Have now flown 14 hrs 37 minutes.

FRIDAY, 9 FEBRUARY

Too windy for flying. Have been put onto Avros now!
Quicker than anyone else by far! Lectures all day and usual
fed upness. Letter from Bunty. Wrote to Mother, Bunty and
Hugh Craig and parcelled up two films to send home to be
developed. Ship (TBD) blown up off the island [Isle of
Sheppey] last night.

In his letter home that week, Jack drew an excellent sketch of the
Curtiss JN.4 8807, with a scarf trailing behind the pilot's head,
and added:

You wouldn't know me if you could see me in the air! No
face to be seen! I sit in the back seat when flying it, the front
being for a passenger or observer. You work her with a
wheel like a car, only it's not for steering with as that's done
by foot. The lever at the side is for bomb dropping. You will

be able to show Aunt Eliza her muffler round my neck. I'm sending two films to be developed. Please don't let Hogg [Alexander Hogg 1870–1939 was one of Belfast's most distinguished early professional photographers] send them to me when finished, it would be better if you would. If the one of me sitting in a machine of the above type comes out, I'd like ½ dozen prints please. If any of me standing in kit come out (beside machine), I can send you some back and explain them. The one in which I'm standing beside a machine is of a Maurice Farman – the sort I learned to fly first. The one of the machine No. 8935 and two chaps in it was taken after I'd come down from a two hours 10 minutes flight by myself. Everyone else was at dinner but as they were Flying School DO [Duty Officer] and time-keeper they'd to wait and straf [chunter/complain] till I came down. The coloured circles are Allied identification marks. I think the Curtiss buses are very fine machines though comparatively slow. The small machine with a chap beside it is a Bristol 'Bullet' and flies at about 85 knots. Then in the picture of the place, the huts on the hill are our quarters. This was taken from just behind the sheds and is a jolly good photo.

What his mother and father must have felt when reading the next few lines can only be imagined – concern mingled with pride and amazement in equal measure:

I saw an airship the other day over Sheerness and was going to examine it, when I thought the better of it, as they fire at you [from the ground] if you're over 3000 feet there. The bumps too have been pretty bad lately. They're not dangerous only one needs to be pretty wide awake, as you suddenly drop perhaps as much as 20 or 30 feet and next minute you're thrown up as far or else you roll from side to side. It's just like a ship in a bit of a sea but I find it rather more amusing. They nearly all vanish at 1000 feet so you only notice them going up or landing. As a matter of fact, flying tractors makes one most awfully sleepy (not in the air!) and also makes one's ears – well you're as good as deaf most of the evening if you've done much flying during the day. So when I get the time in the evening I usually go straight to sleep in a chair and if I don't my hands are usually too shaky to write. I can hardly believe I've done so well! Our water supply has been about one small cupful a day for washing purposes this last fortnight! A bath is a forgotten luxury – and a proper wash. Whenever the cisterns are even a quarter full, the pipes are frozen.

SATURDAY, 10 FEBRUARY

Splendid for flying at breakfast time but a breeze sprang up and in about ten minutes there was a heavy fog and a force six wind. Exam on construction. Went on leave by 12.10 train, had lunch at Lyons and then went up to P—s. Had a ripping evening. Posted my letters home and bought some chocolates for Mary P— as tomorrow is her birthday.

SUNDAY, 11 FEBRUARY

Nice but cold day. Barbara and I went up to see Mr Norton to say good bye as I'm for Cranwell next Saturday with a lot of work for the month ahead of me worse luck. Then in evening ran over to say good bye to Aunt Mary. Missed my train, so spent the night at Belgrave Mansions.

MONDAY, 12 FEBRUARY

Caught 5.50 this morning and arrived at Eastchurch 9 o'clock. Got strafed [told off for being late] then went to navigation lectures. Letter from Father with some War Loan forms to be signed. He's giving me £100 of it. Also the long lost photos arrived tonight and just about time.

FRIDAY, 16 FEBRUARY

I and 10 others are for Cranwell this weekend, worse luck.

CHAPTER FOUR

From Cranwell to Freiston

By 1915 the Admiralty had established a series of air stations around the south and east coasts of Britain and required a central establishment at which officers and ratings could be trained to fly and maintain aeroplanes, airships and kite balloons. Flying training was much in need of standardisation to develop a common curriculum and raise the level of tuition. The probably apocryphal story is that Cranwell was chosen by a young naval pilot who had been ordered to fly around until he found a tract of land that was both large and flat enough to serve the purpose. The site was suitable for expansion in any direction, for feeding the East Coast stations and in the future becoming a War Station for airships. There was plenty of good, open country (free of dykes and ditches), good roads and cheap local labour. It was a short distance by air to the coast for firing practice and there was suitable cheap land. By the end of 1915 the first 2500 acres of farmland near Sleaford in Lincolnshire had been requisitioned and construction begun of huts and hangars.

The RNAS Central Training Establishment, Cranwell, was commissioned on 1 April 1916, under the command of an experienced and eminent officer Commodore Godfrey Paine CB, MVO, who had gained his RAeC Certificate (No. 217) at Eastchurch in May 1912 and who had also been the commandant of the RFC's Central Flying School at Upavon in Wiltshire, before the Royal Navy decided to go its own way with regard to matters aeronautical. It is said that Paine urged the workmen on with the offer of a five pound note to the foreman exceeding the day's quota for pipe laying and that he also made an agreement with the CO of the 4th Battalion, the Lincolnshire Regiment, to prepare for digging trenches in France by marching his men for earth-moving duties on the building site that was to become Cranwell.

Henceforth pilots in the RNAS would commence flying training to the standard of flying 'a moderately fast tractor' at one of four preliminary schools – Eastchurch, Eastbourne, Chingford and Redcar, where they would achieve some twenty to twenty-four hours solo – and would complete their advanced training at Cranwell. This comprised a further twenty hours or so of flying, including cross-country work, familiarisation on fast scout aircraft, bomb dropping, wireless telegraphy and aerial photography. Ground examinations covered such subjects as engines, aircraft construction, navigation, gunnery and wireless telegraphy. After graduating at Cranwell and being promoted to flight sub-lieutenant they would then be appointed to Freiston, also in Lincolnshire, five miles east of Boston on The Wash, which was opened in mid-1916. There they would spend about a fortnight engaged in practical gunnery and bomb dropping.

Pilots streamed onto seaplanes (including those from Windermere) went directly from the four preliminary schools to Calshot, Felixstowe or Killingholme for further specialised instruction. Airship and kite-balloon pilots and observers came to Cranwell following initial training at Wormwood Scrubs in London. Commodore Paine left Cranwell on 31 January 1917 to become 5th Sea Lord and was replaced by Commodore John Luce.

Pilots who had completed their preliminary training joined A or C Flights which were equipped with the Avro 504. After going solo on the Avro, they then progressed to D or F Flights, which flew the BE2c, and embarked on a more demanding programme than simple circuits, including cross-country flights as far afield as Nottingham. Lastly came E Flight on which they would have the pleasure of flying single-seat scouts and so could be identified as suitable for future employment on these or on bombers.

In the course of six to eight weeks at Cranwell some twenty

more flying hours would be flown, giving the student a total of thirty to forty hours solo on graduation, including six to eight hours at Freiston. A few Maurice Farman Longhorns were also kept at Cranwell for miscellaneous duties.

SATURDAY, 17 FEBRUARY

We're told we were to go by 4.30 from Queenboro'. Arrived in Victoria 6.08 and had dinner in Lyons. Have had leave granted till 5 train tomorrow from Kings and so went to Mrs P—s and had a very nice time. Ripping train up to Grantham where we arrived at about 8; no connections so we got leave to stay till 8.30 tomorrow. Awful hunt for rooms, but all right in the end and I had a jolly good sleep.

MONDAY, 19 FEBRUARY

Arrived about 10 o'clock at Cranwell. Got strafed first of all for not appearing last night and a fortnight's leave jambed [stopped]. Lectures all day as too misty for flying.

TUESDAY, 20 FEBRUARY

Rained all day, lectures and squad drill. Wrote and posted letter home; this is some size of a place. Am in A flight and A section for lectures.

In his letter Jack gave his first impressions of Cranwell:

I'm very sorry for not writing before, but from about last Friday morning I've had no time to myself really. Well at any rate this C———l. I arrived on Monday morning after an awful lot of bother etc. The Great Northern trains however are fine. I can't tell you anything really about this place, except that it's colder then E———h and a huge place far larger indeed than E———h. Also we've got *some* work to do. We get up at 7.30 am and knock off again at 7.15 at night. I'm very comfy in a brick hut and am quite fixed up in my room with another chap, who seems to be very nice. He's probably leaving towards the end of the week, so I hope I get someone as decent. If I 'pass out' here I get my ring and sub-lieutenant-ship; but I've got to pass out first and that takes some doing. Would you please let me know when all the birthdays come off and also send me some stamps? I'm keeping very well indeed and hope you are all, too. I hope you've not been anxious about me. I'm sorry Jock's not well and hope he soon will be.

WEDNESDAY, 21 FEBRUARY

Fog again today. Lectures in morning and PTI [Physical Training Instruction] in gym which is a very fine one; also there is a fine swimming bath. Some flying after dinner but none for me worse luck. Wrote to Barbara this evening.

THURSDAY, 22 FEBRUARY

More fog, so lectures as usual; we stop work early on Thursday afternoons so that's a change. Have not got any letters yet but hope to soon.

FRIDAY, 23 FEBRUARY

Some flying both morning and afternoon but it was very bumpy and windy and at 1000 feet I believe the earth was out of sight, so I didn't get up. Am in A flight, Avros. As I'd no lectures this evening from 6.15 to 7.15 pm, I went to the Armament shop and got some instruction, stripping a Lewis gun and a Webley revolver and a Webley Scott pistol. Letter from Mother, P and Kitty. All well at home.

SATURDAY, 24 FEBRUARY

Letter from Father enclosing prints – 10 of them, all good but two. The Mill gave £2025 to the War Loan and Belfast £12,000,000 so we've not done badly in the North. Too misty for flying. Lectures till 11.30 and then off for the day. Wrote home and to Uncle Willy and Bunty. On duty from 2 – 4 in morning.

SUNDAY, 25 FEBRUARY

No flying owing to a heavy mist. Divisions at 10.30 and then we were free for the day. Went a walk round the place after dinner. Had a very bad headache after being up on duty. Slept in till 8.30 am. So didn't get brekker at all. Wrote home, and to Uncle Willy and Bunty.

MONDAY, 26 FEBRUARY
Flying part of morning and of afternoon; got up for six minutes and then came down as the bumps were awful. Wrote to George. Still got a headache so didn't go into supper. Got some handkerchiefs from Mother and a letter and a postcard from Peggy.

TUESDAY, 27 FEBRUARY
Fine day for flying, only a bit hazy. I did 35 minutes dual and then went up solo as follows:-

8.45	Avro 504B 1031	35 min Dual
11.25	Avro 504B 1028	50 min Solo
2.05	Avro 504C 8585	15 min Solo *
2.40	Avro 504C 3302	80 min Solo
4.05	Avro 504C 3302	25 min Solo

*Had my first broken inlet valve and made a very good landing just in front of the sheds. Did one or two nose dives and managed OK. I'm not fond of crash helmets. Letter from Barbara.

The Avro 504 is justly recognised as one of the great aircraft types; it was the standard trainer of the British flying services for fifteen years and early in the war carried out some audacious bombing operations, notably on 21 November 1914 when three Avro 504s of the RNAS attacked the Zeppelin sheds at Friedrichshafen on Lake Constance. Avro 504s were also employed as anti-Zeppelin fighters. Indeed the C variant, of which about eighty were supplied to the RNAS, was specially developed for anti-Zeppelin patrols, with an auxiliary fuel tank in place of the front cockpit, which increased its endurance to eight hours, and it could carry a Lewis gun mounted to fire upwards through the centre section at an angle of 45 degrees. The 504B was a dedicated training version, of which about 190 were built.

WEDNESDAY, 28 FEBRUARY
Put in a good deal more time today. Did several nose dives and enjoyed myself generally. Then an inlet valve went and I had to come down. Still I was up on several machines and

had some good fun. A good many crashes today, though nothing serious.

Thursday, 1 March

Put in about 2½ hours again and had quite a good time. An awful lot of crashes, which wound up by a chap called Daglish coming down upside down from 10,000 ft and killing himself. [Temporary Flight Sub-Lieutenant GRG Daglish was killed at Cranwell that day when the BE2c 8620, which he was flying, crashed.] *I didn't see it, I'm glad to say. It fairly put the wind up everyone. There were either 8 or 10 crashes, one being a collision. Letter from home this morning. I went up to 4000 feet but had to come down as my head went very bad. I hope my nerves aren't going. Got paid £23 so will send a good deal home. No leave as place is in quarantine owing to mumps and then measles. Letter from George at Eastchurch – irony. I'm glad he's doing jolly well at the flying.

Friday, 2 March

No flying in morning as there was a very bad ground haze. But in the afternoon it cleared up beautifully and I got in about 45 minutes. Very bumpy up to about 2500 feet. Made two jolly good landings. One crash today: a Nieuport scout being wrecked. Pilot not hurt. Got a ripping letter from Bunty enclosing my photos.

Saturday, 3 March

No flying as there was a heavy mist all day. Two hours' lectures in the morning. Got hold of a Mandoline [sic] in the afternoon and had quite a good time, it's funny how the chaps gather round! Wrote about six letters, one to Barbara. Nothing of any importance today.

Sunday, 4 March

Funeral service for Daglish, rather touching. Fearfully cold day. No flying at all, so have had quite a good rest this weekend. Wrote home and to Bunty. Letter from Father enclosing some postcard prints of me etc. Quite good. Jock, who had been scrapping, is nearly all OK now.

Jack's letter home revealed:

> I've done a good deal of flying this week, about nine hours, eight and a half of which was solo. This was all on Avros and now I'm done with them and am going on to BEs which are what the RFC use at the front. Then I've only to do fast scouts – like the Bullet I photographed and other machines such as Nieuports and Sopwiths. Then if I pass out in my exams I'm supposed to be a 1st class pilot, in fact, if I don't pass out in exams the RFC will give us a lieutenantship I believe. So, of course, when I pass out I become a Flight Sub-Lieutenant and get my ring [on the sleeves of the uniform jacket]. I hope to pass out of here in a few weeks but where I'll be sent I don't know. I am afraid it may be the Somme [flying Scouts – Sopwith Triplanes or Pups], perhaps Dunkerque [flying the larger Sopwith 1½ Strutters, Nieuport 12s or even 'Old Man Shorts'].
>
> I managed to get hold of a mandoline. I was doing the Perfect Day, Destiny etc and some psalms on it and was doing double stropping and I've got quite a good way of doing it now, in fact, though I know Father won't believe it, it sounds awfully pretty done in my way. I use my finger tip instead of a plectrum and play very softly. I'm on 'workshops' next week (engines and aeroplane construction etc). I don't get any flying so the weather doesn't matter, the worse the better, as it will keep me from longing to be up. Oh, I forgot, thanks very much for the cocoa – I still have an awful supply of Oxo!

MONDAY, 5 MARCH
Workshops. Once more the Renault engine.

TUESDAY, 6 MARCH AND WEDNESDAY, 7 MARCH
Workshops.

THURSDAY, 8 MARCH
Income tax forms from Admiralty. Letter from Mother and also one from George. A good deal of snow.

MONDAY, 12 MARCH

On the BE flight, but there are about 25 others and most of the machines are crashed. However it was washed out today for most of us. One of the junior instructors, a very nice chap called Knight [Temporary Flight Sub-Lieutenant RV Knight] was killed today in a Bullet. He nose dived from 200 feet. He was only about 23 and had a wife and child at Sleaford where he had waved to them out of his bus only about 10 minutes before.

TUESDAY, 13 MARCH

Washed out flying again today. Have a very sore foot and can hardly walk. Did squad drill – drilling the men for an hour this morning. Got a possible in Lewis gun firing; poor at Vickers and Webley pistol. Also did some quite good bomb dropping practice. Letters from Mother and Kenneth.

WEDNESDAY, 14 MARCH

Had to go sick, my foot was so bad, so didn't get any flying. The surgeon was going to put me in a ward; however I escaped and spent all day sitting in an armchair with my foot up! A glorious day so I was fed up listening to the other buses. Wrote to George and Barbara. Got seven letters this evening. Watched several buses up in the sunset; very pretty sight indeed.

THURSDAY, 15 MARCH

My birthday. Still sick; foot not quite OK yet. Only a little flying till the evening when there were several up. Very quiet day for me. Wrote T & K and P & K. Got a parcel with cocoa in it from Mother this evening. Revolution in Russia. Tsar abdicates and Petrograd riots take place.

The February Revolution (Russia still used the Julian calendar, which in 1917 was thirteen days behind the Gregorian calendar) began on 8 March with strikes and riots in St Petersburg, which had been renamed Petrograd. Its cause was the chaotic direction of the war by a divided government, the heavy casualties and the lack of food and ammunition. The Duma appointed a Provisional Government and Tsar Nicholas II abdicated on March 15.

FRIDAY, 16 MARCH

Got into duty again but not into a machine. Letter from Bunty for my birthday; jolly nice of her to remember it. Ordered a new jacket and trousers from Gieves with F/S-L stuff on. Lights went out when I was in Scott's cabin and then went on dimly; cause being Zepps over Norfolk or Kent or somewhere.

SATURDAY, 17 MARCH

Got up for 24 minutes' dual in a BE. Fine, and lovely, up at 4000 feet. 'Sat' down: a great stunt I think. Most uncanny machines. They fly themselves, putting on their own bank when you rudder. Once you're up you can let go of the stick and they look after themselves. Too bumpy a day to practise landings but instructor told me I was very good in the air. Foot still sore so had to hang about a good deal all day. Got some shamrock and a letter from Father.

The inherent stability of the BE2, which first appeared in 1912, was both a blessing and a curse. It was easy and safe to fly but not very manoeuvrable which made it 'Fokker fodder' on the Western Front. Owing to the lack of any suitable replacement, it had to soldier on in the front line well into obsolescence. The RNAS used the BE2c with success not only as a trainer but also for anti-Zeppelin and anti-submarine patrols and as a bomber in the Eastern Mediterranean theatre. Jack added further comments in his letter of 18 March:

I'd a fine sensation when I was up. The instructor shut off [the engine] and [I] came down like a leaf or a feather – floating down horizontally without any directional motion. Looking over the side all was stationary below – we were up at about 4000 feet. The ground wind was about 30 knots but up there, there was none and leaning over the side, one got first a lovely little breath of warm air from the prop. I will probably be sent on a cross-country next week if the weather's good enough. We may go over Grantham, Lincoln and Nottingham or some such trip. I intend taking some note paper up and trying to write you a letter! It would be quite unique, though of course if I'd an observer or someone piloting for me it would be easy enough. We also have to take photos of various places by means of an aerial camera.

I was top in the Lewis gun shooting on the range this week, as I got a possible with three bursts of five rounds in separate magazines. We have to correct our jambs and load and fire in a certain time and I did it four seconds faster. I was hopeless at the Vickers and the Webley automatic pistol though. I did very well at the bomb dropping practice, too, only missing my target once. I'll explain how it's done on the ground in a tower when I see you. They're sending a lot of our chaps to seaplanes at Calshot near Portsmouth, where I believe they have to graduate again. It's for 'sub-hunting'. If I get a 1st Class pilot's certificate I hope they'll put me on a fast seaplane called the Sopwith Schneider. The RNAS is doing far more than people know, both on land and sea.

P.S. I forgot to thank you for the Shamrock which I got last night. It's sprouting in my cabin now!

SUNDAY, 18 MARCH

Bapaume falls at last and also two other towns. [On the Somme battlefield where many Irishmen from the North, 36th (Ulster) Division and the South (16th Irish Division) had given their lives the year before in the attack of 1 July 1916.] Zepps brought down in Paris L39 or something; came down in flames. [Following the raid on Kent by five airships mentioned by Jack above, the L39 (LZ86) was driven off course by strong winds and apparently suffered engine failure; drifting over France at reduced altitude it was hit by anti-aircraft fire and crashed near Compiègne.] Lovely day, but too windy for any flying so am writing several letters. Went on a lovely walk with Scott in afternoon just after dinner round the Zepp shed [Cranwell's shed for Coastal Class non-rigid airships and the great double rigid airship shed were completed in the first half of 1917] and then through some of the woods. Things aren't green yet.

MONDAY, 19 MARCH
Péronne falls and British and French still advancing rapidly. No flying.

TUESDAY, 20 MARCH
Advance continuing. Heavy RFC losses. [In fact, by the brutal standards of the Western Front, 1917 was to prove to be a quiet year on the Somme; it was not until the offensive of 1918 that Bapaume and Péronne were finally liberated. The main battles fought by British and Imperial troops in 1917 were Arras, 3rd Ypres and Cambrai. 'Bloody April' would indeed prove to be a very difficult month for the RFC which sustained heavy losses supporting the Arras offensive.] No flying.

THURSDAY, 22 MARCH
Letter from Mother. Too windy for flying. Also letter from George. Tony's going to join some Forestry stunt for the Hols.

FRIDAY, 23 MARCH
Was up for 12 minutes doing landings and was to have gone solo in the BE, only another chap took up so much time doing rotten landings and take-offs with my instructor I didn't get. Very fed up about it. Another chap put Bullet in on its nose. No letters.

SATURDAY, 24 MARCH
German resistance increases; though we're running up to St Quentin. Was up for 24 minutes' dual this morning in BE2c. Very misty, ground out of sight at 400 feet. Gilligan very pleased with me, I think. He crashed in afternoon and turned right over on his nose and back. Got some ripping prints from home. Letter from Bunty too. Solo next suitable day for me. Got no brekker today.

SUNDAY, 25 MARCH
No flying for me as it is too windy and misty. Someone crashed a Bullet. I think this is Communion Sunday at home. British 5 miles from St Quentin. Turks look like

catching it from both sides. [The forces of the Ottoman Empire were being pressed in Palestine by British and Imperial forces advancing from Egypt and in Mesopotamia, where Baghdad had recently been captured.] Big rumours of riots in Germany.

The weekly letter home noted:

> Your shamrock is still alive in my cabin. George seems to be all right, I don't know whether I told you, he crashed a Maurice [Farman] some time ago. Undercarriage I think, so of course he was all right. I wouldn't say anything to Mrs H [his mother] if you come across her at all. As a matter of fact it's one of the most difficult things to do, to crash a Maurice.

There must have been a question in the previous letter from home as Jack added a postscript.

> I've not looped yet, but at any rate there's nothing in it.

MONDAY, 26 MARCH
Had to get up at 6 am for early morning flying. Snowing, so no one else turned up. Did not get up all day, so was fed up, as usual

TUESDAY, 27 MARCH
Up for early morning flying but nothing doing. Got up for about 50 minutes after tea on my first solo and enjoyed it very much. Think BEs are ripping buses. Put the wind up a lot of 'em as I couldn't get the bus to turn into wind, consequently nearly hit sheds, but hoicked over by 10–15 feet. Then made quite a good landing. Got up to 6000 feet. Glorious sight to see the sunset and the clouds.

WEDNESDAY, 28 MARCH
Was up for 20 minutes before brekker and had quite a good time on a very nice machine. No flying then till after dinner when I went up for about 1½ hrs. Put the wind up myself and a Curtiss chap. Was chasing him at 1500 feet and nearly hit him. Just managed to clear him by hoicking over him. If

he'd done ditto!! Burst a tyre though landing was quite good. Very misty.

THURSDAY, 29 MARCH

Was up again today and had quite a good time. Nothing special happened. There was a good deal of mist so I couldn't go up any height.

FRIDAY, 30 MARCH

Was up before brekker and in fine form. Came down to ask permission to loop. Another chap sent up in my bus and I got a Curtiss BE [a BE2c with a 90 hp Curtiss engine] for the job but as belt was too big and engine missing it didn't come off. Am not to do any more flying as my time on BEs is up except for a cross-country. Long letter from Father and one from K.

SATURDAY, 31 MARCH

Reported at flight to try a loop but no good owing to mist. Also reported after tea but no good as another chap spun a BE and a lot of time was lost. He wasn't hurt though bus was right on its nose. I think I'm the only one of my lot in the flight who has not got wind up or spun one so far. Letters from Mother, Aunt Bessie, Tony and Grandmother; also from Bunty. Saw a new bus Galbraith was flying called a Sopwith Camel: two synchronised Vickers and 130 Le Clerget. Sopwith Triplane arrived in evening. Am on Scouts next week.

SUNDAY, 1 APRIL

Passed out on BEs! Some flying early in the morning, but a snow storm came on. Stayed in all day.

He occupied his time constructively by writing a letter home:

There were only two of us, a Canadian and I, who weren't more or less frightened of BEs. They more or less fly themselves – if you let them, but they've one or two very nasty tricks, one of which is spinning. Well practically everyone did this but luckily no one was hurt this week, but somehow I found no trouble at all in them, nor did the other chap I mentioned. I think they are by far the nicest bus I've flown yet. On my first BE solo – Tuesday evening, I was up at about 6000 feet at about 6.30 pm when the sun was setting, and really you have no idea what scenery is till you've seen that. The clouds are wonderful to be above and where you see the ground it is just a mixed mass of green and reddish brown – ploughed fields. I'm afraid I have a tendency for my head to swim at over 6000 feet. Several chaps find that.

MONDAY, 2 APRIL
Went down to Scout flight before brekker and got up in a Bullet; delightful bus to fly; very delicate indeed. Made quite a good landing.

The Bristol Baby biplane or Scout or Bullet made its first appearance in February 1914, when it made an immediate impact as a civil racing aircraft, particularly in the hands of Irish peer Josh C Evans Freke, the tenth Lord Carbery. It would have been a very efficient fighter in the early period of the war if suitable armament other than rifles or pistols had been available. By the time suitable machine guns firing through the disk of the airscrew were developed, the nimble Bullet had been superceded by faster and more powerful machines, though Captain Lanoe G Hawker RFC won his VC when flying one on 25 July 1915. The RNAS made extensive use of the type in a variety of roles.

TUESDAY, 3 APRIL
Flew a Bullet again and put on some vertical banks. Instructor very pleased with my flying and told me so. America decided for War by tonight's paper. [As the virtually inevitable consequence of the resumption of unrestricted submarine warfare by Germany on 31 January, the USA declared war on 6 April.] Our troops appear to be closing in on St Quentin.

WEDNESDAY, 4 APRIL
Went up in a 1½ Strutter; was up five minutes and lost myself in a fog bank. Finally came down at RFC drome near

Grantham about 20 miles; had quite a good time. They thought me some nut as they do not fly Scouts. Left Cranwell 9.40 and got perfect landing. Lovely machine. Then went up in a Nieuport but couldn't land him at all. Letter from Barbara to say [her little sister] Mary died on Sunday; she was such a nice kid.

As the Sopwith 1½ Strutter played such a major part in Jack's career in 1918, discussion of this type will be left until later in this account. The Nieuport 12 was a larger and more powerful two-seat development of the excellent and famous Nieuport Scout. It gave useful service with the RNAS but not to the same extent as the comparable 1½ Strutter.

THURSDAY, 5 APRIL

Went up in a Nieuport before breakfast, made two landings and crashed the second one. Wrecked the undercarriage, props and wings. No more flying owing to the wind.

FRIDAY, 6 APRIL

Was up early but did not get flying. After breakfast was up for 18 minutes in a Bullet and had quite a good time. Then a wash out – Good Friday till 5 pm. Went up in a Pup! Had 27 minutes – hairy banks etc. Made a priceless landing and was properly congratulated by Donald – 'Very, very good McCleery!' Swelled head. A Bullet and a Pup both crashed on their noses. Swotted in the morning. Letters from Father, Miss Craig, Uncle John and Alec Thompson. Wrote to the Pilkingtons. Pup is some bus. Lovely to land, full of gadgets and does 80 knots level. Hunter Herriot home on leave.

The Sopwith Pup was a classic little fighter and was used extensively on the Western Front by both the RFC and the RNAS, where it wrested the initiative from the German Air Force during 1916–17. Legend has it that the Pup received its famous nickname from an RFC pilot who declared on first seeing one that the larger 1½ Strutter had borne a pup and he had just flown in it! Despite official discouragement the name stuck. At this stage it will suffice to say that it is not surprising Jack enjoyed his first flight in one, as it has been universally acclaimed as a delightful flying machine, the most pleasant to fly of all the British aeroplanes of the Great War.

SATURDAY, 7 APRIL

Too misty early morning for flying and when it cleared up it was too bumpy for Scouts!! Got up for half an hour in a Pup after tea. Up to 9000 feet in 20 minutes, then spiralled down. Lovely bus. Donald, my instructor, said I made a perfect landing. Got a copy of my report – some report. Lovely sight to see clouds at that height, but head began to go light so came down. No crashes today. Swotting after dinner.

Jack enclosed his report with his letter home, which must have made very encouraging reading for his proud parents:

Has flown exceptionally well in the Flight except for one regrettable accident when he upended a Nieuport. Should make a really good Scout Pilot. Very keen, recommended flying seniority. Percentage proficiency of officer under instruction 88% VG 1.

With the honesty that is a shining feature of his letters and which is also a mark of the close and loving relationship, the *joie de vivre* positively springs off the page as he jumps from one thought to the next. Jack began his letter:

I *have* had a week of it! I've now flown every type of machine on the station, and have only crashed one – on landing. I'm bringing the whole ½ of my Nieuport prop home as a memento. I *may* get home this week; I'll not make any promises so that you'll not be disappointed, if I don't. If I do I'll wire and let you know. I was intending and had made some arrangements for springing myself on you while you were at brekker some morning.

I wasn't hurt in the Nieuport just a little shaken. I went up in another machine that evening and got on A1. I can't tell you about these machines in a letter of course but I can tell you that the 'Pup' is a pretty fast bus. I got up to

9000 feet in 20 minutes last night. I hope I get sent on a battleship as a scout. I've not looped yet at all, I'm sorry to say. It's been the finest week I've ever had in my life.

However amid his own happiness, he still thinks of others:

Mrs P's little daughter Mary, an awfully nice child about seven years old, died suddenly last Sunday of blood poisoning. I wrote a letter of sympathy to Mrs P, but I'm not much of a hand at it, I'm afraid. I'm glad Tom McCleane is getting better now and that your stocktaking is now over. Well I think that's all, so I'll close again hoping you'll soon be all right every way and that I'll see you soon.

SUNDAY, 8 APRIL

No flying today at all. Did not get up till 10 o'clock as I was tired out with flying. Letters from Mother, Bunty, and George.

MONDAY, APRIL 9

No flying for me as the graduation exams commence tomorrow. Had a lecture by 'Bunny' White (Commander) on his subjects till 11 o'clock.

TUESDAY, 10 APRIL

Exams
            Meteorology
            Navigation
            Theory of Flight
            Engines
            Construction
Not too hard, except last two which were a bit stiff.

WEDNESDAY, 11 APRIL

            Armament
            Signals
Had a bit of a headache after the WORK. Will know results tomorrow. Hear I've passed Bunny White's subjects.

THURSDAY, 12 APRIL

Have all packed up for home. Heard at 10 o'clock I've passed and was on for landplanes at Freiston, worse luck. Sent luggage on to Boston and left Sleaford by 11.15. Arrived Liverpool 4.50 and went to Birkenhead. Boat didn't leave till 2 o'clock tomorrow morning. Read in bed till 3 o'clock.

FRIDAY, 13 APRIL

Tony's birthday. Was on deck at about 8 o'clock when we were off the Mull of Galloway; lovely morning. Arrived Belfast 11 o'clock and was met by Mother, Father, T & K and P & K. Drove home in car. Went to see Bunty. Had a good time on the bike; it's ripping to be home again.

SATURDAY, 14 APRIL

Mill in the morning; saw the new hoist etc. etc. Went to Ballynahinch in car after dinner to see Uncle Hamilton and Aunt Amy. Road fearful. Clutch slipped very badly coming back, so fixed it. Had a bath. Went to Whitehouse and saw 'em all.

Bunty, Kathleen and their families lived on the north shore of Belfast Lough only a few miles out of Belfast. Whitehouse was a village centred on the mill workers' modest dwellings and other, more substantial, homes of the well-to-do.

SUNDAY, 15 APRIL

Kenneth's birthday. Did as I used to in the morning and jolly glad to. [Back in the old familiar routine.] Walked up in the morning and down and up after tea. *Beaucoup de* handshakes and welcomes etc.

MONDAY, 16 APRIL

Trotted all round and had tea with Mother in the Carlton. All were photo'd in our uniforms after dinner, so was too bored to do a solo one down town! Went to Aunt Jinnie's and Uncle Willy's after tea. Also to Mr Herriot's. Met Doris Smith in town and she said Jack was very well.

TUESDAY, 17 APRIL

Went to Mackie's in morning and Mill. Went and saw Meta 'years since we spoke!' After dinner the Mill and then to Victoria Hospital to see Tom McCleane. Then Meta and I home again. Aunt Jenny and Uncle Ernest came to say good bye. Drove car down to 3.15 boat from Fleetwood and said good bye once more. I hope it's not for the last time. Had supper on board and went to bed at 10 o'clock. Saw a super-sub in the lough. Fairly rough part of the way across.

WEDNESDAY, 18 APRIL

Caught 6.15 am train to Manchester. Then from another station to Retford with two hours wait and then Lincoln. Saw the cathedral and bought postcards and three souvenirs; then went to pictures and had tea there. Caught 6.15 pm to Boston. Arrived at Freiston at 10 o'clock; rotten hole on a sort of a dried up marsh. Am in a big hut with six or eight others, which is splendidly ventilated all over through the walls. Have to use candles as there is no other sort of light on the station. Was asleep at 12 o'clock.

THURSDAY, 19 APRIL

Machine gun on range in morning, and the graticule sight [with cross hairs for aiming] after dinner. Food quite good here. Rotten drome and machines are nearly all crashed or konked. Some of the *officers* are employed at making a road. If there's no flying during working hours we also have to dig potatoes.

FRIDAY, 20 APRIL

Went up to do Very lights [signal flares fired from a short, large-bore Very pistol] on a Maurice Farman 3 times and had to come down each time for engine trouble – the third time one set of exhaust pipes came adrift. No. 1 [the station's second-in-command] hugely delighted with me on a Maurice, said I made the most perfect landing he ever saw on one. Inoculated after tea and then dug seven rows of spuds! What about Harry Tate's Navy?! [Harry Tate was a popular music hall comedian of the period, in contemporary slang it meant amateurish or incompetent – in the

fashion of Fred Karno's Army.] Wrote to George and home.
A bit stiff.

SATURDAY, 21 APRIL

Feeling rotten after being stuck [inoculated] so had to
spend the day in bed. Lots of flying and some day worse
luck. I'm going to apply to fly Pups off the decks of battleships. I'd like to collar a Zepp!

MONDAY, 23 APRIL

Was sent up in an old Maurice again to test it for some other
chaps. Then did Very lights in a BE after dinner, but it was
bumpy. Had another shot at it later but put my hands in my
pockets and merely enjoyed myself. Then a new Avro
arrived and I had a test trip in it. Lovely bus indeed;
practised firing or rather aiming at the target.

THURSDAY, 26 APRIL

Did some more firing in the air. After my first two shots I
managed to hit the target – with my left wing! As I was only
800 feet up I might have had a really bad crash. Also struck
the balloon wire. Kicked about with a rugger ball and am
very stiff. Got my first letter since I came here – from
Mother, all are well.

FRIDAY, 27 APRIL

No flying as there was a gale blowing most of the day. Did
firing on the range etc. etc.

SUNDAY, 29 APRIL

Looks like I'm not going to France but to the Grand Fleet to
fly Pups off a battleship. I'll probably have to learn
seaplanes before I go to the North Sea. If not I'd have been
sent to Eastchurch to be an instructor.

MONDAY, 30 APRIL

Got word to go back to Cranwell to fly Pups. Did 1½ hrs in
them in the evening; got on quite well. One of our chaps is
on notice for Italy – lucky dog! Was with George most of
the afternoon.

TUESDAY, 1 MAY
More Pup flying. A F/S-L called Grundy killed himself on a BE today. [Temporary Probationary Flight Officer HE Grundy died of his injuries following the crash of the Bristol Scout D N5419.] Spent afternoon with George. Put in some good time again. White hat covers from today until Sept 1st.

WEDNESDAY, 2 MAY
Up early flying. Got on OK. Did several quick releases [of bombs].

THURSDAY, 3 MAY
Did a cross-country on my own in Pup this morning. In everyday togs and a helmet, no gloves or goggles. Fine and warm. Lincoln and Grantham and back. Buzzed around Cathedral, which looks very well from above. Saw several army machines up and two big dromes there. Engine began to konk out as I got back. Then back to Freiston. Dropped low bombs and made nearly a possible. Wretched old BE I was in would not turn to the right.

FRIDAY, 4 MAY
Dropped explosive bombs this morning before brekker – 16 lb ones. Exhaust pipes came adrift with me. Then buzzed back to Cranwell. Leave till Monday pm when I'm to go to Calshot. Arrived S Woodford about 7 o'clock. Mrs Herriot there and Hunter turned up. Some day.

SATURDAY, 5 MAY
Saw Hunter. Gorgeous day.

As ever, Jack made sure that his parents were kept fully informed:

I've had some week of it, moving about from one place to another. Last Monday I went back to Cranwell for special scout flying, Thursday went back to Freiston, Friday back to Cranwell. Then I was given leave till Monday when I am to go to Calshot unless I get a telegram to the contrary. I was four days with George. He's changed a good deal and is most awfully quiet. Why I don't know. We had several walks together. He is solo on Avros now and seems to get on very well on them. He's very careful in the air, far more so than on the bike, I'm glad to say.

It is obvious that Jack was worried about the state of mind of his best friend. It must have been difficult for George, who it would seem was finding it not so easy to become a pilot, in contrast with Jack who was a star pupil. Jack continued:

I've had 8½ hours in Scouts in three days – which isn't too dusty. I came down in the train yesterday with a boy who flew a bus in the Freiberg stunt. He didn't like doing it, he said and you needn't trust too much in what the papers report.

On 14 April, Sopwith 1½ Strutter bombers and fighters of No. 3 Wing RNAS had carried out a bombing raid on Freiberg in Germany. Two tons of bombs were dropped and also leaflets which claimed that the two raids carried out that day were reprisals for the torpedoing of the British hospital ship *Asturias* by a German U-boat. This caused a certain amount of discussion in the press and Parliament. According to Jack's photograph album Handley Page O/100 heavy bombers also took part in the raid, so his companion on the train may have given these to him along with first-hand information about the sorties.

CHAPTER FIVE

Calshot and the Isle of Grain

RNAS Calshot, which was originally established on 29 March 1913 by the Royal Flying Corps, was located at the end of Calshot Spit and operated mainly as an experimental and training station for seaplanes and flying-boats. After the start of the war, the station's role expanded to take on the protection of shipping in the English Channel with anti-submarine and convoy protection patrols. Its landing area was sheltered by the mainland, to the west, north and east, and the Isle of Wight a few miles away to the south on the other side of the Solent.

MONDAY, 7 MAY
Left S Woodford by 12.10 train and arrived Calshot 8 o'clock! Lovely spot and quite good quarters – AND grub. Had a good sleep. Seems to be a fine place. Lovely weather. Our place is really Warsash, where we live in former Coastguard cottages and we cross to Calshot by tender.

TUESDAY, 8 MAY
Crossed to Calshot in 9 o'clock boat – a motor launch. Got up in 160 hp Short and did about two hours after about five minutes' dual. Awfully soggy, but nice to taxi and land. Got on OK. No banks. Wrote home. Lovely day.

This is further evidence that Jack was a naturally gifted pilot, taking control of a large and cumbersome seaplane after only five minutes. Taking off required a different technique from landplanes in that it was necessary to hydroplane or skim along the surface of the water before it was possible to get 'unstuck'. Depending upon the strength of the wind, the state of the water, the power of the seaplane's engine and the weight carried, 'unsticking' could take quite a while. He wrote home that evening and referred to his new 'bus' in less than effusive terms:

> Seaplanes are like flying traction engines – awful!

WEDNESDAY, 9 MAY
> Misty day till about 11.30. Did about 35 minutes in 160 hp Short. Wrote to George. Americas are some buses. [Curtiss H.8 and H.12 'Large America' flying-boats had a crew of four, an endurance of six hours, could carry up to 460 lbs of bombs and four machine guns.] Lovely evening.

THURSDAY, 10 MAY
> First flight in Baby Sopwith; mono engine. Enjoyed it very much as there is very little between it and a Pup, except wheel control. Hairy banks.

The Sopwith Baby single-seat scouting and bombing seaplane was a development of the Sopwith Schneider, with a more powerful engine and a synchronised Lewis gun installed above the fuselage. In RNAS service Babies flew from a dozen or more bases around the coast of Britain and aboard seaplane-carriers operating in the North Sea and the Mediterranean, undertaking bombing missions in the Aegean, Italy, Egypt and Palestine, as well as flying fighter patrols from Dunkirk. Operational needs often required the diminutive Baby to carry two 65-lb bombs, the Lewis gun (or even two thereof) and ammunition, a carrier pigeon, drinking water and a sea anchor – the concern caused to pilots by this dangerous overloading was alleviated by the introduction of a more powerful 130 hp Clerget engine. Most pilots found the Schneider to be a pleasant and lively aeroplane but the Baby was a joy to fly.

FRIDAY, 11 MAY

More time on Baby – 55 minutes. Got on OK. Up to about 4000 feet. Lovely day – no bumps and very clear. I could see for miles. I like being over the sea very much. Letter from Mother. They had a fire at home the other day and had to call out the Fire Brigade.

SATURDAY, 12 MAY

Didn't get up as the weather was too bad till after lunch and then Jackson [F/S-L WD Jackson] crashed the machine. Heard poor old Penny has been killed; poor chap. We had been with each other up to Freiston. [Probationary Flight Officer DE Penny was killed in the crash of the Avro 504E, 9283, on 9 May 1917 at Chingford.] Great flashes in the sky tonight. Letter from Mother and a letter and photo from Meta.

SUNDAY, 13 MAY

Gorgeous day after about 10.00 am; very misty before. Letter and three films from Father; all are well at home. I'd no flying, today (none indeed until Saturday next).

THURSDAY, 17 MAY

PFO Simms killed at Freiston, same as Penny. Choked mono Avro and stalled.

SATURDAY, 19 MAY

Visit by DAD. [Rear-Admiral Charles Vaughan-Lee, Director of the Admiralty Air Department] Was up for first flight in FBA. [The FBA Type B was a small, two-seat flying-boat, some 116 of which were used by the RNAS for training purposes only.] Went with instructor and put the wind up some people on the beach at Lee-on-Solent by zooming at them. Rotten buses but very amusing, as you never quite know where you will be two minutes later. Put in three hours today. Letters from Father and Mother.

Sunday, 20 May

Lecture at Warsash on battleships by No. 1. No flying owing to mist; up at 4.45 pm – wash out. Letters from George and Barbara.

Jack's letter home dwelt at some length on the recent fatal crash:

George is flying BEs and seems to like them very much. Penny was at Chingford and was going to fly a machine up to Freiston. Hunter [Herriot] was just going up with him for a joy flip, when he had to go and censor a mail, and so did not get in, luckily for him, though he would most likely have escaped, as the passenger seat was the back one in this bus. Penny must have been very unfortunate as George says his [crash] was a much worse one and he got out all right.

Jack added some comments on his first experience of flying-boats:

I've been flying FBAs or 'boats' this week, that's to say yesterday. They really are a very ugly and peculiar sort of boat, with wings attached. They're very funny in the air, as it's quite as good as gymnasium to fly one and they are decidedly eccentric in their movements. To get them down *nose* first you have to practically nose dive them! They'll come down tail first if you let them, but it's advisable not! I did three hours on them yesterday and was jolly stiff after it.

And he had a serious question to ask:

By the way, please don't laugh too hard, but who am I insured with, is it the Ocean and what was the date of joining it? Also will they cover air risks?

He concluded with some more war news, which underlined the pride he felt in being part of the Naval Air Service:

It appears that out of 40 enemy machines brought down during the week before last in France, 29 were strafed by the RNAS! That's not so bad.

The fighter squadrons of the RNAS had indeed been putting up a great show. The first Sopwith Triplanes to see active service were those of No. 10 Squadron 'Naval Ten' towards the end of 1916. To begin with they flew Channel patrols but following the heavy losses suffered by the RFC during 'Bloody April' in 1917, they joined the fight on the Western Front. B Flight, commanded by Flight Commander Raymond Collishaw, had at its core five redoubtable Canadians, including Collishaw himself. The flight's Triplanes were specially painted – the engine cowling, wheel disk covers and forward fuselage decking were black with the individual aircraft names in white lettering – *Black Maria* (Collishaw), *Black Death* (F/S-L JE Sharman), *Black Sheep* (F/S-L GE Nash), *Black Roger* (F/S-L EV Reid) and *Black Prince* (F/S-L WM Alexander). During June and July the highly aerobatic and fast climbing Triplanes of three RNAS squadrons (1, 8 and 10) took on the hitherto triumphant Albatros D-III *Jastas*, gave the Germans a dose of their own medicine and provided a much-needed boost to British morale. Black Flight alone claimed no fewer than eighty-seven of the enemy destroyed or forced down for the loss only of Nash in *Black Sheep*. Collishaw eventually became the top-scoring RNAS ace of the war with sixty victories.

MONDAY, 21 MAY

> Doubtful weather in early morning. Letter from Meta. Got up in a Baby this morning. Nearly did myself in, when taking off, as I got in the wash of a ship. Great thunderstorm tonight; lightning simply wonderful.

Jack described this in more detail in a letter to his father wishing him a happy birthday:

> I and my cabin mate or vice versa sat at the window for long enough watching the lightning. Simply enormous flashes, lighting up the ground all round most vividly. As I write tonight I see a most peculiar thing on the Solent. There's a bit of mist on, but in one spot the water is quite lit up red, presumably from the sunset, though you can't see the sun or any rays from it through the haze. It looks just as

if an enormous red lamp was under the water!

TUESDAY, 22 MAY

Didn't get up as it was a hopeless sort of day. Wrote to Father before going to bed.

WEDNESDAY, 23 MAY

Father's birthday. Misty morning, but it got better. Went up in a Baby for 1½ hours. Did a few stalls – mild variety. Got up to 6000 feet but couldn't climb any further. Then made a topping spiral down to 1500 feet. Anti-aircraft bursting quite close to me: unpleasant. One shell just missed the quarters at Calshot; one man luckily ducked his head in time or he'd have been strafed by the fuse. Wet night. Watched RFC man doing spins, loops etc in 110 hp Bristol monoplane.

THURSDAY, 24 MAY

Rotten day, so did no flying. Came over to Warsash. Lecture from Number One. Then slept on grass most of afternoon. Saw a big two-engined Avro. [Possibly an Avro 523 Pike, though he did take a photograph at Calshot of the only AD Admiralty 1000 twin-engine seaplane, so it may have been this one instead.]

FRIDAY, 25 MAY

Did 1¾ hrs this morning in a Baby. Chased round clouds and had a splendid time. Did several spirals and stalls. Went up again after lunch for 50 minutes. Engine missing [misfiring] so came down. Very bumpy at any rate.

SATURDAY, 26 MAY

No flying owing to dud weather. Lectures as usual. Letters from home. Very big air raid on Dover last night by aeroplanes: 76 killed and 146 injured in first account. Three were strafed by RNAS pilots at Dunkerque.

On 25 May 1917, twenty-three Gotha G.IV heavy bombers set out for a daylight raid on London, but two were forced to turn back over the North Sea owing to mechanical difficulties. Poor weather forced the remaining bombers to divert to secondary targets at the Channel port of Folkestone and the nearby Army camp at Shorncliffe. The raid resulted in ninety-five deaths and 195 injuries, mostly in the Folkestone area. In Shorncliffe, eighteen soldiers – sixteen Canadian and two British – were killed; ninety were wounded. Nine RNAS Sopwith Pups engaged the returning bombers near the Belgian coast, shooting one down.

SUNDAY, 27 MAY
  No flying. Wrote home and to George. Rained mostly.

Jack's comments on the Gotha raid were interesting and showed an independence of mind:

> That was a fine raid on Dover, and evidently got everyone asleep, though what's puzzling us all here is why do the papers talk about 'Murder in the Air' etc. Dover's a naval base as everyone knows. *And* the RNAS it was, who accounted for three of them, so it wasn't one sided in the end.

Presumably Mr and Mrs McCleery were getting used by this time to the hair-raising nature of some of Jack's flying tales. I would suspect, however, that the following breezy paragraph, which starts innocuously enough, raised a few eyebrows at the breakfast table.

> I had a most gorgeous trip on Friday in a 'Baby' Sopwith. There were a lot of clouds about, so I went up and tore around them and over and in between them. It was ripping. I was up for 1¾ hours and enjoyed myself immensely. I tried to put on my safety belt [doing it on the water before take-off would have been a better idea] when in among the clouds – about 3000 feet up; to see if I could do it. I had to keep her level by pressing the wheel forward with my head. Well when I did look up again I saw the earth nearly right over me! I'd put on a vertical bank without knowing. It's very amusing, not to look out or at your instruments for about a minute, and then to look over and see where the

earth is! It's hardly ever below you in its proper place. The clouds looked quite pretty from above. I got up to 6000 feet in the same machine a few days before and she wouldn't go any higher, no matter how I tried pushing her nose down a bit and then giving it a big pull back; the fabric was a bit old and what we call 'soggy'. When she was new she did 13,500 feet one day.

While Jack's confidence and developing skills are to be praised, it would not be at all surprising if a parental caution came back by return of post, reminding him that 'Pride goeth before a fall'. Moreover, if Jack had shared his cheery memories of this experience with one of the instructors at Calshot, he might well have been given a word or two of timely caution and advised that, as is well known to airmen: *There are old pilots and bold pilots but there are no old, bold pilots.*

Be that as it may he was certainly doing something right, as he was selected for further training at the Isle of Grain and his promotion to flight sub-lieutenant was granted with six weeks' backdated seniority to 3 March. At Grain, according to the biographer of one of the pilots detailed to go there:

> A brilliant and popular pilot, Flight Commander EH Dunning DSC, would gather around him a group of pilots who were, wrote Squadron Commander FJ Rutland,
> 'Certainly second to none in the RNAS. They exercised at Grain in both seaplanes and Sopwith Pups and when *Furious* commissioned in June 1917 with these superb pilots, the effect was exhilarating. They raised the standard of flying to that obtained on the Western Front.'

Another contemporary later wrote:

> Grain always seemed to be home-from-home for the 'bloods' of the naval flying community and besides one met there the pilots who were to become the star-turns of the future.

Jack was a junior member but he was undoubtedly picked to be part of an elite group.

TUESDAY, 29 MAY

Passing out today. After a lot of bother, got 4.30 train from Swanwick. Caught 8.45 from Euston to Kingstown and got boat at 2.30.

WEDNESDAY, 30 MAY

Arrived Belfast about 10 o'clock. Went to Mill and surprised Father as he didn't know I was crossing. Then took bike to Stewarts and then up home and surprised Mother. Saw Meta in afternoon. Also Mrs Herriot. Dunmurry after tea.

THURSDAY, 31 MAY

Got wire approving leave till Sunday pm. Wired for extension till Tuesday pm. Saw Meta. Went to Whitehouse.

FRIDAY, 1 JUNE

Leave extension granted! Went to pictures to see 'Sons of the Empire' (RNAS etc), went with Mother, Father, Mrs H and George who arrived this morning. I'd gone to meet him in the car, but missed him. Saw Meta again.

SATURDAY, 2 JUNE

Down town most of the morning, then went up and saw Meta. Also got prints of photos from Calshot etc. Drive in car after tea; went to Whitehouse and lost an eagle! [Presumably one of his uniform buttons given as a keepsake.]

SUNDAY, 3 JUNE

Chose the hymns! Some jolly good ones, too.

MONDAY, 4 JUNE

Said good bye at the Mill in morning. Had my photo taken at Hallidays. Came home with Aunt Jenny. Took Meta to Picture House after dinner. Ripping orchestra. Crossed by Fleetwood 8.15. Had a decent sleep.

TUESDAY, 5 JUNE

Travelled all day except 2½ hours in London I spent at Strand cinema. Good journey, masses of red hawthorn. Arrived at Grain 8 o'clock. Quartered at Yacht Club on a landing with Jackson. Very comfortable. This is a fine place, bigger than I thought! Just missed being in a big air raid over this place by 1 hour. [This was the second Gotha bombing raid on Sheerness.]

The Isle of Grain is in north Kent, at the eastern end of the Hoo peninsula opposite Sheerness. In March 1912 a seaplane base was established there, chiefly for experimental purposes. It was the second naval air station to be created. From the beginning the war regular patrols were made along the Thames estuary from Grain, as part of English Channel defences, a Nore War Flight being established in April 1916. In 1914 Port Victoria, adjacent to the station, became a Royal Navy aircraft repair depot and subsequently was the home of the Experimental Constructive Department. About a dozen pilots destined for *Furious* had been assembled under the command of Squadron Commander Dunning, though as he was away in Newcastle very often on work associated with fitting out the ship, much of the day to day activity was coordinated by his deputy, Flight Commander WG Moore.

WEDNESDAY, 6 JUNE

Too windy for flying. Saw round the place. Very big place, mostly experimental. Saw the 'Kitten', a very tiny bus.

To meet a requirement for a lightweight, single-seat airship interceptor suitable for operation from platforms on relatively small ships, the depot at Port Victoria produced the PV 7, Serial N540, to the design of WH Sayers, which became known as the Grain Kitten to distinguish it from a competing design of the RNAS Experimental Flight at Eastchurch (which accordingly became known as the Eastchurch Kitten). The PV 7 was an extremely small sesquiplane (where one wing set, usually the lower, is much smaller than the other) powered by a 35 hp ABC Gnat two-cylinder engine. Armament consisted of a single machine gun mounted above the wing centre section.

Difficulties were experienced with the engine from the start of flight testing in June 1917, the aircraft being tail-heavy and its performance disappointing. A series of modifications was introduced, but the PV 7 was not flown again.

THURSDAY, 7 JUNE

Left at 1.30 in a 150 Short [Short 827 seaplane with 150 hp Sunbeam Nubian engine] to take it to Calshot; very bumpy round N. Foreland. Arrived at Dover. Landed outside as I couldn't find the hangars and taxied in behind a launch. Filled up with petrol and oil, but found engine wouldn't open up. So had to spend night in Dover. Tea at Strand Hotel and then King's Hall picture house. Very good pictures indeed. Wrote home and to Meta when I got back. Bed at 10 o'clock. Peace.

A letter on the notepaper of The Grand Hotel, Dover, was soon on its way to Ava House on the Old Cavehill Road in Belfast in which Jack informed his parents that he passed the time there watching the latest Charlie Chaplin film.

I don't usually like him, but oh, *he was funny*. The scenes were in a café and then at a skating rink, so you can guess what it was like. Also a splendid one called Miss Adventure which had everyone in fits.

FRIDAY, 8 JUNE

Got up at 8 o'clock and had brekker. Then went round to hangars. Got carburettor etc overhauled and cleared off about 10.30. Saw 2 Blimps and an SS. [RNAS coastal patrol airships; there would have been two bases on Jack's route at Capel, near Folkstone and a little further along, Polegate in Sussex.] Saw ship that had evidently just been torpedoed, thought I saw wash of submarine but had no signals on board, so wash out. Glorious trip round coast, Beachy Head, Brighton etc. Saw British submarine near Isle of Wight, running awash. Arrived Calshot 12.45. Saw George & spent afternoon with him. Car to Swanwick for 6.10 train. Dining saloon. Arrived London 10 o'clock pm and went to Ivanhoe Hotel in Bloomsbury St.

SATURDAY, 9 JUNE

Woke up at 10 minutes to 10! Then went to Gieves and cashed cheque £28. Left luggage at Cannon St and went to Mrs P—s. Met Mr P— for the first time. Caught the 5.30 train back and arrived Grain at 7.10 pm. Seems years since I was at home, but it's not a week. Lovely day.

SUNDAY, 10 JUNE

Lovely day. Had to take up Short with passenger; couldn't get off. Managed it after dinner. Then Schneider – lovely bus [very like the Baby] and finally Pup. Stalled latter and started to spin! Some sensation. Wrote home [requesting] 'a pocket case for letters, stamps etc like Uncle H gave me some years ago, as it was going to pieces down the sides'. Keeping very well. Letters from home. Frank Barnie RFC missing; poor chap. Hope he's alive.

Jack made no diary entries for this week but fortunately his letter home fills in the gap:

I was up after those Huns the other day. [On June 13, the third raid by Gothas was the first daylight raid on London, causing 162 deaths and 432 injuries. Among the dead were forty-six children killed by single bomb falling on an infant school in Poplar. This was the deadliest air raid of the war, but no Gothas were lost.] I was trying to get near them but only saw one and I wasn't sure of it as it was about 17,000 feet up and I was in a seaplane which wouldn't go over 10,000 – 11,000, so it was a wash out as far as I was concerned. It was a priceless day up but as I was up for nearly two hours at that height, with just ordinary, everyday wear – no helmet, gloves or muffler, I began to feel chilly a bit. Finally my engine konked, no petrol, and I came down about a mile out, and had to be towed in! The RNAS were up in force that day! It was some raid, I'd tell you more only I can't!

At the back of the diary Jack lists the aircraft in which he flew during 1917, one of these was the Short Bomber, 'Old Man

Shorts', which he noted had a 250 hp Rolls-Royce engine and a wingspan of 85 feet. In this letter he goes on to write:

> I was over old Eastchurch twice the other day in a *very* big land machine. It was as bad as physical drill flying her, as it was awfully hot and the bumps were simply weird – and sickening my passenger thought! Also my goggles blew off and are now 'somewhere in Sheppey!' It's too hot to wear a helmet or muffler nowadays for ordinary flying, so we go up bareheaded. It saves an enormous amount of Brilliantine! I've taken up several chaps – mechanics, lately who haven't been up before and they seemed to like it very much. One of them today was quite excited when I got into a few mild bumps and so as there were very few real ones about, I manufactured one or two for him which seemed to impress him very much. I'm keeping very well; castor oil [the engine lubricant] seems to agree very well with me, though *not* my clothes! The mosquitoes here are awful. They keep you awake all night strafing them till about 6.30 am, when they more or less – chiefly less, ease off. They're simply humming in the room now.

FRIDAY, 15 JUNE
Did no flying as there were no machines for me. Had about five air raids after dinner but saw no Huns. Hooters going all the time. Most amusing not being able to go up in anything at all.

SATURDAY, 16 JUNE
Nice day but hazy. Did some stalls, and I came out sideways twice on purpose. Tried to spin 6 times; only managed twice for about two runs each. I couldn't hold her into them. Letters from home and Kathleen.

SUNDAY, 17 JUNE
Nothing special today. Lovely day and was up in 150 hp Short. Wrote home.

MONDAY, 18 JUNE

Duty Officer. Not much to do. Wrote to George and Meta. Had a couple of flips in Baby Sopwith 3804, which is a ripping machine. [A modified Schneider with an enlarged fin, with ailerons replacing wing warping controls, and a new tail and float.] 100 hp Gnome Monosoupape doing 1200! [engine revolutions?] This level at 85 kts!

TUESDAY, 19 JUNE

Returning Officer. Had to march men up at 5.30, and the rain and lightning was awful. Got soaked and no way of changing or drying till 8.30. Up in Baby 3804 again and quirked around Southend in it and also in a Short with passenger. Letter from Meta.

WEDNESDAY, 20 JUNE

Nice day. Put in a lot of time on Short taking up three passengers. Had ripping time over Southend zooming at yachts etc. Also ditto in Baby, in which I put in a lot of time. Our ship to sail on 1st July. Poor chance of even rotten leave. Letters and ripping pocket book from home. Also proofs of photos; not bad. Very windy tonight; have mosquito net rigged up on my bed. Good show of pictures in C shed tonight.

Jack was delighted with his new pocket book and wrote in his letter:

Just a *very* hurried line to thank you very much for the absolutely priceless pocket book you sent me. It's really a lovely one with tons of room for everything. Also I expect to be home next week, *probably* on Tuesday morning. Ship sails on 1st which is Sunday. I just missed crossing tonight worse luck.

However, there must also have been a word of admonition from his mother in her letter, which presumably referred to the visit to the cinema with Meta on 4 June, as Jack added:

Mother needn't worry about me in regard to her letter. I've only done it once and have no intention of making a hobby of taking girls to picture houses.

SUNDAY, 24 JUNE
   Was Duty Officer today. Nothing to do. Had two flights.

Jack left Grain with a report from Wing Commander ET Briggs
which stated that Jack had conducted himself to his entire satisfaction and was a keen and capable officer and seaplane pilot.
Briggs was a pre-war naval pilot who had also seen service in
France and Belgium in 1914.

MONDAY, 25 JUNE
   Peggy's birthday. Crossed home by Dublin.

FRIDAY, 29 JUNE
   Crossed back by Larne. Arrived 12.45 and stayed night at
   Carlisle in the County and Station Hotel.

CHAPTER SIX

The Development of Naval Aviation before HMS *Furious*

Before rejoining Jack as he embarks on HMS *Furious* for the first time, it would be worthwhile to examine how the Royal Navy had arrived at this point of sending to sea the first aircraft carrier capable of operating efficiently with the battle fleet. *Furious* has been regarded as a revolutionary ship in the annals of naval aviation but it is really more accurate to regard her genesis as part of an evolutionary process based on the empirical knowledge gained over the previous eight years.

The first official mention of aviation in the Royal Navy goes as far back as July 1908, when it was proposed that the new post of Naval Air Assistant should be established at the Admiralty. This was despite a very brusque dismissal given to the Wright brothers the previous year, 'Their Lordships are of the opinion that aeroplanes would not be of any practical use to the Naval Service.' Initial thoughts chiefly concerned lighter-than-air craft. In August 1908 a letter from the Admiralty invited Messrs Vickers, Son & Maxim of Barrow (which as part of BAE Systems is still to this day a major firm for UK government armament work) to tender for a rigid airship comparable to or better than current German airships. The original idea was for a long-range scouting and gunnery direction platform to assist the main battle fleet, equipped with wireless telegraphy (WT) – which was as much in its infancy as aviation. In February 1909 the Committee of Imperial Defence recommended that £35,000 should be spent on a rigid airship project for the Royal Navy. A construction shed was built at Cavendish Dock, Barrow-in-Furness, and it was agreed that the design would be by a consortium of naval officers and Vickers engineers. There was little technical knowledge available; therefore construction was very much on trial and error lines. It was a highly ambitious project, with a length of 512 feet and a beam of 48 feet; it was as large as any of the Zeppelins constructed so far, of which LZ3 and LZ4 had made a very successful series of flights in late 1908. Despite Louis Blériot's remarkable feat in the early hours of 25 June 1909, when he completed his crossing of the English Channel in his monoplane in a time of thirty-seven minutes, contemporary, heavier-than-air aeroplanes were frail and unreliable mechanically. The airship offered much greater range, endurance and carrying capacity in respect of crew, weapons, fuel and the wireless telegraphy set.

The framework of His Majesty's Airship No. 1 was to be fabricated from an entirely new and untried alloy, duralumin. Captain Murray Sueter was appointed Inspecting Captain of Airships to oversee the design and production of the airship and so assembled a team of technically minded and promising officers.

On 22 May 1911 Naval Airship No. 1 (familiarly known as the *Mayfly*) was taken from its shed, for handling and mooring trials. It was moored to a 38 feet mast erected on a pontoon in Cavendish Dock. This was the first time a rigid airship had ever been made fast to a mast. The trials were successful in that the airship withstood winds of up to 45 mph. Moreover, engine tests were conducted, and a considerable amount of handling experience and data was collected by the nine officers on board. But it soon became clear that she was overweight and incapable of static flight. Gross lift was estimated to be 19.665 long tons (44,048 lbs), with the weight being 19.589 tons (43,876 lbs), not including fuel or crew. The resulting disposable lift of 0.076 tons (170.24 lbs) was utterly negligible. The options were to insert another bay and increase the lifting capability or to lighten ship. The latter was chosen, and the external keel and many other

items were removed – including the anchor! The disposable lift
was thereby increased to 3.21 tons (7190 lbs), which would be
enough for trial flights and training.

On 24 September 1911 she was taken out of the giant shed
again, tail first. Just as the nose was clearing the hangar doors, a
strong gust of wind caught the massive airship and rolled *Mayfly*
virtually on her beam-ends. Shortly after righting herself, the
hull of the airship abruptly tore apart forward of the rear car.
Her back was broken – overstressed without the stiffening and
support of the keel. No. 1 was a wreck, and became the subject
of much negative publicity about being a waste of taxpayers'
money. Fortunately there were no fatalities; most of the crew
had managed to dive overboard as the airship reared and
plunged. The report of the Court of Inquiry into the accident no
longer exists. The First Lord of the Admiralty, Winston
Churchill, censored publication at the time and all known copies
have been lost or destroyed, so the precise findings are never
likely to be known. The great airship frame was broken up, the
Admiralty lost interest in rigids for the time being and in
January 1912 the Airships Section was disbanded. No. 1 was
certainly not a success but the story is not one of total failure as
valuable knowledge had been gained.

It was not until 1918 that a rigid airship with a Royal Naval
crew, the R.26, would carry out any effective patrols. In contrast
to this almost total lack of success, some 200 smaller, non-rigid
SS, SSZ, Coastal and North Sea class 'blimps' undertook very
valuable and unsung anti-submarine and convoy escort duties
from RNAS stations around the coasts of Great Britain and
Ireland throughout the war. Experiments were made but these
non-rigid craft were not suitable for operations far out to sea
with the Fleet.

If aircraft were going to support the Grand Fleet's battleships,
battle cruisers, cruisers and torpedo boat destroyers then they
would have to be taken to sea by ships. The initial steps in the
process of trialling heavier-than-air machines on board ship
were taken in 1912, when on 10 January, the first take-off from
the deck of a British warship took place. This was accomplished
by Lieutenant Charles Rumney Samson flying the Short S.38 T2,
fitted with floatation bags to its undercarriage. He flew from an
improvised platform, the construction of which he had designed

and supervised at Chatham, on the forecastle of HMS *Africa*, then anchored in the Medway off Sheerness, landing safely at Eastchurch. A few months later, on 2 May, came the first take-off from a ship under way, again by Samson, with the Short S.38 T2, which had been refitted with a 70 hp engine. The ship was HMS *Hibernia* and the location Weymouth Bay. Samson landed some six miles away near the coast at Lodmore. The next day he took off from the water in Portland Harbour in the Short S.41 H1 and 'flew round the Fleet in harbour, 3 miles in 4 minutes. First time I have been off water and landed on water.' Both *Africa* and *Hibernia* were *King Edward* Class battleships.

Further organisational progress was made on 13 May 1912 with the formation of the Royal Flying Corps, which consisted of separate Naval and Military Wings. The Naval Wing was commanded by Samson. In the words of the Military Wing's CO, Lieutenant Colonel Frederick Sykes, 'Very early a rift appeared between the Naval and Military wing, which gradually widened until two rival bodies emerged, competing against each other for men and material.' In September 1912 the Admiralty set up an Air Department to administer the Naval Wing; by the end of that year it comprised sixteen aircraft of which three were 'hydro-aeroplanes'. The term seaplane was not introduced until the following year – a word which was apparently coined by Winston Churchill. Progress was swift: by 1913 experiments in bomb dropping, spotting submarines, night flying and wireless telegraphy took place; an aircraft with wings which could be folded for easier stowage on board ship was developed (the Short Folder); naval air stations were established at the Isle of Grain, Calshot, Cromarty, Felixstowe and Great Yarmouth; and naval aircraft took part in fleet manoeuvres. On 28 July 1913 the Caudron G.II biplane amphibian, serial No. 55, was flown off the temporarily converted cruiser, HMS *Hermes*, by Flight Lieutenant FW Bowhill, the first naval aeroplane to fly from a ship specifically equipped to operate them. *Hermes* had been fitted with a forecastle ramp, as well as canvas hangars fore and aft. The Naval Airships Branch was reformed and, in October 1913, airships became the sole responsibility of Naval Wing. *Hermes* became the parent ship of the Aeroplane and Airship Section of the Naval Wing.

At the beginning of 1914 there were over 100 trained naval

pilots. In July 1914 the Naval Wing was renamed the Royal Naval Air Service. The first Director of the Air Department of the Admiralty was Captain Murray Sueter CB. This was shortly before the Royal Fleet Review at Spithead which was held from 18 to 22 July 1914. Seventeen fixed-wing seaplanes (Shorts, Farmans and Sopwiths) from Grain Island, Dundee, Yarmouth, Felixstowe and Calshot, twelve fixed-wing, land-based aircraft (BEs, Bristols, Sopwiths and Avros) from Eastchurch and four airships from Kingsnorth and Farnborough also participated. Further technical innovations were made. Only a few days later on 28 July, Lieutenant Arthur Longmore made the first successful torpedo drop from the air flying the Short Type 81 Folder seaplane, No. 121, at Calshot. Moreover, firing trials were carried out by Lieutenant RH Clark Hall with a 1½-pounder gun mounted in the nose of a Short Gun-Carrying Seaplane, No. 126.

At the outbreak of war in August 1914 the RNAS consisted of 130 officers and some 700 petty officers and ratings. Its aircraft strength was a total of seventy-eight, of which forty were land-planes, thirty-one seaplanes and seven were airships – not all of which were fit for any type of operational duties.

Hermes' ramp had been removed before she was sunk by a torpedo fired by *U-27* in the Straits of Dover on 31 October 1914 when transporting two Short Folders to France. Steps were taken to convert a number of vessels for service as seaplane carriers from a variety of merchant ships; these are listed at Appendix 2. There were three main problems in using any of these vessels. Firstly, none of the assorted ships had a sufficient turn of speed to keep up with the Fleet; secondly the seaplanes had to be hoisted out for take-off from the sea and hoisted on board again after landing, for which the ship had to stop, thus taking it further away from the protection of the Fleet; thirdly seaplanes could only operate in fairly benign sea states.

There were some successful operations. Even before the arrival of sea-going platforms, however slow and cumbersome, the RNAS carried the fight to the enemy by air raids from land bases in Belgium and France – the first strategic bombing missions. On 22 September, a motley collection of four aircraft from Wing Commander Charles Samson's force at Dunkirk, flown by two Royal Marines, Major Eugene Gerrard RMLI and

Lieutenant Charles Collet RMA and two RNAS officers, Squadron Commander DA Spenser Grey and Flight Lieutenant Reginald Marix, set off to attack the Zeppelin sheds at Düsseldorf and Cologne. Collet in the Sopwith three-seater, No. 906, was the most successful, actually seeing a shed and dropping a couple of 20-lb Hales bombs in its general vicinity. A few weeks later, on 7 October, Spenser Grey and Marix tried again, flying a pair of Sopwith SS1 Tabloids. Grey in No. 167 set off for Cologne, while Marix in No. 168 attacked Düsseldorf. Grey was unable to find the shed and dropped his bombs on the railway station instead but Marix made no mistake and succeeded in destroying the Zeppelin LZ25. Collet, Grey and Marix were all awarded the DSO.

A more ambitious scheme was then planned, with four Avro 504s being shipped under a cloak of secrecy to Belfort in France, near the border with both Germany and Switzerland, followed closely by the pilots. The top-secret target was the Zeppelin construction sheds at Friedrichshafen on Lake Constance. Three of the Avros, serials 873–75, flown by Flight Commander John Babington, Squadron Commander Edward Featherstone Briggs and Flight Lieutenant Sidney Sippe, respectively, carried out the daring long-range (250 miles there and back) raid on 21 November. Remarkably, it was the maiden flight for each aeroplane and none of the pilots had ever before dropped a bomb. Little damage was caused but a concept had been tried and shown to be possible. DSOs were again awarded all round, though Briggs had to wait for his, as he had been made a prisoner of war, having been forced down at Friedrichshafen.

Then on Christmas Day 1914 the seaplane carriers, and former cross-Channel steamers, *Empress*, *Engadine* and *Riviera*, supported by the Harwich Force, a group of cruisers, destroyers and submarines commanded by Commodore Reginald Tyrwhitt, carried nine Shorts seaplanes (four Type 74s, three Type 81s and two Type 135s) to a position ten miles north of Heligoland Island, where they were made ready for launching from the water. Seven of the nine took off on what would become known as the Cuxhaven Raid. Not a great deal of damage was done by the small quantity of bombs dropped; nevertheless the raid demonstrated the feasibility of attack by ship-borne aircraft and showed the strategic importance of this new weapon. The following year, on 12 August 1915, the former Isle of Man packet *Ben-my-Chree* carried the Short 184 seaplane, No. 842, flown by Flight Commander CHK Edmonds, which made the first successful attack by aerial torpedo while operating in the Dardanelles. The *Ben-my-Chree*'s captain, Squadron Commander C L'Estrange Malone, wrote the following prophetic words in his report, 'One cannot help looking on this operation as being the forerunner of a line of development which will tend to revolutionise warfare.'

The next step was to see if by fitting detachable trolleys to the floats of a seaplane, successful take-offs could be made with war loads from a ramp fitted to the foredeck of a seaplane carrier. The ramp had to be of sufficient length to allow the aircraft a reasonable run to build up speed and lift and the vessel had to be fast enough to create sufficient headwind when steaming into the wind to allow the heavily laden warplane to take off with a reasonable expectation of success. HMS *Campania* was a former Cunard liner and therefore was capable of greater speed than a packet ship. Her flying-off deck was 100 feet in length and on 6 August 1915, while steaming at 18 knots, she successfully launched the Sopwith Schneider, No. 1559, flown by Flight Lieutenant WL Welsh. This appeared to be the solution to one part of the problem but seaplanes would, of course, still have to land on the sea and be winched on board the stationary mother ship. Moreover, it was an undoubted fact that the weight and drag of a seaplane's floats, struts and bracing wires severely reduced both the performance and load-carrying capacity when compared with its landplane equivalent and as for being able to climb fast enough to intercept a high flying Zeppelin – that was a different matter again.

The work involved in flying off and recovering a seaplane on board *Campania* was described in detail by her Senior Flying Officer, Wing Commander Richard Bell Davies VC:

A seaplane could be lifted out of the hangar by either derrick and put on the launching deck or swung over the side. Spreading the wings could be done on the launching deck or, if going into the sea, the seaplane could be lowered temporarily on the boat deck and the wings spread there. For recovery of seaplanes at sea, there was a swinging boom about 50-feet long hinged at upper-deck level some distance forward of the derrick on either side. A long wire with a hemp tail on its outboard end and known as the seaplane wire was rove through a block at the boom-head. The inboard end of the wire was controlled by a steam winch on the upper deck.

At sea the *Campania* always had two destroyers in company. When a seaplane returned from reconnaissance the three ships turned into wind; the destroyers then steamed ahead at high speed to break up the seas and make a slick. When the slick was long enough the seaplane was signalled to land. The pilot tried to touch down about a quarter of a mile ahead of the ship. When the seaplane was down, the ship was manoeuvred so as to bring one of the seaplane booms over the aircraft, the pilot meanwhile holding the seaplane head to sea with the engine. Two men went out along the boom, one holding the hemp tail of the seaplane wire, the other a steadying line attached to the hook of the derrick purchase wire. As the boom passed over the seaplane, the pilot stopped the engine. The observer climbed on to the nose of the inboard float where the first boom-head man threw him the hemp tail of the seaplane wire. When he had hauled in the end of the wire and attached it by means of a snap hook to a becket on the nose of the inboard float, the slack of the wire was hove in and the seaplane was in tow from the boom head. Meanwhile the pilot had climbed on to the top plane. The second boom-head man swung the derrick hook to him and he hooked it on to the slings. The seaplane could then be hoisted in, the seaplane wire acting as a guy to hold her clear of the ship's side. Two men holding long bamboos with padded heads also stood by on the upper deck to bear her off if she swung.

There were many refinements. Derrick topping lifts and purchases had long spiral springs introduced to absorb shock. Special hooks had been designed both for hoisting in and out. The efficient working of these arrangements depended almost entirely on the team spirit of the handling party, and there can seldom have been better team work than that in *Campania*.

I timed the operation of recovery several times during exercises at sea in moderately fresh winds. The average, from the signal to land till telegraphs were put to ahead, was about 4½ minutes.

As early as July 1915 Admiral Jellicoe reported to the Admiralty that seaplanes were not going to be effective as Zeppelin interceptors and stated:

I regret that I am unable to propose any means of meeting this menace, unless it be by the use of aeroplanes [landplanes] rising from the deck of *Campania*, capable of climbing above the Zeppelins, and able to land on the water and be supported sufficiently long by air bags to allow rescue of the pilots.

It was decided to experiment with launching a landplane from the deck of a ship, the first of which was the Bristol Scout C, No. 1255, flown by Flight Commander BF Fowler from the seaplane carrier HMS *Vindex* on 3 November 1915. The aircraft was fitted with flotation bags, as unless it could reach dry land again it would have to land in the sea – which would inevitably damage the aircraft but not, hopefully, the pilot. The take-off was filmed for later analysis. The Scout, however, was not the answer as it lacked both performance and suitable armament for the role.

While Sopwith Babies were used effectively in the Mediterranean on bombing raids from the parent ships *Ben-my-Chree* and *Empress* in 1916; proof of the limitations of using seaplanes in the strike role came on 4 May 1916, when out of eleven Babies which *Engadine* and *Vindex* attempted to launch, only one succeeded in bombing the target, the Zeppelin sheds at Tondern.

Only one aviation-capable ship took part in the Battle of Jutland, the seaplane carrier *Engadine*, whose captain was Oliver Swann (who had changed the spelling of his name from Schwann). Only one aircraft was hoisted out and launched from the sea, on 31 May 1916. This was the Short 184, No. 8359, flown by Flight Lieutenant FJ Rutland, with Assistant Paymaster GS Trewin as his observer. A report was quickly sent on the position and movements of German ships. History was made, as this was the first time wireless communication was established between an aircraft and ships engaged in a fleet action. In the assessments following the battle it was considered that more aircraft and more ships capable of carrying them, with a performance sufficient to keep up with the fleet, was a highly desirable aim both for reconnaissance and anti-Zeppelin duties.

The German High Seas Fleet failed to either destroy or seriously reduce the effectiveness of the Royal Navy's Grand Fleet at Jutland. If Germany was going to win the war at sea by choking off the supply of materiel from across the Atlantic then it would have to be by recourse once more to war under the sea. On 1 February 1917 the Imperial German Government declared the resumption of unrestricted submarine warfare, which had been tried before for three months in 1915. U-boats were now, however, available in quantity and this time not only Allied shipping but also neutral vessels (such as those on the US register) would be sunk on sight in the eastern Atlantic and the approaches to British ports. This was an enormous gamble, as America would inevitably enter the war (the USA declared war on Germany on 6 April 1917) but could the Allies be starved into submission before sufficient reinforcements and materiel could arrive to break the deadlock on the Western Front? The Chancellor, Bethmann-Hollweg, assessed the situation facing the Germans:

> On the whole, the prospects for the unrestricted U-boat war are very favourable. Of course, it must be admitted that those prospects are not capable of being demonstrated by proof. We should be perfectly certain that, so far as the military situation is concerned, great military strokes are insufficient as such to win the war. The U-boat war is the 'last card'. A very serious decision. But if the military authorities consider the U-boat war essential, I am not in a position to contradict them.

The initial impact cannot be understated. In the first three months, over 1000 merchant ships were sunk. The situation was perilous. Winston Churchill later wrote:

> At first sight all seemed to favour the Germans. Two hundred U-boats each possessing between three and four

weeks' radius of action, each capable of sinking with torpedo, gun fire or bomb, four or five vessels in a single day, beset the approaches to our islands along which passed in and out every week several thousand merchant vessels. Of all the tasks ever set to a Navy none could have appeared more baffling than that of protecting this enormous traffic and groping deep below the surface of the sea for the deadly elusive foe. It was in fact a game of Blind Man's Buff in an unlimited space of three dimensions.

This would indeed prove to be one of the most critical campaigns of the war until it was won by means of the introduction of the convoy system, the laying of minefields, the introduction of improved detection technology, the provision of adequate numbers of escort vessels and the successful use of airships and aircraft for patrol and spotting duties. If the Grand Fleet had been destroyed or severely weakened and the High Seas Fleet had been able to leave harbour with impunity and attack the convoys, then it is likely that the war would have been lost – Britain would have been starved into submission.

In the meantime the Royal Navy continued with its blockade of the sea routes to Germany and so severely deprived the German people of vital supplies. By virtue of its geographical position Britain could place a block on German access to the oceans of the world via the North Sea or the English Channel. If the High Seas Fleet could not intervene to prevent this strangulation of Germany's seaborne commerce, then what was its use? The Grand Fleet by its very existence prevented this and rendered the High Seas Fleet impotent. That is not to say, of course, that important lessons were not learned at Jutland regarding the timely provision and use of intelligence, communication between the C-in-C and his subordinate commanders, the inadequacy of British ship design and the poor destructive quality of the explosive shells supplied for the fleet's great guns.

Admiral Sir David Beatty, who succeeded Admiral Sir John Jellicoe as C-in-C of the Grand Fleet, set up an Aircraft Committee in January 1917 to consider the lack of continuous aerial reconnaissance over the North Sea to give warning of enemy units at sea, the provision of anti-U-boat patrolling by air ahead of the Fleet and the establishment of reliable, sea-borne, anti-Zeppelin interceptors. The committee reported that the *Campania*, with six fighter and six reconnaissance seaplanes had done valiant service but was ageing and unreliable, while *Manxman* and *Engadine* with eight seaplanes each, were too slow to keep up. New aircraft carriers and new aircraft were needed urgently. One solution was the former Italian liner *Conte Rosso*, which had been requisitioned while still on the stocks at John Brown's shipyard on the Clyde. It was in process of being converted into the first flush-deck aircraft carrier, but would not be ready for service until late 1918. A solution to this urgent requirement was needed within a much shorter timescale. As regards aircraft the committee recommended that for attack on enemy Zeppelins, the Sopwith Pup would be the most suitable type and for close reconnaissance, the Sopwith 1½ Strutter. It should also be noted that at about the same time as the committee was reaching its conclusions Commodore GM Paine RN was appointed Director of Air Services and Fifth Sea Lord, the first to hold an appointment which would enhance the promotion of air power within the Board of Admiralty.

CHAPTER SEVEN

HMS *Furious* – the 1917 Conversion and Operations from Rosyth

In March 1917 a large warship was nearing completion at the Walker Naval Yard at Newcastle-upon-Tyne, owned by the famous firm of Armstrong Whitworth. She was one of a class of three vessels ordered in 1915, the others being HMS *Courageous*, also built by Armstrong Whitworth, and HMS *Glorious*, which was constructed at Harland and Wolff's in Belfast. They were the brainchild of Admiral of the Fleet Lord Fisher, who wanted them as the spearhead of an assault on Germany by means of a landing on the Baltic coast in Pomerania. The specification included the necessity of high speed (32 knots), heavy armament and shallow draught. As a result of this they would be fitted with much less protective armour than was normal for ships of this size – they were to be over 140 feet longer than the battleships *Iron Duke* and *Queen Elizabeth* and more than 1000 tons heavier than HMS *Dreadnought*. *Furious* was laid down in June 1915 and was built with great secrecy, being launched on 18 August 1916. As her main armament, single 18-inch guns (the largest ever installed in a British warship) would be mounted fore and aft. The three ships were designated as 'large light cruisers' or 'light battle cruisers'. In July 1916, the carriage of two small, single-seater seaplanes had been approved and provision made for a small hangar forward. Now much more extensive work was ordered.

Following on from the recommendations of the Grand Fleet Aircraft Committee and endorsement by Admiral Beatty, which were sent to the Admiralty early in February, on 15 and 31 March 1917, the Director of Naval Construction issued orders that *Furious* was to be fitted to carry four two-seater reconnaissance seaplanes and four single-seater fighters, which would be fitted with land undercarriages. This was to involve the following:

- The foremost 18-inch gun and mounting were to be removed.
- A large new seaplane hangar was to be built, using the space thus provided, with weather doors forward and special arrangements for ventilation, heating, and lighting.
- The shell room could be turned over to bomb storage.
- A flying-off platform 228 feet in length and 50 feet wide was to be made on the top of the hangar.
- Carpenters' workshops would be required, and stowage for 600 two-gallon cans of petrol.
- The Captain would be instructed that it would not be possible to drive the ship at maximum speed without injury to the flying-off deck except in fine weather.

Top priority was to be given to completing the ship with these substantial alterations and remarkably she was ready for commissioning by Captain Wilmot S Nicholson on 26 June 1917. The ship's company numbered 796, in addition to which there were fourteen officers and seventy ratings of the RNAS under Squadron Commander EH Dunning.

Edwin Dunning was born in South Africa on 17 July 1892, the second child of Sir Edwin Harris Dunning of Jacques Hall, Bradfield, Essex; he was educated at Royal Naval Colleges at Osborne and Dartmouth. He would have been twenty-four years old when Jack met him for the first time but was already an airman of distinction. He had flown Sopwith Type 807 and Short Type 135 seaplanes from the seaplane carrier HMS *Ark Royal* in the Dardanelles in 1915 and was regarded by Arthur

Longmore as one of his best night pilots, flying a Bristol Scout in the War Flight, when under his command at Eastchurch. In March 1916 he had been awarded the DSC for 'exceptionally good work as a seaplane flyer, making many long flights both for spotting and photographing.' During the previous few weeks when the aircrew selected for *Furious* had trained at Grain, he and the others designated as scout pilots had practised deck landing Sopwith Pups on a dummy deck constructed there.

SATURDAY, 30 JUNE
Got up at 10 o'clock. Had brekker and went round town; saw outside of Castle and inside of Abbey. Very nice day. Caught 2.18 pm for Newcastle. Train packed full the whole way. Arrived on board *Furious* 6 o'clock. Some ship. Great rag in hammocks.

SUNDAY, 1 JULY
Spent most of day in gunroom [the junior officers' mess]. Wrote home, George, Tony and Meta.

Jack described his first experience of hammocks:

We're sleeping in hammocks and of course had the usual rough house for the first night. Mine stayed up but I brought another chap's down when getting into mine! One hammock was down five times! Still they are very comfy really. I'd a bath this morning – hot! We should be very comfy on board as far as I can see, but will be very busy, I suspect.

MONDAY, 2 JULY
Went to South Shields with Dickson to fetch Short. She didn't turn up. Lorimer and we returned in evening.

TUESDAY, 3 JULY
Left Newcastle at 2 o'clock; arrived at Rosyth about 8.30. Very calm. Had two destroyers as escort. Letter from Meta. Gun tests: Long Tom (18-inch) makes some disturbance.

Firing the 18-inch gun made a strong impression, the projectile could be seen for a long time as it flew up to thirty miles away.

The effect of the recoil on the lightly built ship was tremendous; in Flight Commander Moore's cabin, which was directly beneath, he experienced a snowstorm of sheared rivet-heads coming down from the deckhead each time it was fired. Its usefulness as a weapon was, however, doubtful.

Rosyth on the north side of the Firth of Forth and in the shadow of the great Forth Railway Bridge since 1890, was in today's parlance the 'forward operating base' of the battle cruisers and faster, more modern battleships. It had been so for a strong detachment of heavy units since December 1914, as it was strategically necessary to have a substantial force within closer range of the German fleet to deter opportunistic raids on British coastal towns and, as so nearly happened at Jutland, to draw the Germans into the waiting guns of the Royal Navy's battleships. Rosyth offered considerably greater attractions for young officers, being close to the restaurants, cinemas and other delights of Edinburgh.

WEDNESDAY, 4 JULY

Left Rosyth for Scapa Flow. On watch from 8 to 12.30 this morning. Rotten cold job. Also tonight from 8 to 12. Calm all the way. Ship did about 31 knots in speed trials.

Lying some 200 miles to the north of Rosyth, Scapa Flow, the great natural harbour in the Orkney Islands was the war station of the Grand Fleet, to which it had come in the last days of July 1914. Even though it had first been identified and recommended to the Admiralty as 'a rendezvous for Line of Battle Ships' as early as 1812, it was not until the first decade of the twentieth century that the quickening pace of the Anglo-German naval race ensured that its potential as a base dominating access to the Atlantic Ocean between Great Britain and Norway should be explored. In the years before the outbreak of the Great War the isolation and peace of the anchorage was disturbed more and more frequently by the flotillas and squadrons of the Royal Navy. Separated from mainland Caithness by the often turbulent waters of the Pentland Firth, where the North Sea meets the Atlantic, Scapa Flow is a magnificent, almost landlocked, natural harbour. It measures fifteen miles in length from north to south and eight miles across from east to west and covers 140 square miles, with three main entrances, Hoxa Sound, Switha Sound and Hoy Sound.

THURSDAY, 5 JULY
Watch 12.30–4 day, and 12–4 middle. Spent most of day on flying deck at derricks.

The three Short 184s and five Sopwith Pups (later four Shorts and three Pups) with which *Furious* was equipped would have needed winching on board. The Pups would have been brought across from the shore by lighter and the Shorts could have taxied alongside. The derricks did not prove to be completely satisfactory as they were too short with the booms set too low. They were powered by electricity rather than steam and were rather unreliable, being prone to tripping as regards the overload switch. Raising and lowering aircraft from the hangar was also fraught with difficulty as there was not much clearance through the foredeck hatch.

FRIDAY, 6 JULY
Watch 4–6 day. Admiral Beatty came on board to inspect the ship. First aircraft flew off deck.

SATURDAY, 7 JULY
Mother's birthday. Nice day. Still in the Flow. Had to take picket boat to depot ship for some gear. Wind up, force umpteen. Letters from Mother, Meta and George. Meta sent me a jolly nice blue hanky.

Jack wrote to his mother to wish her a happy birthday but was unable to relate any other news apart from the fact that the gunroom had a very good gramophone, which was getting plenty of use.

SUNDAY, 8 JULY
Was up in Short after lunch; engine oiled up three times with me. Very good bus. Night watch 8–12; awfully cold. Heard a Captain tell our Skipper, 'This will be the most useful ship in the service, of that I feel sure'! Eh what, boys! Wrote to home, Meta and George.

During his first period of service in *Furious* Jack was specifically a seaplane pilot and the type which he flew was the Short 184. It was a large, single-engine, rather ungainly-looking seaplane, carrying a crew of pilot and observer. It was armed with a single Lewis gun aft and either a 14-inch torpedo or up to 520 lbs of bombs. More than 650 were built. Its looks belied its utility and it gave valuable service from first to last. In home waters its main tasks were anti-submarine patrols and also bombing attacks on enemy North Sea coastal bases. A pilot of the time, Flight Commander AH Sandwell, commented:

> It was a physical impossibility to fly a Short at much more than 75 miles an hour. It was, however, the pilot's dream for putting in hours – docile, stable, obedient, and thoroughly deserving its affectionate nickname – Home from Home.

In the opinion of the doyen of World War One aviation historians, Jack Bruce:

> The type would not have won any beauty contest, and it had no list of individual victories to its credit. Yet it served throughout most of the 1914–18 war, and beyond – stolid, unspectacular, and unobtrusively gallant. They that went down to the sea in Shorts did indeed faithfully occupy their business in great waters.

Such was the secrecy that surrounded *Furious* as she worked up there was little of substance that Jack could report in his letters:

> I'm afraid I'll not be able to say much as there's nothing of any interest happens that I may tell you. I'm getting on very well here – more or less, and it is fairly hard work. Do you think you could arrange for me to send my dirty linen to grandmother to get sent to the laundry, as we've got no means of doing it on board? PS If Mother could knit me a Balaclava helmet in blue, it would be very useful. If so, I'd like it a fairly tight fit, so that it wouldn't be sloppy on me.

These were very busy and stressful times for *Furious*, her captain and officers and men. Amongst the huge assembly of battleships, cruisers and destroyers at Scapa Flow there were at this time only two vessels available for air support of the Fleet; the old *Campania* and the slow *Manxman*, which were capable of carrying eleven and eight seaplanes respectively. *Furious* was better armed than any other carrier in existence, was larger and more capable of putting to sea in all weathers, was 10 knots faster and had a flight deck big enough for any seaplane or aeroplane of the day to take off, so was therefore an important and vitally required reinforcement. To work up any new ship to full efficiency is always strenuous, yet for the men there were the additional complications of learning the new technique of handling aircraft; constant calls for experiments, official and unofficial; problems arising from a complicated system of higher organisation for the manufacture and supply of spare parts by the Ministry of Munitions; and above all the urgent need to become ready as soon as possible for war operations. For the remainder of July and all of August they were kept hard at it, exercising either under way in Scapa Flow or at anchor.

The pilots also had to assimilate much new information with regard to serving on board a ship – many of them had never even been on a warship before but as they wore the full executive curl on the gold braid of their monkey jackets and drew an officer's pay, they were now expected to play a full part as sea officers on active service. Flight Commander Geoffrey Moore later recalled the kindness and consideration of the regular and RNVR 'salt-horse' officers from the captain downwards, who exercised great patience and charm when showing the newcomers the ropes.

> I remember particularly well the Commander, Buckle, by naval tradition always known to the crew as the bloke, and two watch-keeping officers, both Lieutenants, Flynn and Poland. The latter two would take us down to their cabins at night and tell us all the things we wanted to know, and what to call things – a scuttle for instance and not a porthole; a deckhead not ceiling etc – and how to behave in general aboard ship. Also they would tell us about the traditions of the Navy, all in the nicest possible way. So it was throughout the ship's company.

MONDAY, 9 JULY

Two Pups flew off the deck this morning. Wish I'd stayed on in 'em now. Was wakened at 12 midnight by Dickson – 'Battleship blown up and sub in harbour'. Sure enough HMS *Vanguard* had blown up: 20 officers and about 3 men saved out of 800. Spent night on bridge; very cold indeed. Complete turret found in a field about 2–3 miles away.

Take-off was assisted by means of a ball welded to a bracket on the Pup's tail skid. This was fixed into a slotted tube mounted on a trestle. The tail was thereby kept up in a flying attitude so that none of the deck available for the take-off run was wasted getting the tail up. The engine was run up and as soon as it was showing satisfactory revolutions the pilot raised his hand and a member of the crew pulled a lanyard to release the cable attaching the aircraft from its mounting and away it went. Landings were made at a small airfield which had been established at Smoogroo Bay on the north-western side of the Flow. The Pups were returned to *Furious* by picket boats towing little rafts made from old seaplane floats over which planking had been laid.

Just before midnight on Monday, 9 July 1917 at Scapa Flow the battleship HMS *Vanguard* suffered an explosion. It was probably caused by an unnoticed stokehold fire heating cordite stored against an adjacent bulkhead in one of the two magazines which served the amidships gun turrets P and Q. She sank almost instantly, killing an estimated 843 men; there were only two survivors.

TUESDAY, 10 JULY

Had a very slack day & a very cold one. No flying.

WEDNESDAY, 11 JULY

Spent most of day in hangar. Very nice day indeed, Letters from Father and Tony.

THURSDAY, 12 JULY

No flying. On shore for a couple of hours. On bridge for some time as we were doing gun practice. Kept fairly busy.

FRIDAY, 13 JULY

Nothing doing in morning. Was in hangar all afternoon. Sibley [F/S-L RGD Sibley was killed when a flight commander with 210 Squadron in France when his Sopwith Camel, D1883, crashed on 1 October 1918] flew off the deck in the Short for the first time; finally crashed as derrick gave way when hauling it in. On bridge at midnight.

SATURDAY, 14 JULY

Barbara's birthday. Lovely hot day. Up in Short for 12 minutes; engine konked. Rowed ashore with Thyne after tea. Shot revolver at puffin; good shots but no bulls. We went up and stroked it in the end!

The pilots and observers also learned to sail whalers and other boats from *Furious* and took part in picnics ashore on the islands surrounding Scapa Flow, either cooking their own sausages over an open fire or visiting the hospitable islanders in their crofts for tea, home-made oat-cakes and potato bread – and other local delicacies which would have been familiar to a good Ulsterman like Jack.

SUNDAY, 15 JULY

Very slack day indeed. Very warm. Put on 2½ hours' notice.

MONDAY, 16 JULY

Grand Fleet put to sea 5 o'clock am. Negative *Furious* and one or two other (!) light cruisers. Did gun practice and fire drill all day.

TUESDAY, 17 JULY

Lovely day. 5.5-inch (3-pounder) practice. Good shooting. Got new uniform from Gieves; jolly good fit. Short flew off deck, on its nose. Much wind up but got off OK. 12–4 watch.

It would appear that Jack's laundry problem had been mostly solved as he was able to report in his letter:

My laundry has gone ashore somewhere and will be sent to me with the rest of the ship's when done, so that's all right.

Do you know if I left my thin underpants at home, as I seem to have only one pair here? I am very sorry to tell you that I lost the gold tie pin Mother brought me from Crieff last time she was there. I don't know what has happened to it and I've searched everywhere for it.

THURSDAY, 19 JULY

Given my action station: I'm in charge of starboard 5.5-inch guns. We went into Pentland Firth and did practice. Row was awful. Can see myself in action – I don't think! Full charge 18-inch. Some splash, not much row, but whole ship jumps forward.

FRIDAY, 20 JULY

Had another trip today, doing about 80 minutes with Lieutenant Poland; got on very well indeed and made three very good landings; 240 HP Sage Short. Letters from home and Meta.

SATURDAY, 21 JULY

Not up in forenoon – lovely day and awful slack. After lunch had the honour of taking up Capt BV Brooke of light cruiser HMS *Southampton*, who got it hot at Jutland. Went up to 6000 feet and did spirals. Lovely view; up 110 minutes.

HMS *Southampton* was the Flagship of Commodore WE Goodenough, Second Light Cruiser Squadron, and was in the thick of the action at Jutland, with casualties of thirty-five killed and forty-one wounded. She torpedoed the cruiser SMS *Frauenlob*, which subsequently sank. His flight with Jack was Captain Brooke's first trip aloft, which was described by Jack:

I took him to 6000 feet and then went through a very thick cloud to see how he would like it – he didn't tell me as we came out at a most astonishing angle! Then I spiralled down and gave him a few bumps. He seemed awfully pleased about it though. We had a gorgeous view as it was very clear up.

There was still an underwear crisis, however, as he appended a plea to the top of his letter:

Please send me any thin underpants you can find.

SUNDAY, 22 JULY
Lovely day. Took up a Commander Caby. Lost my prop after landing. Mists coming up round the Flow.

MONDAY, 23 JULY
Did not get up today. Short and Pup went up off deck. Misty day and generally unpleasant. Very slack.

TUESDAY, 24 JULY
Went on shore and walked with Acland [F/S-L Wilfred Dyke Acland who would be one of Jack's best friends in *Furious*] and padre for 4½ miles; had tea at a nice little school house and walked back. Several seals on shore close in but they cleared off when we appeared. Also found a mat of PK flax! [PK flax was a brand name with which Jack and his father would have been familiar.] Water logged. Mist came up so had to pull out to ship in whaler.

WEDNESDAY, 25 JULY
Flew off deck for first time. Ship in Orphir Bay. Dunning very pleased and said it was the best one done yet, especially as the engine was dud. Did visibility tests from 1000–6000 ft. Also Lewis gun tests and wireless and light to [the light cruisers] HMS *Dublin* and *Cardiff*. Nice up, though fearfully heavy ground mist at first – no visibility at first at all, so much wind up.

THURSDAY, 26 JULY
Slack day. Letters from Meta, Bunty and Kenneth.

FRIDAY, 27 JULY
Went off deck to do spotting for 18-inch gun; 'Long Tom'. Fearfully bumpy and as bus was ditto tail heavy, I nearly collapsed when I got back! Very good practice with 18-inch

at 6 miles. Priceless splash. Also Lewis gun practice. Rough sea for landing. Letters from Mother and Meta.

SATURDAY, 28 JULY

On afternoon watch. Slack morning. Went up after lunch for nearly two hours with Douglas as passenger; quite a good trip. Zoomed at various ships and boats. Engine running poorly.

SUNDAY, 29 JULY

On afternoon watch. Nothing to do. Slack afternoon.

He did, however, write a letter in which the underpants saga continued and in which he also noted reaching a flying milestone:

First of all I must acknowledge the pair of underpants mother sent me. Are there any more? I had my worst trip so far, a few days ago. Three hours and BUMPS! Can you imagine a traction engine coming down the Cavehill railway line full out? Well that would be about ¼ as bad as I had it! I was feeling giddy for two days after it, and I was absolutely fit for nothing when I landed – and then I just missed being seasick! Anyhow I've got my *100 hours* in and only 7½ of it dual control, which isn't bad. Some chaps who joined last August are only 10 hours at the most better then me. I forgot to thank you for the chocolates which were very acceptable and will continue to be so! By the way if father could send me a small Watmans block sketch book, I'd like it very much.

MONDAY, 30 JULY

Spent a morning trueing up a Short on flying deck. Afternoon went for a sail in a whaler for about 2½ hours. Rather dirty weather and got pretty wet. Fine sport. Enjoyed it very much. Watch 6–8.30.

TUESDAY, 31 JULY

At gun drill in morning, part of time; nothing much doing. Under way for turning angles. Got a fine helmet [presumably the knitted, blue balaclava] from Mother.

WEDNESDAY, 1 AUGUST

Went for a sail in a skiff (sprit-sail) with Lieutenant Pyke RNR. Had to be towed back as we couldn't beat up into the wind enough. Letter from Father.

THURSDAY, 2 AUGUST

Under way to Pentland Firth. At 11.00, with the ship steaming at 20 knots, Sqn Com. Dunning made the first landing of any machine on any deck – on a Pup. We all caught hold of him as he was stationary in the air, till he settled down. Heavy swell on and had our usual screen of two TBDs with us. On watch 8.30–10. Went for a pull in the whaler after tea: priceless! On bridge in morning.

It had been Dunning's belief that, with a ship capable of steaming at 31 knots, sufficient wind could be generated over the deck to allow a successful landing on the fore flying-off platform. He planned to fly parallel to the ship to port and then sideslip the aircraft past the superstructure and onto the deck. Being able to launch and recover aircraft from a ship that didn't have to stop would transform the provision of air support for the Fleet. There was a great deal of interest in Dunning's experiment and on the day in question, Flight Commander Moore reported that the ship was, 'weighed down with brass hats and gold braid, as there were many admirals and generals on board to see these experiments.' That morning the conditions were excellent; there was a strong and steady wind of 21 knots. *Furious* steamed into the wind at 10 knots. Dunning was able to manoeuvre his Pup, N6453, at a very slow relative speed of about 30–35 knots without getting too dangerously close to stalling. White lines were painted on the deck to show the pilot his position and correct his drift. When over the centre line and square and clear of the hangar hatch coaming, he cut his engine and dropped. As he touched down lightly, a party of waiting officers, including Jack, rushed to catch hold of the machine and bring to a complete halt. It was a quite remarkable feat and a historic moment (especially considering the short length of time *Furious* had been in commission) in which Jack was most fortunate in being a witness and a participant.

Dunning wrote to his friend Wing Commander Arthur

Longmore, describing how he achieved the landing. Longmore later recalled:

> I replied that it was a fine show as a stunt and had proved it could be done by an expert pilot, but what we wanted was a flush-deck carrier to make it a practicable proposition. I concluded by hoping that he would not try it again.

MONDAY, 6 AUGUST
Very hot day. Started DO [Duty Officer duties] in hangar – rotten job. Dead body found ashore; Walker went and fetched it alongside the ship: horrible sight, what I saw of it. Good deal of Pup flying after lunch. Developed a very good film.

It is probably fortunate that Jack could not reveal to his parents any details of the experimental flying on board *Furious*. It is likely that the information given in that week's letter was exciting enough for them,

> I got a letter from George too the other day. I wish I could get off this packet and go to Westgate [a seaplane station in Kent] with him. I flew several machines there from Grain when I was at the latter place, so he will probably be up in some of the same ones. [Sopwith Babies in all likelihood.] He'll not be able to treat them as badly as I could as we had to stunt them at Grain and they are not allowed to at Westgate – not within sight of the station at any rate. Those were fine days, when we did little else but stunt all day! I'm hopelessly out of practice now, worse luck.

The staid and sober Short 184 was definitely not a machine for stunting or any other extravagant aerial manoeuvres which Jack so obviously enjoyed. On a more domestic note he advised that:

> I forgot to tell you before, I got my laundry back all right the following week, and also I found my gold tie pin in one of my sea boots! I've had three letters from different girls this week in successive posts, so I've not done too badly this week at all.

One can only speculate as to whether or not his mother thought all this female attention was any safer than stunting.

TUESDAY, 7 AUGUST

> Ship under way after lunch. Sqn Com Dunning landed a Pup on deck and smashed elevator and rudder. Tried another Pup and after four attempts, tyre burst and he went over the side into the water. Engines hard astern and out cutter [swing out the cutter and lower it in to the water], but he was dead when we got him: horrible sight. He must have been stunned, when he hit the water, by the cross bar, as his belt was fastened. Machine badly smashed. Several photos taken of machine. We were doing about 25 knots at the time, and wind speed of about 38 mph.

Dunning did not take his friend's advice. The weather on the fateful day was more gusty and unreliable. He took off at 13.40 and made his second deck landing in N6453 at 13.54 hours but at the cost of damage to the tail of the aircraft as the handling party of officers grabbed the specially sown on rope toggles with a little too much gusto, which meant he changed to N6452 for his third attempt, ousting the waiting Moore from the cockpit. He took off at 14.40. As he approached at 14.51, he was a little higher and he was still in the air as he crossed the line painted across the deck which marked the furthest point for a safe touch down. Seeing this, Dunning opened up the throttle to go around again, waving away the deck party. Then the engine choked and stalled. It landed heavily on the starboard wheel and tumbled over the ship's side before the landing party could rush forward and catch hold. It was not until 15.25 that a recovery of pilot and aircraft was made, by which time it was too late. He was only just twenty-five years old. The ship's log noted his death in sparse official terms, 'Accident, aeroplane plunging into sea while flying.' Dunning was buried in St Lawrence's Church in his home town of Bradfield, Essex. Inside the church is a memorial plaque displaying the Dunning family coat of arms and a citation which includes the lines:

> The Admiralty wish you to know what great service he performed for the Navy. It was in fact a demonstration of

landing an Aeroplane on the deck of a Man-of-War whilst the latter was under way. This had never been done before; and the data obtained was of the utmost value. It will make Aeroplanes indispensable to a Fleet & possibly revolutionise Naval Warfare.

Longmore commemorated the all-too-short life of his friend by donating a silver cup to be awarded each year to the officer who had done the most valuable work in advancing fleet flying and cooperation. The winner in both 1917 and 1918 was Frederick Rutland.

Dunning's replacement as senior flying officer was Squadron Commander FJ Rutland, known to posterity as 'Rutland of Jutland'. He was born in Weymouth in 1886 and had joined the Royal Navy as a boy entrant in 1901. He was commissioned in 1913 and learned to fly in 1915. After his memorable experiences at Jutland, he had participated in experimental work leading to the launching of landplanes from seaplane carriers. On 29 April 1917 he took off from the deck of HMS *Manxman* in the Sopwith Pup 9918, in search of Zeppelins over the North Sea. He later wrote of this exploit:

Well, you might suppose that I would be thrilled by this golden opportunity. Having worked hard to get [land] aeroplanes into the fleet and having succeeded, as yet in one ship only (*Campania* had not yet taken on board her Sopwith Pups) we were now to carry out an operation which I considered was beyond the powers of aeroplanes. The orders meant that I would be out of sight of the Fleet for over two hours. I could carry fuel for only two and a half hours. There were no navigational instruments and the compass was notoriously unreliable. For the greater part of the flight I would be flying over enemy minefields. If my engine failed and I had to come down in them, there was not the smallest chance of being picked up. Apart from the probable losses of pilot and machine, I foresaw an even more serious consequence. If the operation proved a failure, someone would almost certainly take what I regarded as the retrograde step back to seaplanes and all our efforts would go for nothing.

He carried out the dangerous operation but had to ditch in the sea off the coast of Denmark, where there was no waiting British warship to pick him up. After a number of adventures, including a meeting with Queen Maud of Norway, he arrived safely home in England.

Undeterred by this experience, he pressed ahead with the idea of fitting take-off platforms on the foremost turret of light cruisers and made the first such successful flight from HMS *Yarmouth* in Sopwith Pup 9901, on 28 June 1917.

This therefore was the man who would arrive to replace the popular and charming Dunning, saying of him:

> His death meant the loss of a really first-class pilot. I was certainly not as good. But I had had more experience at sea and more experience of working from ships.

In the meantime Flight Commander Moore assumed temporary command for a few weeks and noted his great pleasure at being in charge of the flying element of 'the show-piece of the whole RNAS.' He enjoyed an excellent relationship with Captain Nicholson, who was sensible enough to know that he knew little about flying and used the time to pick Moore's brains over pink gins in the captain's cabin. Alternatively, when Moore reported in the early morning with the weather brief, he would find the captain in his bath, with his feet up on the end and reading a newspaper.

WEDNESDAY, 8 AUGUST

Nothing special happened. We had a talk by Captain Nicholson last night on Dunning's death. Very cut up. In hangar all day. Just when going to bed I heard firing, and going on deck I found a TBD or light cruiser was firing across us at a target with 1-inch stuff. They were whistling over us close down, and we got down behind the 18-inch turret. Several lit close to the hangar. Finally we signalled them to stop. Lovely sunset.

THURSDAY, 9 AUGUST

Gorgeous day. Most of morning in hangar, part of time at gun drill. Went off in whaler at 1.30 pm to *Borodino* – Army and Navy Stores ship and bought some grub; got back about 4.30. Saw a dead body in water but didn't pick it up; it looked like an officer's jacket, what we could see of it. Ordered to get full steam up and be ready to sail immediately. Another Pup put on board at midnight – 3 o'clock. Light cruiser squadron went out, negative *Furious*. Great excitement.

On board the SS *Borodino*, the Junior Army and Navy Stores vessel, officers and men could buy 'anything from an elephant to a shirt-button' from immaculately white-coated shop assistants presiding over their well-laid counters. A laundry and gentlemen's hairdressing facilities were also provided. However, not all customers were satisfied:

Some few officers considered that we should keep everything on *Borodino*. One demanded sheet music! Another was indignant when informed that we kept neither screws nor bolts! A captain once enquired for picture frames, and considered that *Borodino* should have a large selection, 'as every officer in the Fleet has the picture of a girl in his cabin.'

FRIDAY, 10 AUGUST
Misty and uncertain day. Went up for two compass courses in morning in Short – could hardly see anything, certainly not the ship. Got back OK. F/S-L Dolman crashed into Smoogroo hill in a thick fog, knocked machine to pieces absolutely; he was hurt about the head and doctor thought his ankle broken. Taken straight away to hospital ship. Two letters from home and cheque book from bank.

SATURDAY, 11 AUGUST
Nothing doing today; too misty for flying. Spent morning in hangar as usual. Got two pair underfugs from Father. Submarine reported five miles NE of main gate about 9 o'clock tonight. Still it can't get in; jolly plucky men. Letters from Meta and Barbara.

SUNDAY, 12 AUGUST

Was tried before breakfast this morning for racing whaler's crew. Fine pull, also ditto appetite. Wrote home and to Meta (enclosing photo). Divisions and Church as usual, accompanied by harmonium and ship's band. Spent about two hours after dinner shipping petrol empties into the stores ship alongside.

All that Jack could say to his parents about the sad event of the week was:

We've had a very unfortunate week of it and I'm very glad it's over. I can't tell you why of course.

But he was able to write about some of the natural life of the Flow and its relationship with the strangers in their midst:

The water around the ship last night was simply full of fry and I never saw anything like the number of eggs (fish) that were there. The birds, which will eat out of the men's hands and will allow you to come right up to them provided you don't touch them, were enjoying themselves greatly with the fry. We've a steam jet which comes up out of the forecastle and it's very funny to see the birds sitting all round this. Suddenly it spouts up and they fly off. When it's stopped they all gather round in the steam till it starts again. I hope to get some good seagull photos and should have lots of chances, as they all gather round every meal hour when the slops are going over.

MONDAY, 13 AUGUST

Quite a nice day. Stood by machine at 9.30 am. Flew off deck in Flow at 10.30; they said it was the best take-off so far: I was off 2/3 of way down. Dropped wheels by picket boat. Did W/T and visual signalling to ship, HMS *Superb* and Scapa station. Started vertical bank by mistake (reversing controls). Was pretty well over! Also tried rolling machine which did OK. Observer fired Lewis gun at targets. Made a very fast landing. Went up expecting to crash – I don't know why, and so chucked her about so as to forget. Up two hours seven minutes. Lovely up. Light Cruiser Squadron came back in afternoon. *Borodino* alongside. Letter from Mother. Another dead body.

Dropping the wheels from the Short's floats was a bit of a nuisance so in due course a new system was devised whereby the four-wheeled trolley was fitted with a projecting arm which ran down a groove in the deck. It was arrested at the end of the deck and remained on board as the seaplane took off. The early trials for this were undertaken by Flight Lieutenant Arthur Gallehawk and Warrant Officer Dan Flemming. These were not without incident, as on an early run the buffer at the end of the groove punctured the floats. After the flight the seaplane had to be hoisted up and left suspended to drain before being returned to the hangar deck.

TUESDAY, 14 AUGUST
Very nice day. In hangar all day. Pulled again before brekker in racing whaler's crew. Some pilots ashore flying Pups. Also pulling at 6 this evening in same boat.

FRIDAY, 17 AUGUST
Pulled in racing crew after tea at 6 o'clock. Fearfully hot and sweaty. Pulled quite well on the whole. Letters from no-one tonight.

SATURDAY, 18 AUGUST
Cold day. Spent day in hangar as we were to have got under way, and one Short and two Pups would have gone off deck, only as there was no wind it was washed out. Letter from Mother this evening. Ordered a Banjoline.

SUNDAY, 19 AUGUST
Very cold day. Church in morning and wrote letters after lunch. Nothing special doing except freezing.

MONDAY, 20 AUGUST
Full calibre practice; used my new ear defenders with great success. Shooting better than previous days, but not good, one gun only fired two shots out of eight. Pretty well

smothered in smoke and cordite. Got something in my eye during GQs [General Quarters or Battle Stations]. Took some photos from fore top.

TUESDAY, 21 AUGUST

Up at 6.30 and flew off deck to do torpedo spotting. Then anchored astern of HMAS *Sydney* [a light cruiser which had gained fame in November 1914 defeating the German cruiser SMS *Emden* in an epic ship-to-ship duel]. Floats leaking so tried to get away, but couldn't start engine, so was towed into Scapa. Found F/S-Ls Boyd and Macro (great friend of George's) there! Invited 'em on board. My eye very sore, so saw one of the doctors and had it bathed. Letter from Mrs P—.

WEDNESDAY, 22 AUGUST

My eye very painful so went to sick bay. PMO [Principal Medical Officer] found a piece of something embedded in the cornea. Had 3 tablets of cocaine in my eye and then they took a tiny piece of metal (?) out. Very sore. Off duty, so stayed in gunroom. Had asked Boyd and Macro to dinner tonight, but too much sea running, so cancelled. Jack Smith wounded.

THURSDAY, 23 AUGUST

Battle Cruiser Squadron came in last night: *Renown*, *Repulse*, *Lion*, *Tiger* and *Princess Royal*. Enormous ships, especially when you see them for the first time. My eye all right again today. Letters from Mother and from Meta.

FRIDAY, 24 AUGUST

Wet, miserable day, with usual mist. RA Phillimore on board during lunch. [Rear Admiral Richard Phillimore was the Flag Officer Commanding Aircraft in the Grand Fleet. 'Fidgety Phil' was an experienced and very competent officer who gave good service throughout the war.] Spent day in hangar. Letter from Bunty. Somebody brought a Zepp down in a Pup off the *Yarmouth*. Sqn Com Busteed came on board. Also F/S-L Addis who is on the *Tiger*. Thomson is on *Renown*.

On 21 August, Flight Sub-Lieutenant BA Smart had flown his Sopwith Pup, N6430, from the platform on HMS *Yarmouth*, which was cruising off the Danish coast. He intercepted and shot down the Zeppelin L23. There were no survivors from her crew. Smart spent the next forty-five minutes looking for his ships and was on the point of landing in Denmark when he sighted their smoke. He ditched near two destroyers and was picked up by HMS *Prince*. For this feat he was later awarded the DSO.

Jack would have known of Squadron Commander Busteed as a senior officer when he was training at Eastchurch. He was on board *Furious* in connection with trials he was carrying out at the Isle of Grain where he was testing Pups fitted with wheeled and also skid undercarriages on the dummy deck. Busteed had come to England from his native Australia in 1911 and had worked pre-war for the Bristol company as an instructor and test pilot, being to a large extent responsible for the development of the Bristol Scout. He also survived the torpedoing of HMS *Hermes*.

Saturday, 25 August

Wet misty day. Got a Short up and Acland flew off deck; nearly had a crash as his controls were locked. Then engine konked and he was towed back. Spent rest of morning cleaning up hangar as VA Pakenham coming on board tomorrow. [Vice Admiral Sir William Pakenham had succeeded Beatty in command of the Battle Cruiser Force.] Got soaked on flying deck. *Repulse* and *Renown* now beside us here. Went on board *Renown* to dinner with Thomson. Glorious big ship, though she's only about our length she seems much bigger. 15-inch guns and some triple 4-inch. Had to wait in picket boat from 10.30–11.15 pm, beside *Repulse*, for Captain.

Sunday, 26 August

Dull day, but dry. VA Pakenham came on board & inspected us. Was very pleased and said he expected great things of us.

Jack's letter home included details of the minor but painful injury which he had suffered:

Well what I really set out to say was that I managed to get something in my eye. It was awfully painful on Tuesday and at night I couldn't sleep, though the doctor said I'd nothing in it. Next morning, however, with the aid of a lens they found something embedded in the cornea. So they gave me cocaine in my eye in tablets (that was as sore as the rest) and got it (the piece of stuff) out. I had to wear a bandage over it and most of my head, so that I wouldn't use the eye. It's OK now though. I've met two of the chaps on board one of our finest ships and I was on board one of them to dinner last night. Could you send me some more thick woollen socks (black), all my black ones have got holes in them and I'd be very glad to have some more, please. The other day (before I hurt my eye!) I saw four rainbows in the sky at one time! It was very curious. Some lovely sunsets to be seen, too.

MONDAY, 27 AUGUST

Had Thomson and two others to dinner tonight from *Renown*. Dirty weather. Went off in filthy weather at 8 am to spot torpedoes for *Lion* and *Princess Royal*.

TUESDAY, 28 AUGUST

Very dirty weather, quite a swell on in Flow and ship could be seen rolling. Nothing special happened.

WEDNESDAY, 29 AUGUST

Dirty weather, and kept busy in hangar all day trying to keep place dry. Letter from Meta tonight. Battle cruisers left this afternoon to go South [back to Rosyth].

THURSDAY, 30 AUGUST

Left Flow at 5.15 pm presumably for Rosyth. Different course to usual. Lot of vibration aft. All gear in hangar had to be lashed up. Most gorgeous night. I walked up and down quarterdeck for about an hour; a slight roll on, but very pleasant. We kept up 25.8 knots most of the way; no escort! Vibration very uncomfortable for sleeping.

FRIDAY, 31 AUGUST
Arrived Rosyth about 8 am. Nice but dull morning. Anchored between *Courageous* and *Glorious*, outside Forth Bridge. Work in hangar as usual.

Rosyth would now be the war station for *Furious*, her aircraft and her crew for the rest of the war. According to the revised Grand Fleet Battle Orders of August 1917 her aircraft were to be used for scouting, supplementing the work of the light cruisers and for intercepting and shooting down enemy aircraft before they could give away the position of Royal Navy vessels.

SATURDAY, 1 SEPTEMBER
Nice day; nothing doing much out of the ordinary; in the hangar all morning. To have flown, but couldn't get Short off water owing to calm and also bad revs. Took AD boat to station above Bridge for overhaul. Cox'd picket boat under Bridge. Saw some very fine 'K Class' submarines – just like TBs [torpedo boats] on surface.

K-Class fleet submarines were designed to operate with surface units and were powered by steam engines on the surface, which gave a maximum speed of 24 knots. Diving entailed shutting down the boilers, folding down the funnels and then going through the normal diving procedure – all of which took about half an hour. In service they gained a reputation for being somewhat accident prone.

SUNDAY, 2 SEPTEMBER
Lovely day. Divisions as usual. Vice-Admiral [Trevelyan] Napier came and inspected us; he shook hands with all RNAS officers including myself! He is in command of 1st Cruiser Squadron (that's *Glorious*, *Courageous* and *Furious*).

Jack's father must have written that he and Jack's mother had been visiting Tony at Merchiston and taken him for tea in Edinburgh as Jack was able to drop a hint in his letter:

Owing to having been at sea again, I've only got one letter this week – from Father. We have had better weather on the whole this week, though it's cold where we are at present, not 1000 miles from where you and Tony had tea the other day [Edinburgh]. I'm not surprised Hunter disliked scouts, as I don't think he's got the right temperament to fly them well. (I hope that's the way to express it!) He'd be much more useful flying seaplanes. He's very probably at Portland. If you get his address I'd be very glad to have it.

MONDAY, 3 SEPTEMBER

Light cruisers came back after having strafed four Hun mine layers off Jutland. Nice day, but cold. Went off in Short, but couldn't get off for a long time; finally did, but machine very tail heavy indeed.

TUESDAY, 4 SEPTEMBER

Nice day. Usual ships going in and out. Spent day in hangar. Lovely night, and show of searchlights in Firth. Tried to get off in Short but wouldn't lift. Camel came over ships and did some loops and verticals.

WEDNESDAY, 5 SEPTEMBER

Left Rosyth about 10 o'clock this morning with four TBDs. We are going on a stunt of some sort. *Lion* and other ships coming after us; Commander says 'we're off to look for trouble and will probably find it'. Lovely weather. Most priceless sight, all the TBDs. Believe they saw two enemy light cruisers, but not sure.

THURSDAY, 6 SEPTEMBER

Slept in till 7 am. Then GQs and was up on gun deck; very hungry. Then spent an hour on the quarterdeck. Could see *Lion*, *Princess Royal*, *Tiger*, *Repulse* & *Renown*; also *Pegasus* [seaplane carrier] and a host of light cruisers and TBDs. Fairly good visibility but no Zepps so far.

(Later) No excitement at all except when we saw our own K boats and thought they were U-boats! About 22 ships out, but no Huns. Object of manoeuvres Plan K – and to 'ascertain if German fleet makes any attempt to interfere with the operation!' Only saw two other vessels – a Belgian Relief steamer and a Dutch ketch. *Lion* just missed by torpedoes by a few yards.

FRIDAY, 7 SEPTEMBER

Returned to Rosyth at about 8 o'clock. Had an excellent sleep. Then went up to hangar and hoisted two Pups and Short onto deck. Nice, very warm day – touched up some sketches I made yesterday. No mail.

SATURDAY, 8 SEPTEMBER

Wet day, got Pup off deck and did usual work in hangar. Battle cruiser HMS *Inflexible* in, also *New Zealand* and *Australia*; both very ugly big ships.

Jack was feeling that he was not getting enough flying as he wrote home:

> I'm afraid I'm beginning (and also another of my lot) to get touches of nerves – not on account of too much of my work, but the very opposite. I feel like a quirk doing his 2nd solo on Maurices nowadays. It's a common complaint in this particular branch and there's only one cure – more of the business or else leave and that's most unlikely.

His letters were a useful safety valve and no doubt helped to alleviate his worries and any feelings of homesickness that assailed him. He would have been interested to learn that just as he was writing this letter trials were being carried out at Grain which would have an impact on his future flying career. A pair of Sopwith 1½ Strutters (9377 and 9390), which had been fitted with hydrovanes and flotation gear, were making successful practice landings in Sheerness Harbour.

SUNDAY, 9 SEPTEMBER

Very nice day. Were going out again this morning but it was cancelled. Service as usual. Went to Burntisland after dinner and walked to Aberdour; lovely walk, about five miles. Destroyers went out tonight, about 15 of them.

MONDAY, 10 SEPTEMBER
Left for North Sea at 10.30 this morning. Very misty, but clear at 3 o'clock and very calm really. Submarines and mother ship – a destroyer – went out first.

He hadn't managed to post his letter so continued:

At sea again. I'm sorry you'll not get this letter till late but I couldn't get it off. This is a lovely day, pretty calm, in fact unusually calm and fairly good visibility. I got one leg down into a manhole this morning and fell down till I reached the deck and so can hardly walk just at present. I twisted it a bit but I suspect it will be all right tomorrow. Please excuse this writing, but it's nearly impossible to write decently at all, under the circumstances. Priceless air out here and it makes one's face burn – unless one has to sleep on the deck and then it's far from setting fire to one! I got 'Carry me back to Old Virginny' for the gramophone and every time one comes into the gunroom that's what is being played! It's the most popular record we've got. [The American soprano, Alma Gluck, recorded the song in 1916 and it sold more than a million copies.]

TUESDAY, 11 SEPTEMBER
Up at 4 o'clock, near North Dogger Bank. Very dirty morning; had two cups of ship's cocoa to keep me alive and then went and slept in the gunroom – where I was wakened at 7.30 to get Pups up, as a Zepp had been sighted. Flight Commander Moore up but saw nothing so landed by TBD Mystic; bus lost. Another sighted at about 12; also an enemy submarine Very dirty weather, TBDs catching it.

Moore had searched among the broken cloud at 10,000 feet for an hour or so but had found no trace of the Zeppelin. On descending he discovered he was over land – was it Holland or Germany? He flew out to sea and getting very short of fuel, he was beginning to feel worried. He saw in the far distance some 'white cotton threads on the water' which didn't look natural. He flew for these and discovered they were the wakes created by a large force of warships. He ditched close to five destroyers, was thrown a line by the fifth to pass him and hauled on board with great rapidity. He was offered dry clothes by Number One, the second-in-command, but no sooner had he come up on deck again in his borrowed finery than he was soaked once more as the destroyer jinked to starboard. He thereafter stayed below until they were back in the calmer waters of the Firth of Forth.

Jack's serially completed letter resumed:

Quite an interesting day. Rather dirty weather and the ships being chucked about a little but in a ship this size it doesn't affect us much. I'm very glad I'm not in a TBD today. They are catching it. I'm going to try and get a bit of caulk (sleep) now, as I was up at 4. My hands are very cold now and that's what's making the writing even worse.

WEDNESDAY, 12 SEPTEMBER
Anchored at Rosyth about 7.30. Very nice day but bitterly cold. Wrote home.

THURSDAY, 13 SEPTEMBER
Went ashore to dockyard to return umpteen stores. Took 20 matelots. This at 1.30 pm. Got stranded and wasn't met by PB [picket boat] till 9 o'clock No tea! They'd no water but filled in about ¾ from hose as pumps weren't right. Then konked out beside a TBD with choked condenser caused by weeds getting in. Got back at 12 o'clock midnight.

FRIDAY, 14 SEPTEMBER
Nice day. Went with FL Gallehawk to Rosyth to try and get rid of Short N1630 [a Type 184]. Crashed into rocks and messed up elevator; they had no room so went to *Pegasus* [a seaplane carrier]. They hadn't. We got tea there with Trace and Arnold. Then tried *Nairana* [another seaplane carrier], with same result. Then we smashed starting gear! Had to be hoisted on board (he and I) by crane! Got going again and couldn't stop engine, so returned to *Furious* about 8.30 pm (went off at about 1.30)!

SATURDAY, 15 SEPTEMBER

Flew with Acland about 50 miles down the coast. On way back his engine gave out and we both came down at Eyemouth. Weight off my aerial gone. (I nearly did myself in just after leaving deck, as my pressure dropped (Renault-Mercedes engine) got clear of ship however in time). Crowds met us on beach. We had to wade in (clothed) to turn buses. I drifted on rocks and couldn't get going for about 2 hrs! Coast guards got me off into the open and I got off. Bus terribly tail heavy. I nearly collapsed when I got back. Made a priceless landing, I was told by Flight Commander Sibley. Acland left stranded! Absolutely done after two hours flying when soaked up to my waist!

Jack was a little unfortunate as Short 184s with 240 hp Renault-Mercedes engines were generally thought to be very reliable when compared with those powered by a 260 hp Sunbeam. In his weekly letter home he wrote about his mishaps:

Twice this week I've had no food for 12 hours! One time of these two I was soaked to my waist nearly five hours! There's absolutely no need to be anxious though. I'm fear-fully behind with my letters, I simply can't keep them up at all now as I'm kept pretty busy.

He went on, presumably in answer to a question:

About spinning, to take a machine out the usual way (it doesn't work in some kinds where you simply let go of everything and wait!) you merely take off rudder and put your stick forward again and she comes out – in a nose dive of course, but that's rather a nice feeling really. I've done it a good many times and there's 'nothing in it.' You can do it safely at 1000 feet in a Pup. We've got Cavatina on the gramophone now. It's awfully good. [Possibly Beethoven's 5th movement of his String Quartet No. 13.]

SUNDAY, 16 SEPTEMBER

Another buzz. We are going out at 2.30. Where? No-one knows. Very tired and stiff after yesterday's performance.

Had to fly Sunbeam Short from Rosyth. Couldn't go over bridge, so managed to fly under it! In spite of net wires! Awfully bucked I got through!

A letter to his Uncle Hamilton gave a few more details of this adventure:

Today I was up again and was to have gone over the [Forth Railway] bridge. My engine was failing so I had to go under it! I was *awfully* bucked when I got through without doing the bus any harm.

Monday, 17 September

Up at 2.45 am to get Shorts on deck. Weather too dirty, so had to wait until about 5. Gallehawk went off and did reconnaissance, landing again beside *Pegasus*. Fine sight to see whole Grand Fleet steaming in a bit of a sea. Got some very excellent photos of various ships. Airship broke adrift (engine failure) so Sibley had to go and look for it. Got going again all right. [He took off at 17.30 and found the NS3 within fifteen minutes.] Lovely sunset. Stripped one of our turbines.

Tuesday, 18 September

Came to anchor well above bridge and Rosyth. Had to go up in Short 1630 with Lieutenant Miller. Stayed up about 40 minutes and then came down as it was extremely bumpy. Doing right hand banks in left hand turns etc. etc! Letter from George. Smart awarded DSO for bringing Zeppelin down off the Yarmouth. Wrote four letters.

By this time Moore's temporary command had come to an end with the arrival of Squadron Commander Rutland at the end of August, who discussed the events leading up to Dunning's tragic loss with his pilots. They had seen the two successful landings and were keen to continue experimenting. Rutland was much more sceptical, as he believed it was too risky to carry on unless some means could be devised of holding down the aircraft automatically as soon as its wheels touched the deck, asking Admiral Beatty's Flag Lieutenant, Seymour, to convey his

robationary Flight Officer Jack McCleery in 1916.

MF Longhorn 8935
at Eastchurch in
early 1917.

80 hp Bristol Bullet
Eastchurch in 1917.

90 hp Curtiss JN.4
at Eastchurch.

'Old Man Shorts' – The Short Bomber at Eastchurch.

Machine gun practise at Freiston 1917.

Jack warming up a BE2 at Freiston in 1917.

Not one of Jack's better landings! Turnhouse 1918.

Jack flying a 'Touch and Go' on the foredeck in a Sopwith 1½ Strutter.

opinion to the C-in-C. Showing a considerable amount of courage, he decided that the only way to come to a firm conclusion was to try it himself:

I came in about four feet above the deck and my wing-tip was within two feet of the conning-tower. Blipping my engine, I landed only a couple of fuselage lengths from it. The airspeed of the ship was approximately twenty-five knots; I sat there for perhaps ten seconds, with the tail up, literally flying the plane with my wheels on the deck. Then I flew off, landing at the aerodrome. Next day I issued probably the shortest report ever rendered. 'I beg to submit,' I wrote, 'that, with training, any good pilot can land on the *Furious* flying-off deck. But I estimate that the life of a pilot will be approximately ten flights. I shall need tests under sea conditions to determine whether this average would be appreciably less.'

His verdict was accepted and there were no further attempts to land Pups on the flying-off deck.

A conference of the captain and officers was chaired by Rear Admiral Phillimore that day. Its conclusions were that only the most skilled pilots could be expected to land a Pup on *Furious* by side-slipping onto the flying-off deck but that a pilot of moderate ability should be able to land safely on a long flush deck in any fighter or reconnaissance aircraft. Additional recommendations were made; a landing deck of full width, not less than 300 feet in length, should be constructed abaft the ship's funnel. To accommodate this, the after 18-inch gun, turret, mast and torpedo control tower should be removed. Lifts should replace the cumbersome system of hatch and derricks for bringing aircraft up from the hangar deck. Captain Nicholson was not too keen to lose his 18-inch gun as he wished *Furious* to remain, at least in part, a fighting-ship. However, the Gunnery Captain of the Fleet persuaded him that one single big gun was almost as bad as no gun at all. Rutland was in favour of a flush deck from stem to stern with the funnel placed horizontally. He was told that such a major change would be technically much more difficult, if not impossible, and in any case would take up too much time. It was noted that removing *Furious* from the Fleet for any length of time while these experimental alterations were being carried out was not ideal. The report was then sent up the chain of command.

WEDNESDAY, 19 SEPTEMBER

Nice day. Slacked most of the day. Got my prints dried; all very good indeed. See Sqn Com Bettington, CO Flying School at Eastchurch, has been killed. Heard he had been stunting as usual; probably in mono Bristol. Also Flight Com Deville, CO School at Calshot injured; probably stunting in Baby.

Acting Squadron Commander AF Bettington was just twenty-two years old when he was killed at Eastchurch on 12 September in Avro 504B N6150.

THURSDAY, 20 SEPTEMBER

Dirty wet day. Was going to Edinburgh but put it off till tomorrow. Young Bridge now reported 'presumed killed'. [F/S-L BH Bridge and AM2 Jones had failed to return from a patrol from Cattewater in Devon in Short 184 N1099 on 9 August 1917.] Wrote to Kathleen and Rex. Make and mend in afternoon.

FRIDAY, 21 SEPTEMBER

Went to Edinburgh with Sub Lt Walker by 12.00 boat. Arrived 1.30. Lunch at North British Hotel [still a city land-mark but now the Balmoral Hotel] and then walked up and down Princess Street looking for shops. Tried to buy rock for P and K – not being made due to lack of sugar! Then up to Castle and down Cannongate to Holyrood and Back. Caught 6.00 train back after one hour in the picture house. Very dud show.

SATURDAY, 22 SEPTEMBER

Went to Edinburgh again and to picture house. Quite nice day and had a good walk. Went with Acland, Dickson, Smart and Douglas. Rough on coming back to ship.

SUNDAY, 23 SEPTEMBER

Had to take Sunbeam Short to Engadine – taxied as engine was popping very badly. Took Lieutenant Miller as passenger. Lunched on ship and then walked from Rosyth docks to Charlestown – about 7 miles. No picket boat, so had tea in hotel and then got off in *Glorious* PB with their PMO. Lovely day.

MONDAY, 24 SEPTEMBER

Regatta day. Officers' crews: 2nd (Warrant Officers) and 3rd (ours). Seamen's cutter first, rest 2nd and 3rds. Had Mrs Thyne and some other lady on board to lunch; very good lunch indeed. Wrote home and started another but got fed up so didn't bother to go on with it. Zepps expected. *Vindex* sent up and lost Pups and Short Seaplane. Poor chaps, it must be rotten in the North Sea in a Pup tail in this weather. Great band – drums, gramophone (Wee MacGregor etc). Played the kettle drum with fair success.

When writing his letter home Jack noted at the top of the page that this was one of fourteen he had written recently, so he was trying hard to catch up on his correspondence. He also had some not-unsympathetic but also fairly candid remarks on a death noted in his diary entry of the 19th:

I see the CO of Eastchurch has been killed. He was a very fine pilot, though he drank a good deal. His machine evidently went to pieces in the air owing to his engine flying to pieces and cutting it up. He was most popular with everyone who knew him and was a regular giant.

TUESDAY, 25 SEPTEMBER

Rotten day. A new Pup, 9940, arrived; got it on board and into hangar. Make and mend in afternoon. Am log officer and have about 20 books all at least two months behind to try and get up to date by Friday. Rutland is a rotter.

It appears from other memoirs that Rutland was not as popular with his pilots as Dunning had been. He was a good ten years older than most and according to F/S-L William Dickson, who was a particular friend of Jack's:

> No one likes to feel that time is passing him by and he became rather a lone wolf. For our part we admired him for his record and for his undisputed 'guts'. But we really did not get to know him or he us. He seemed too busy and engrossed to take us into his confidence and inspire us as Dunning had done.

There may also have been an element of snobbery too, as Geoffrey Moore admitted that the pilots did not like being bossed by an ex-lower deck – however valiant. He added that Rutland was greedy with the limelight and did not permit his officers to speak to senior visiting dignitaries. Rutland's biographer also commented that he did not really see eye to eye with the captain, which was not a good career move.

WEDNESDAY, 26 SEPTEMBER
Went ashore to Donibristle. To fly! Flew a BE for first time in about 4–5 months; enjoyed it immensely. Very bumpy up and very hazy. Stayed up 25 minutes with Warrant Officer Ross. Got back to ship at 5.30 pm.

Donibristle, between Inverkeithing and Aberdour on the coast of Fife, on the northern shore of the Firth of Forth, was a ships' aeroplane base in 1917–19. It was used again in World War Two, when it was commissioned as HMS *Merlin* and finally paid off in 1959.

THURSDAY, 27 SEPTEMBER
Very dirty day. Was to have gone ashore to fly but it was washed out. Took Duty Sea Boat for first time round fleet above bridge. Very heavy sea for Picket Boat and had my bones well under several times. No lunch – 4th time! Got soaked right through. Four letters tonight! Something must have happened.

FRIDAY, 28 SEPTEMBER
Was to have gone to Donibristle but it was washed out owing to dud weather. Went ashore to Edinburgh with Acland. Went to all the pictures in Princess Street! Had

quite a good time and came off by 10 o'clock boat. Saw Lightbody and Thin, who were at Merchiston with me, and are now officers. Didn't recognise them till too late and so didn't speak.

On this day the C-in-C, Admiral Beatty, completed his evaluation of Rear Admiral Phillimore's report of 18 September and forwarded his recommendation to the Admiralty endorsing the conclusions reached.

SATURDAY, 29 SEPTEMBER

Only RNAS officer on board as I was DO and others had gone to fly. Worked derrick for the first time – quite successfully. Pretty busy day of it. Rotten weather. Hear we are probably going to Newcastle to refit with probably two months there at least. That ought to mean at least a month's leave! Probably getting two 15-inch guns. [Unsurprisingly, news and unsubstantiated rumours travelled fast around the Fleet.]

MONDAY, 1 OCTOBER

Speed trials again with repaired turbine. Did 31 knots. Enormous wash over quarterdeck. Acland went off deck. Dirty weather. Kenneth went back to school tonight I believe.

Squadron Commander Rutland was away from *Furious* having been assigned to carry on with his experiments regarding the launching of landplanes from major surface units of the Fleet. On this day he took off in the Pup N6453 from a ramp fixed on B turret (the second from the bows) of the battle cruiser HMS *Repulse* and landed ashore. The purpose was to ascertain if fighters could be carried on capital ships to act in the 'air superiority' role, being launched when required to drive away and, if possible, shoot down enemy aircraft and airships engaged on surveillance activities in the vicinity of British warships. A week later he flew the same aircraft off Y turret (the aftermost). A total of twenty-six battleships and battle cruisers, as well as twenty-two cruisers and light cruisers were eventually fitted with ramps for the operation of aircraft – generally Sopwith Pups, Camels and Ship Strutters (navalised 1½ Strutters with hydrovanes, detachable wings and floatation bags). It should, of course, be noted that on none of these ships could the aircraft land back on again. In the event of being launched, the pilot had either to find dry land or ditch his aircraft somewhere near a vessel or face a watery grave – as was the case for Flight Commander BD Kilner who was lost at sea at the end of September. He took off from HMS *Vindex* in Sopwith Pup 9927 in the pursuit of a German airship and was never seen again. It should be noted, of course, that the North Sea was cold and inhospitable even on a summer's day.

TUESDAY, 2 OCTOBER
> Went ashore to fly, but as weather was far too bad, washed out. Went with Smart to Edinburgh, in our old gear. Bought a shirt, collar and stick, and changed there! Went to two picture houses as it was dud weather.

Jack's letter this week was fairly brief, for which he apologised. He thanked his parents for a parcel containing socks, films, chocolates and Horlicks. He commented how quickly the time had come around to remove white cap covers again and that it was funny to be without them. (RN officers wore white cap covers for part of the year and removed them for winter.) The main news item was:

> We've a lovely little kitten now as a gunroom mascot. We call it 'Erk and it's just one month old! We get some great fun out of it.

WEDNESDAY, 3 OCTOBER
> Went ashore to take up RN Officers in BE. Dud weather so washed out. Had a trip with Sqn Com Fowler in his car – a Maxwell, to drome and through Earl of Murray's estate. Lovely spot. On to Aberdour, Burntisland and back to tea at Crescent.

THURSDAY, 4 OCTOBER
> Went into Firth with *Glorious* and *Courageous*, and 6th Light Cruiser Squadron (LCS) for practice torpedo firing. Flew off deck. Saw two torpedoes; shot down a balloon (observer

did) and one of our own anti-drift wires. Got absolutely soaked in oil, as tank seemed to be burst, or some pipe jammed. Up four hours five minutes. Tail heavy and left wing heavy. Landed by *Pegasus* and had tea. Lovely day up. Letters from K, P and K.

He described this experience at some length in his letter home:

On Thursday I had my longest trip – four hours five minutes, and I'm really afraid I wasn't in a fit state to talk to! I was doing some fairly important work, and consequently there had to be engine trouble. After the first hour I began to be unable to use my goggles owing to the oil getting on them, so they had to come off. Well, it's impossible to see about one without goggles on a cold day and this was the coldest day we've had so far, but when oil began to come over my observer and myself in a *deluge*, it was getting to be about the limit. He had a new flying coat on for the first time. It was soaked *right through* both sides. You'd have thought his head had (without the slightest exaggeration) been dipped in a bucket of oil, and I was as bad. Both of my shoulders (in my old flying jacket – not a leather coat) were soaked through. When we turned to go back, as we were both nearly totally blinded, I had to fly low and under the Forth Bridge. I nearly ran into the bottom of one of the supports, and would have only that he [the observer] saw what was happening and stood up with his hands at either side of me and guided me through it! For the same reason I made a very dud landing. When we got alongside a [seaplane] carrier (the ship was out) they all burst out laughing at the sight of us, and that about put the lid on it! About 24 piston rings had gone! I'd no oil left (except on the sides of the fuselage, and on our persons) and only eight gallons of juice.

I managed to shoot down a large balloon that was sent up (or rather my observer did), at the same time shooting away one of my anti-drift wires which I didn't like. [These wires were positioned on both sides of the fuselage with a view to alleviating the stress on the wings and so prevent them folding backwards.] They were rather pleased about us sticking it for so long.

Jack's mother and father may by now have been used to reading of his escapades but it may be imagined that this letter may have provoked a few feelings of parental anxiety.

FRIDAY, 5 OCTOBER
Up at 5.45 am and fetched N1272 from *Pegasus* [the oil leaking Short 184]. Very cold, but nice morning. Letters from Meta and Bunty.

SATURDAY, 6 OCTOBER
Went ashore with Gallehawk to fly. I went as his passenger, to East Fortune; very fine big drome. On the way back we flew over Merchiston playing field about 100 feet up and circled round it. There was what looked like a Second's rugger match on. I thought I saw Kenneth but couldn't be sure. Fearfully cold up topsides.

East Fortune, which is situated in East Lothian on the south coast of the Firth of Forth, began operations with RNAS landplanes in September 1915 and was commissioned as an airship base in August 1916.

MONDAY, 8 OCTOBER
Admiral [Sir Frederick Tower] Hamilton's funeral. [He had been C-in-C Rosyth.] Had to go, and took sword with me. Got soaked and then had to buzz off to Edinburgh with observer Adams for East Fortune. Soaked again. Spent night at Royal British Hotel.

TUESDAY, 9 OCTOBER
Arrived at East Fortune. Flew BE and Avro. Good weather but bumpy.

FRIDAY, 12 OCTOBER
Flew over school again in BE and chased cows in various fields. Also women workers on the land.

By the end of this week, the Department of Naval Construction, under its Director, Sir Eustace Tennyson-d'Eyncourt, who had been responsible for the original design of *Furious*, having considered the views of Admirals Beatty and Phillimore, submitted its technical appreciation and proposals to the Admiralty.

SATURDAY, 13 OCTOBER

Flew over school several times. Saw K; also match in progress. Then began to run out of oil, so landed at Donibristle and filled up. Took photo. Saw Moore up in new torpedo bus. [In all probability the prototype Sopwith T.1 Cuckoo, N74, with which type the Torpedo Aeroplane School at East Fortune would soon be equipped.] Played billiards with Dickson after tea.

SUNDAY, 14 OCTOBER

Flew over ships and town in BE. Took about eight photos. Also one of some other town. Nice day but misty over Edinburgh. Photo of school with K.

MONDAY, 15 OCTOBER

Good trip with Adams in BE. Stunted round and over Berwick Law; a lot of girls were on it. Also over Haddington, New Linton, N Berwick and Dunbar. Also took up a mechanic. Returned by 6 o'clock train and 10 o'clock boat. Saw Charlie Chaplin in 'Palace'; very good.

TUESDAY, 16 OCTOBER

Off on another stunt. Going to try and catch minelayer and its five TBD escorts somewhere off Germany; also Zepps. Pretty rough; a lot of men sick. I wasn't happy till after lunch time and then was OK. Up at 2.30 am to get seaplane from *Pegasus*. Couldn't get it off so turned in again.

WEDNESDAY, 17 OCTOBER

Still pretty rough though not so bad. *Courageous* and escort joined us during the night. Duty officer. Two Pups and Short on deck. I was to take the latter and my chances of getting back to England as there were no carriers out to pick me up. About 250 miles out. Sighted a derelict. TBDs opened fire but couldn't sink it, though they'd several hits. Wish the Huns would appear, but not much. The Baltic's much safer.

Furious and her two unconverted 'sister ships', *Courageous* and *Glorious*, were part of a large force (twenty-seven light cruisers and fifty-four destroyers) which sailed from Rosyth, Scapa and Harwich to look for the German ships which carried out the raid on what became known as the *Mary Rose* Convoy. Two 3,800-ton, 34-knot German minelaying light cruisers, *Bremse* and *Brummer*, both armed with four 5.9-inch guns, steamed at high speed through all the patrol lines and, early on the morning of 17 October, surprised a convoy of twelve merchant ships, sailing from Marsten in Norway to Lerwick in the Shetland Islands, escorted by the destroyers *Mary Rose* and *Strongbow*. Both destroyers and nine of the merchant ships were sunk. *Furious* was within striking distance of two German cruisers but permission for her to launch an aerial attack was refused on the grounds that the weather was too bad to recover the Short 184s from the sea and the Pups were needed on board in case Zeppelins approached the British ships. With some luck, and a little more foresight, the German ships could have been intercepted as they made their retreat; unfortunately it was not to be and both escaped.

THURSDAY, 18 OCTOBER

Not so very rough today, but nothing doing. We are returning tonight as our TBDs haven't fuel.

FRIDAY, 19 OCTOBER

Arrived back. Went ashore to Donibristle to fly and did 55 minutes in a BE and got up to 5000 feet, where we were both frozen stiff. Could see the mountains covered with snow in the distance. Letters from K, Mother and Meta.

On the same day as Jack was flying his BE2c, the Controller of the Navy, Rear Admiral Lionel Halsey and Armstrong Whitworth Ltd submitted to the Admiralty their agreement regarding the further conversion of *Furious*.

SATURDAY, 20 OCTOBER

Went to Edinburgh and to school. Saw K and a lot of chaps I knew, mostly, or all, in khaki. Match on and we won. Saw most of the masters too, and the school. Took some good photos from topsides. Saw Mr and Mrs Mann and boys. The two German Light Cruisers we were out for sank nine neutral ships and two British TBDs old class, off Shetland. Zepp raid on London by about seven or eight of 'em. Five reported brought down.

The raid had been made by eleven Zeppelins and did indeed end in disaster with five being lost due to adverse weather conditions at the extreme altitude they were forced to fly to evade British anti-aircraft fire and fighters.

SUNDAY, 21 OCTOBER

2½ hours' notice. Church and divisions as usual. Nothing much doing except buzzes.

MONDAY, 22 OCTOBER

Duty Officer. Very slack day. Very dirty weather, wet and wind force five. Letter from Father. Nothing special today, except Battle Cruiser Fleet has come down and we may have to go below the bridge.

TUESDAY, 23 OCTOBER

Wet and windy day so nothing doing; spent afternoon in gunroom reading. Photo of school has come out very good, also self in machine.

WEDNESDAY, 24 OCTOBER

Was to have flown Short, but no engines would start. One Short left at quarter boom and I had to be in it when towed back. It was very rough and stormy abeam of the ship so I'd a job – in pitch darkness – to get alongside. She nearly went over twice. I was told I should have worn a lifeline, but I didn't. I was in it for two hours with two air mechanics and it was awful. I felt very done when I did get out.

THURSDAY, 25 OCTOBER

Very cold day; mostly blowing a gale. Got machines up on top to give room for concert. Latter a great success and some very fine performances indeed by the men. Turned in 12.15 am.

FRIDAY, 26 OCTOBER

Very cold day indeed; snowed off and on most of the day. Much calmer though. Got three letters, receipt and two writing pads from home. Setting machines back into the hangar again; crashed one streamlining on the axle of a Pup when shifting.

SATURDAY, 27 OCTOBER

Duty Officer today; nothing special except general clean up of hangar. Snowed off and on most of the day, and bitterly cold. Letter from home. Drew a Bristol on one of the mechanic's albums for him.

SUNDAY, 28 OCTOBER

Up at 6 o'clock. Not quite so cold today. Service as usual in fo'c'sle deck. Very cold indeed. Wrote home.

It would appear that Jack's letter of 14th was lost in the post, as he comments on its non-arrival in his letter of 28th. It is a testimony to the efficiency of the naval postal authorities and the GPO that this was such an unusual occurrence. It also shows the dedication with which Jack kept up his steady flow of letters. He enclosed the programme for the 'Grand Variety Entertainment' held in the 'Hippodrome HMS *Furious*' on Thursday evening at 7.45 pm 'by kind permission of Capt Wilmot S Nicholson CB, RN and Officers'. Jack marked the handbill in pencil with his brief comments on the performers; the comedians, W Treagust, W Turner, George Tillard and Dan Ryan received 'VG', while the 'Eccentric Comedian', Jack Cranston, was 'Excellent' and the 'Humorist', Will Vale, was 'Very Excellent'. He also gave this high accolade to the 'Speciality Dancer', John Bamford and the 'Club Manipulator', C Hucklesby. The various baritones, ragtime vocalist and elocutionist were not graded and one act, which will remain anonymous, was marked 'Rotten'. The evening was rounded off with a doubtless hearty rendition of God Save the King. Apparently, several of the ship's company were professional artistes before the war. Further good news was that Messrs Armstrong Whitworth had offered to present a cinematograph to the ship.

Jack went on to describe his unhappy experience on the water of the previous Wednesday:

> I'd a very rough trip some days ago – or rather nights ago trying to get a seaplane which was made fast to our quarter boom, up to our starboard boom, with a very heavy sea running on our starboard beam and in pitch darkness. I was towed round of course, but I and two mechanics had to be in the bus. The waves were coming green over her and the men were soaked through as they hadn't brought oilskins. I had and I was soaked. A seaplane is never very seaworthy and twice I was just about to jump for it when I thought she was going over. We should have been wearing lifelines but weren't. Anyhow a picket boat was standing by to pick us up if anything had happened. I was two hours in her to get her only a few hundred feet. When I got out I was quite wobbly! The machine was practically intact however, and none of us any the worse for our spree.

MONDAY, 29 OCTOBER

Went off in Short [Renault-Mercedes 184] N1224 to do PZ [anti-Zeppelin patrol] practice, W/T and visual, with fleet in harbour. No revs, so altered petrol system and she got off. Then she konked out first outside the Bridge at 2000 feet; by again altering the petrol system, picked up at 500 feet. I was at just 800 feet and going to cross bridge when some liquid started spraying on me. Switched off pressure – engine began to konk, switched on again with very little result and found radiator pipe burst. Just missed bridge by 50 feet – wind up. Got to 80 feet up across wind so slid round with hard left rudder and landed. Towed back. Hear two *Pegasus* chaps have been killed in a Short. Cheery life!

TUESDAY, 30 OCTOBER

Fine day, but very windy. Torpedo bus [the Sopwith Cuckoo] came on board from the base in the evening. No letters – mistake, one from Peggy, very well written.

On 30 October, the Board of Admiralty under the First Lord of the Admiralty, Sir Eric Geddes and the First Sea Lord, Admiral Sir John Jellicoe (who had been the first admiral to fly when taken aloft by Arthur Longmore in a Borel monoplane in 1913, from Cromarty Air Station out to the flagship in the Moray Firth), gave its final approval for the work on *Furious* to be set in hand – some forty-two days after the original meeting on board, which, in the circumstances, was a reasonably swift decision-making process. The following instructions were given:

1. The after 18-inch gun, turret, and top ring of armour to be taken out and also the Torpedo Control Tower.
2. The mainmast to be removed.
3. The 5.5-inch guns, now to be the main armament, to be rearranged, those on the shelter deck aft being moved to the lower level of the forecastle deck. Although at first a reduction to eight guns was proposed, later alterations resulted in the loss of only one, leaving ten instead of the original eleven.
4. On the space thus made available, an after landing deck 26 feet above the quarterdeck was to be built, extending from the funnel to a spot 75 feet before the stern, 300 feet long in all with a minimum width of 50 feet at the after end.
5. Another hangar, 70 feet by 38 feet was to be made under this flight deck.
6. Electric lifts, 48 feet by 18 feet, to be provided forward and aft. [The captain considered that these were the most important modifications of all as the hatch and derricks previously used were slow and cumbersome. In the event the Waygood-Otis fore lift was hydraulically operated and the aft lift by electricity for comparative purposes.]
7. To reduce the risk of aircraft over-running into the funnel, a structure somewhat resembling a large football goal was to be built, with strong rope nets hanging from the cross-

piece. Wires, with sandbags attached, placed athwart ships were also tried but were found to be too unpredictable.

8. Fore and aft wires were to be rove to keep the aircraft straight, for which purpose they were to be fitted with skids. Dog lead catches to pick up these wires were also tried.

9. Narrow gangways, 170 feet long and 11 feet wide, were to be built on either side of the superstructure and funnel to connect the flying on and flying off decks.

She would in future be able to carry eighteen aircraft, Sopwith Pup and Camel fighters and 1½ Strutter two-seater reconnaissance types. Seaplanes were no longer part of her complement, although they could occasionally be operated.

Her original building and alterations to date had by now cost just over £6,000,000. Additions in weight for the flying decks and their supports totalled 1481 tons, but 2758 tons had been saved by the removal of the two turrets and guns, mainmast, net defence and by the provision of smaller boats now that they must be hoisted by davit instead of derrick.

An incidental but useful advantage arose from the building of the high flying deck aft, since from now onwards the ship carried considerable weather helm. This meant that she practically steered herself, even at slow speed, when dead into the wind's eye for flying on or off. No bad helmsmanship need worry the approaching pilot after he had lined up.

The work was to commence as soon as possible and be completed within six months.

WEDNESDAY, 31 OCTOBER

Fair day with slight showers. Spent most of the day in the hangar. Received *Motor Cycle* from Barbara, but no letters. Have just finished a very good book by Merriman called *The Sowers*.

The Sowers, which was written in 1895 by Henry Seton Merriman, was a romantic adventure yarn of plotting and corruption largely set against the panorama of Imperialist Russia but with some of the skulduggery taking place in the major capitals of Europe. It was his biggest bestseller and was reprinted thirty times.

FRIDAY, 2 NOVEMBER

Went off deck in Firth. Engine konked three times, and each time I got off again – nearly breaking my prop each time. Came back to *Nairana* and had tea. Taxied back like a Pains' firework show – sparks, flames etc. Derrick crashed with machine level with flying deck, floats hit torpedo net rail and broke off. One man broke his leg and t'other only was soaked. They were lucky to get off alive. Machine deleted. Most of my flying gear lost. Torpedo bus flew off deck and attacked ship, but torpedo sank. It was picked up later.

SATURDAY, 3 NOVEMBER

Went to base with Sub-Lieutenant Walker to fetch a new Short to replace last night's effort. His first time up. Never had been flown – even tested, and I couldn't get her off more than 10 feet and then she konked out in fairway with strong tide running. Wound prop for 1¼ hrs with only backfires. Cause was one magneto loose in holder strap and also auxiliary mag timed wrong in BTDC and not ATDC. Towed back by picket boat from *Malaya* [*Queen Elizabeth* Class battleship]. I'll soon have been towed back by every ship in the Grand Fleet! Rumours of scrap by TBDs. Got my banjoline safely. Priceless instrument.

He described his new acquisition in his letter and also commented on his promotion prospects:

You will be very surprised to know I've got a new musical instrument. It's called a banjoline and it's like a mandolin only it's got a banjo face – the strings are like a mandolin's. It's a lovely gadget, and has a beautiful tone – not tinny at all. I can play two strings now in a sort of a way. It's pretty heavy though. One of our WOs has one and he can play it most beautifully – three or four strings at once. We have now two mandolins, a fiddle and this gadget and another of the officers is getting one like it. I suppose Hunter will have his second ring up now or very soon. Instructors get on very easily at home. It will probably be another six or eight months before my turn comes but I will at least have been on active service.

SUNDAY, 4 NOVEMBER

Fine but misty day. Service as usual – very cold. Some of our TBDs chased some Huns up in the Kattegat [the sea area between Denmark and Sweden at the entrance to the Baltic Sea] – an armed liner and some armed trawlers. 65 prisoners taken.

MONDAY, 5 NOVEMBER

Went ashore to fly. Did 30 minutes in a BE2e (first attempt) and I got up to 4000 feet where I stood still in a gale. Came down to 2000 feet and got into a thick fog. However by coming low and missing trees I got back and made a very fast landing. Took Sub Lieutenant Walker up to 5000 feet for ½ an hour in evening. Up above clouds. Acland took torpedo up in new bus and nearly had a bad accident owing to engine trouble.

The BE2e was a refined version of the faithful old BE2c. It was slightly faster and a little lighter on the controls. The main structural differences were single bay wings with blunt raked tips, the upper being considerably larger than the lower wing, a raked back tailplane and a larger, more curved vertical fin. Some ninety-five of these were used by the RNAS for training.

WEDNESDAY, 7 NOVEMBER

Two Shorts on deck. I don't know why but I've had wind up all day, and was very glad I didn't fly. We were to have gone out only it was postponed for some reason or other. Pretty dirty weather.

THURSDAY, 8 NOVEMBER

Duty Officer. Shorts and Pup hoisted on deck and lashed down for sea. Very dirty weather. Out with *Princess Royal*, *Lion*, *Tiger*, and *Repulse*. 2nd LCS and 6th LCS and umpteen destroyers. Two TBDs couldn't keep station owing to sea and rammed each other. I think they got back alright; no casualties.

FRIDAY, 9 NOVEMBER

Very dirty weather indeed. Am Duty Officer again and having an awful time. Pup and two Shorts on deck. At about 2.30 am a TBD rammed us on our port beam. I was on flying deck and saw it all. Their men all thrown on their faces. We have a decided list to port, but are OK. Her bows all bashed up and can only steam 14 knots. Two hands on watch on deck – awful job. Turned in 7.45 but owing to vibration I couldn't sleep.

SATURDAY, 10 NOVEMBER

Nice day. Returned about 7.30. Letter from Father to say George has had an accident which he thinks has been fatal. He was only about 10 days back from leave. Pray God he is still alive; am not going to write to his people till I get more definite news. I got an awful shock when I heard it. Saw the hole in our blister today. A very big gash. Ship is being heeled to starboard so as to examine it.

He wrote back immediately and was obviously in a state of shock from the stressful last few days and now the dreadful news:

I've just received Father's note and don't quite feel like writing, but I'm off this afternoon and may as well. The news has come as an awful shock to me, but as I have seen nothing in the papers I'm hoping he's still alive. I would have had your letter earlier only I've just got back from sea after some pretty bad experiences. You needn't be at all anxious though, we're all well I'm glad to say, but I was never as near it as we were yesterday, and that was only the second bit of the programme! We had very dirty weather and the nights have been as black as I've ever seen them. I did not suffer from seasickness at all. Somehow I feel as if I can never be quite the same again if George has gone. It is very strange but on Wednesday (I don't know if it happened then); I had the wind up the whole day. I was going to fly, but it was washed out and I was very glad indeed. I never felt so blue in all my life as that day and it seems a strange coincidence.

Flight Sub-Lieutenant George H Herriot died of his injuries after a crash while flying from Westgate in Kent on Tuesday, 6 November in Fairey Hamble Baby Seaplane N1327, which was so badly smashed up that it was damaged beyond repair.

SUNDAY, 11 NOVEMBER

It is true about George. How I will miss him if I get out of this war. He was the finest, straightest and best hearted friend I've ever had or ever can hope to have. I couldn't sleep last night much for thinking of him, the times we had together and the times we were both looking forward to and now he's gone. There is a blank in my life now and it will take some filling.

MONDAY, 12 NOVEMBER

Have just heard of two RNAS men being killed when flying over Edinburgh Varsity grounds. They were F/S-L Clive and PO Reardon. A dud pilot and an excellent PO. [TFS-L RD Clive and PO TCM Reardon were killed when their BE2c 8724 crashed on 11 November.] Also another seaplane came down in flames off St Abbs Head; machine from Dundee; pilot called Andrews, both killed. [This was Short 184 N1661 which crashed killing F/S-L E Andrews and Air Mechanic GW Bickle.] Grand Fleet have all gone out. We were de-ammunitioning and had to fill up again.

TUESDAY, 13 NOVEMBER

Went off one hour's notice at 11 o'clock. I went ashore with the Torpedo Gunner's Mate and two hands to bring off 18-inch torpedo from drome. Managed all right. Langton nearly killed himself flying off the deck in Pup; stalled machine which stood on its nose with engine revving. Finally went into ditch [the sea] and he climbed up the tail. Acland and I only F/S-Ls left on board.

WEDNESDAY, 14 NOVEMBER

Got under way at 6.30 am. Very fine bright day, but poor visibility. Doing a steady 26 knots. Expect to fly off deck before we get into Tyne for our refit. Will leave machine at South Shields [RNAS seaplane station and depot] if it gets as far as that! Expect 14 days' leave in a few days; am not in such a hurry as if George's accident had not occurred. Wonder will we bump a mine or get mouldied [torpedoed] on the way down! [Three seaplanes took off at 12.24, 12.42 and 13.00.] Flew off for 10 minutes. Cut Gallehawk out by landing slap up to the slip; he had to taxi for about 20 minutes! They all had the wind up, I was so close. Priceless landing.

This was to be Jack's last flight in a seaplane; it would have been a Short 184. It seems that his nerves had recovered and that he was able to enjoy a bit of fancy flying. From July to November 1917 *Furious* had steamed some 5500 miles, including one sortie of 1000 miles between 16 and 18 October. She had shown her potential, giving assurance that henceforth the fleet would have eyes reaching further ahead than the screening cruisers and that enemy aeroplanes and airships would not go unchallenged.

THURSDAY, 15 NOVEMBER
All flight officers left ship except Sqn Com [Rutland] and myself. Spent whole day at derrick hoisting out gear and shifting stores about. Sqn Com seems to take no interest in it and leaves me to do it all alone. Had 40 seamen and 30 of my own hands to look after.

FRIDAY, 16 NOVEMBER
Busy as ever. Sqn Com went to London and left me in sole charge. Lot of work to get through by Monday but I think we can do it. Wrote out night order book! About 35 seamen today. Making WOs do duty officer tomorrow so I won't be so busy I hope. Worked derrick and also used beach crane. Loaded four trucks.

SATURDAY, 17 NOVEMBER
Still busy. I spent most of day sending stores from turret down to shell room. Getting along OK but no time for a caulk.

SUNDAY, 18 NOVEMBER

Worked till 2.30 and then had nearly everything clear except a few oddments. Let liberty watch go ashore at 3 o'clock. Had a stroll around dockyard. Saw very big K boats and small E type [one of a large class of more than fifty submarines, the backbone of Britain's underwater fleet during the war] also new LC, the *Rodney* [more likely this was the *Anson* which was planned as a sistership for the famous battle cruiser, HMS *Hood*, but which was not completed] and Q boats. [One of the RN's secret weapons in the anti-submarine war – merchant vessels, with naval crews, fitted with concealed armament to lure a U-boat to close range and then destroy it before it could escape. U-boats preferred to sink merchant ships on the surface with gunfire rather than waste scarce torpedoes.]

Light Cruisers have had a scrap in the Bight. They were evidently doing our stunt and got what they were after; lucky blighters and us in dock. *Glorious* burst one of her 15-inch guns in the scrap. *Renown* did 35 knots and got right into it. They put up a smoke screen and got away – Admiral Phillimore on *Renown* refused to obey Ad Pakenham's signal to return and went slap through the mine fields after the Huns. Like Nelson's blind eye! We had some casualties, but not many.

Because of the requirement to be in Newcastle to begin the major programme of work Jack and the rest of the crew of *Furious* just missed taking part in a sharp naval encounter in the North Sea.

In November 1917 minesweeping in the Heligoland Bight to keep U-boat base approaches free from British mines was the Imperial German Navy's most important task. The mine-sweepers had to sweep further and further out to sea until eventually they were operating some 150 miles from home, covered by destroyers and cruisers who themselves, from time to time, needed battleship cover.

An ambitious sortie was planned for 17 November, involving a considerable array of vessels: the 1st Cruiser Squadron, of *Courageous* (the flagship of Vice Admiral TDW Napier) and *Glorious* but minus *Furious*, with four escorting destroyers; the 6th Light Cruiser Squadron, consisting of *Cardiff* (the flagship of

Rear Admiral ES Alexander-Sinclair), *Ceres*, *Calypso* and *Caradoc*, with four destroyers; the 1st Light Cruiser Squadron, of *Caledon* (broad pennant of Commodore WH Cowan), *Galatea*, *Royalist* and *Inconstant*, with two destroyers; and the 1st Battle Cruiser Squadron, of *Lion* (the flagship of Vice Admiral Sir W Pakenham), *Princess Royal*, *Tiger*, *Repulse* and *New Zealand*, with nine screening destroyers.

The plan was to steam across the North Sea to a position about halfway along the western edge of a large British minefield in the Heligoland Bight and, having reached a rendezvous point, turn north-west and drive before them any German forces they found, either destroying them themselves or forcing them into the path of the 1st Battle Squadron, of six battleships and eleven destroyers, which was lying in wait in cleared water between the eastern edge of a German minefield and the top north-western limit of the British field.

It was an ambitious but practicable scheme and it should have worked, but by that stage of the war the waters of the North Sea and the Heligoland Bight were infested with minefields laid by both sides. Full knowledge, even of the British minefields, was not available to all the British admirals. In fact, only Beatty, the C-in-C, and Pakenham had detailed and up-to-date charts. The others, particularly Napier, knew only of some fields, which would prove to be the cause of a lack of forceful leadership amidst uncertainty.

All of the ships involved in the operation had sailed by the afternoon of 16 November and just before dawn the next day, the leading cruisers were steaming east-north-east at 24 knots towards the mine barrier, *Courageous* was in the van, ahead of *Glorious*. The battle cruisers were about ten miles behind. Visibility at first was poor. The Germans were also out in strength, in support of a major minesweeping operation, including the light cruisers, *Nurnberg*, *Konigsberg*, *Frankfurt* and *Pillau*. Two battleships, *Kaiser* and *Kaiserin*, were lurking near Heligoland to give support. The early morning mist dissipated a little as the sun climbed higher and *Courageous'* lookouts first sighted the enemy at 7.30. *Glorious* signalled 'Enemy in sight bearing due east' four minutes later.

Courageous and *Glorious* both opened fire with their 15-inch guns but they were afforded only brief glimpses of the enemy, appearing and disappearing in the lingering murk. Confusion ruled the encounter, Napier was later accused of not being decisive enough and of failing to press home the attack and make full use of the superior speed and firepower of his two main ships. Moreover, despite the huge quantity of shells fired by all the British ships, the damage to the enemy was slight. Poor marksmanship and faulty explosive in the shells was also blamed. By 10 am the action was virtually over and within the hour a dense fog had descended. Given the poor visibility it is unlikely that aircraft from *Furious*, had she been available, would have made any difference. In the end it was a highly frustrating missed opportunity to give the Germans a bloody nose. *Furious* had, however, given ample proof over the past few months that in the event of a fleet action, her aircraft had the potential to be the eyes of the C-in-C at a much greater range than could be provided by a traditional screen of light cruisers and, moreover, that German Zeppelins could not roam unchallenged over any seas patrolled by *Furious*.

It is likely that Jack's experience working in the Mill stood him in good stead while *Furious* was being de-stored. He wrote a fairly brief letter to his parents on Sunday and explained:

> I'm afraid I've had no time to write this week and haven't now even. We're in dock for a refit and I'm in charge of our section as about half the hands and all the officers are away. So at present, I've been having a fearful time dispatching stores and shifting stuff about. I spent about two days working a manhandled derrick – no joke as there are so many guys, blocks and the purchase winch to look after. However all seems to be nearly clear and I *hope* to be home this week for 14 days' leave. From *Flight* [magazine] George seems to have spun a Schneider. Please excuse this scribble – I've been busy all day and am hurrying up so as to get to bed as I'll be up early again and there's still some work to be done. I'll wire when I'm crossing.

MONDAY, 19 NOVEMBER

Joppa fallen to Allenby. [General Sir Edmund Allenby who commanded the British forces in the successful campaign against the Turks in Palestine.] Minesweeper sunk yesterday and two Hun light cruisers damaged. Got rid of the last of our stores today by sending hydrogen cylinders to South Shields. Only cleaning up to be done now.

Kitty, who was six years old, wrote to Jack on 19 November, in ink, in her very best handwriting:

Dear Jack, I hope you are quite well. Jock is a very good dog now. One day he saw a motorbike and he thought it was you and he barked at the man who was on it because he thought it was you. I have written a letter and a postcard to Kenneth. With love from Kitty xxxxxxxxxxxxxx

TUESDAY, 20 NOVEMBER
Got away in the evening for 14 days' leave. Passed night in Newcastle. Dud show.

WEDNESDAY, 21 NOVEMBER
Started off for home by 10 o'clock for Carlisle. Then on to Preston. Preston is a hopeless place; from there to Fleetwood and so on.

THURSDAY, 22 NOVEMBER
Was met by everyone except Kenneth, in the car. Jock knew me. [It is a very human touch that Jack was pleased enough to record his pleasure that the family dog hadn't forgotten him.] Saw Mrs Herriot. She is in a pretty bad way still.

SATURDAY, 24 NOVEMBER
Went to Dunmurry on bike. Great ride.

SUNDAY, 25 NOVEMBER
Got nervy in Church in evening and had to retire! Felt awfully bad so went to bed as soon as I got home.

Jack's grief over George's death probably only really hit him when he was back in his old, familiar surroundings, which would have brought back many poignant memories of happy and carefree times shared with his friends.

Sunday, 2 December

Stayed at home all day as I was still uncertain of my head. Lit both fires. Heavy snow.

Monday, 3 December

Went to Mackies in morning and in the evening.

Wednesday, 5 December

Should have crossed back but port closed.

Thursday, 6 December

Port still closed. Ripping ride to Whitehouse in the evening. Got pretty wet coming back.

Friday, 7 December

Crossed by *Princess Maud* – Larne to Stranraer ferry.

CHAPTER EIGHT

Flying from East Fortune and Grain

The pilots from *Furious*, who had accumulated hours of hard won experience in operating from this unique vessel, were being kept together while waiting for the ship to be further converted and were billeted close to East Fortune in order to keep their flying skills current. They would have gone to the Isle of Grain but there was no room there at that time.

SATURDAY, 8 DECEMBER
Arrived Carlisle at 1.15 or so in morning. Woke up at hotel at 11 am! Got 1 o'clock train to Edinburgh. Lovely ride over hills. Arrived digs about 6.30. Very nice digs with Gallehawk, Dickson and Acland. [The Elms, Bayswater Park, Dunbar – a quiet seaside holiday and golfing resort on the coast of East Lothian some thirty miles east of Edinburgh and on the railway line to East Fortune, which was ten miles closer to Edinburgh.]

SUNDAY, 9 DECEMBER
Church in evening. Sermon on Elijah and also some good hymns.

MONDAY, 10 DECEMBER

Did just over two hours today. (East Fortune). Lovely day but cold; tried sideslipping. [A method of losing height without increasing the forward speed of the aeroplane. By moving the control stick to the right, the right aileron moves upwards and the left aileron down. The right wing drops and the left rises. This is called banking. The machine slips downwards and to prevent the nose dropping left rudder is applied. There is very little forward speed but if correctly done, the aircraft remains under control.]

Jack appears to have fully recovered from the indisposition suffered while at home but it had worried him, as he wrote in his letter of Tuesday 11 December:

It has been bitterly cold in these last two days and I've done about four hours in the air. I never felt better in the air, so I'm very pleased. I went up alone the first time in case I wasn't happy but I was full out – chasing sheep, cows and people. The latter usually on golf courses! These digs are very comfy and we're well looked after. We train up and down to EF and have a car sent for us on Sundays if the weather is good enough for flying. We're forbidden to fly over Edinburgh now, so there's not much chance of getting up to see K. Thank you very much for the chocolate.

Due to *Furious* being in dock, her ship's company missed the action of 12 December, when some twenty-five miles off the Norwegian coast the Germans once more assaulted a Scandinavian convoy of five neutral merchant vessels escorted by two British destroyers. Within the space of forty-five minutes all were sunk, except one of the destroyers, by a superior German force. Admiral Beatty dispatched battleships, battle cruisers and cruisers to intercept but the four German destroyers escaped. Henceforth it was decided that the convoys should be larger, less frequent and with a much heavier escort. As we will read below, Jack very nearly took an active but potentially very hazardous part in the proceedings.

Saturday, 15 December

Duty Officer again. Wasn't up in morning but took Lieutenant Gallehawk to Portobello in a BE in order for him to go to Edinburgh. Very thick up. Went to pictures in evening – only live place in Dunbar but full of Tommies. 9½ hours flying this week – pretty good going.

The flight to Edinburgh was somewhat stressful as Jack was looking for a suitable field in which he could land his passenger. The ground was practically invisible from 500 feet. Eventually he found one and Gallehawk was able to complete his journey by tram. He was able to report on what could have been a very nasty accident in his letter home:

A pilot the other day swerved in a BE just as he was getting off the ground. He missed a hut by a few feet and went slap through about 10 telegraph wires on our side of the railway; carried away two of the lower ones on the other side and crashed on his nose in a neighbouring field! It was rather a sticky sight but he was quite unhurt and went straight up again in another bus. The 10.30 Express was due, too, so if he'd got on the line there'd have been a railway smash. As it was they had to hurry up and clear the wires away. He was only straight up from Cranwell and it was his own fault. Unfortunately I hadn't my camera at the time.

He added somewhat mysteriously:

Acland and I had quite a unique chance of getting DSCs [Distinguished Service Cross] this week but unfortunately I can't tell you about it.

Sunday, 16 December

Dirty morning, so did not have to go EF. Went to Parish Church in morning, the sermon, hymns, psalms and prayers were all 'Jerusalem'. Organ and organist very good, a funny old man with a red face and very white hair. Had a long walk after lunch. Tea with Commander and Lieutenant Poland.

Monday, 17 December

Dirty day, but tested a BE2e after dinner. Nothing much doing. Put in for leave but was not passed.

Tuesday, 18 December

Wasn't up for a decent trip in morning – only 15 minutes. Went to Portobello and had an awful trip back – bumps, clouds etc. Was scared stiff, and very glad to get back OK.

Sunday, 23 December

Went up in car to EF. Up for 50 minutes, very nice but 50 knot wind at 2000 feet, so hard to fly against. Came back about 3.30. Church at 6 o'clock.

Jack was therefore due to spend his second Christmas in a row away from home and no doubt was thinking nostalgically about his family and fireside when he wrote that evening:

I am sorry to hear Peggy and Kitty have managed to get measles – especially at this time, but suppose they will be able to eat all right! I'll not be able to get home for Xmas as none of us are being allowed for some unearthly reason or other. I've been trying to buy Xmas presents but it's hopeless here to get anything. I sent you a small parcel which I hope you got all right. Tony and Peggy and Kitty were beyond me altogether so I'm just sending POs [Postal Orders] to do what they like with.

He then revealed the mission which might have earned him a medal:

Acland and I were to have gone out and bombed those destroyers that day, but the weather set in too foggy and though we were both very full out to go they wouldn't let us. The telegraph wires have again been carried away! Not by an aeroplane though. I saw a very fine Hun Albatros the other day; [one of the leading German types in both two-seater and single-seater versions] an RFC pilot was in it and rolled it twice about 100 feet up! I'm enclosing a piece of fabric, not doped, that we use. I believe it is a standard strength we use in all machines but I'm not sure. I've got a bit of Zepp fabric too and quite a decent piece of Zepp framework.

Monday, 24 December

Misty day, but I had to fly up to Montrose [on the coast of Angus between Dundee and Aberdeen, this was Britain's first operational military airfield, set up by the Royal Flying Corps in 1913] with a carpenter, to try and get some details of the rigging of a 1½ Strutter. Got there and back on a very doubtful engine. Flew most of way by compass over sea, touched other side at Arbroath. On way back strong tail-wind, first saw land again about 3 miles off May Island [at the mouth of the Firth of Forth]. Got up to 6000 feet above the clouds. 1¼ hours going, 40 minutes coming back. Then tested another engine for a few minutes.

Tuesday, 25 December

Stayed in Dunbar all day; rainy at first but fine later, went for a walk in the morning and to tea with Observer Lieutenant Miller. Chicken and plum pudding for dinner! Would have been much happier flying though.

Wednesday, 26 December

Flying as usual, though I managed to be DO again and had to stay on the ground most of the time. Slept in drome.

Thursday, 27 December

Flew up to Portobello with Lieutenant Gallehawk. On the way back I got up to 10,000 feet altitude in an hour; not bad for a BE. It was warmer up there than at 3000 feet, strangely. At least I only felt cold when I was about half way down. I don't love BEs high up as the sides are too cut away. Did formation flying in the morning for 1½ hours.

Friday, 28 December

No flying all day, as the weather was too bad, so indulged in lectures on armament, ships, signals and W/T. Got Nash to play the piano in intervals so made merry. Letters from Mother and K.

SATURDAY, 29 DECEMBER
Very wet morning so no flying. Unloaded three 1½ Strutters from trucks in the afternoon and also did 20 minutes in the air on a BE2e with a WO doing W/T. Went over Dunbar in thick clouds. Nice trip otherwise. Letters from Father, Peggy and Kitty and Barbara. Also four *Motor Cycles* [magazines].

His last letter of the year noted a change in the status of *Furious* and included thanks for the gift of a new diary:

We are to be a flagship when she recommissions again and are to have an Admiral and Wing Commander etc, etc. Thank you very much for getting me the diary and for going to so much trouble about it. It doesn't matter in the least about the colour, thank you.

His Walker's Pocket Dairy for 1918 was bound in red leather and on the first page is written 'JM McCleery, 1.1.18, RNAS East Fortune'. Jack also wrote the following on the memoranda page at the front:

George's Epitaph 'It is not the length of existence that counts, but what is achieved during that existence, however short'

Killed Nov 6 1917

TUESDAY, 1 JANUARY 1918
Duty Officer again. Slept in very decent single cabin with a Bastion radiator. Have an extremely bad cold and feel very rotten. Did about two hours in the air. Fine but very cold day. Flew a BE2e (not knowing) with tail skid broken and tailplane wires broken.

WEDNESDAY, 2 JANUARY
Dickson broke a landing wire in the air in a BE2e today – plane began to shake. Did about 1½ hrs in the air, nothing very special doing. Letters from Kathleen and Bunty.

Thursday, 3 January

One of Acland's king-post wires broke today in the air same as yesterday. It is the limit. Did photography, very cold at 3000 feet.

Aeroplanes of the Great War were constructed using much piano wire and cable for bracing and control. Jack's note book, in which he recorded details of the technical lessons he received at Eastchurch, contains the following information, particularly with regard to BE2s and Farman Longhorns but also with a general relevance. Control wires linked the ailerons and elevator to the joystick and the rudder to a foot bar; king-posts on the ailerons and elevator were connected to the control wires. Broadly speaking the wings of biplanes were braced with two sorts of wires, flying wires and landing wires, arranged diagonally between the upper and lower planes. Flying wires held the wings in position in the air; landing wires took the weight of the wings when the machine was standing on the ground. The wings were also supported by interplane struts often fashioned from spruce. Wires also braced the undercarriage. The internal structure of the wings, tailplane and fuselage was a framework of spruce, ash and steel tube, again braced with wires and covered in doped and varnished Irish linen. The swivelling tail skid made of ash with a metal shoe kept the tail off the ground.

Friday, 4 January

Fine day. Went down coast by myself in a BE2e as far as Eyemouth [past St Abbs Head and towards the border with England at Berwick-upon-Tweed], where Acland and I had the unpleasant time in the Shorts. Flew back over the Lammermuir Hills where it was a bit bumpy. One of Acland's flying wires carried away in the air on his BE and he had a forced landing. That's four dud wires in the one bus! No-one is to fly her again till cable wires have been put in.

Saturday, 5 January

Fine day but very thick fog up. Was going to Donibristle in a BE2e but had to turn as the ground was out of sight at

2000 feet near Edinburgh. Letter from Mother. Came back to digs at 2.30 as it was a make and mend. Smith came round for a few minutes before I'd my tea, but didn't stay for any tea. I amused him (?) with the banjoline. CP went up in forenoon and for a change didn't crash.

SUNDAY, 6 JANUARY
Fine day. Went to Church in morning and afternoon. Latter was the intercession service commanded by the King. Very fine service and a big lot of troops at it. Last post was played for those killed belonging to the Church. Wrote home, and to Aunt Amy and Barbara.

It appears that Jack made good use of one of his Christmas presents in particular, though he expressed great gratitude for them all:

The zig zag puzzle [akin to a jigsaw] is quite a cure for the going to bed early craze. It occupied two of us from 8 o'clock one night till 1.20 the following morning and then we had about a dozen pieces we couldn't fit in. However, Acland managed to do it yesterday in about 2½ hours.

The going to bed early craze may have been due to the fact that flying was a fairly tiring occupation or it may possibly have been because there was not a great deal to do in Dunbar of a winter's evening. Despite almost a year's experience as a pilot, Jack could still be surprised in the air, even on a seemingly routine flight:

I got a *very* bad bump a few days ago when flying around the side of Berwick Law [a conical hill at North Berwick, on the coast to the north of East Fortune]. Without exaggeration, we must have dropped 80–100 feet – first up and then the drop. My observer was thrown right up from his seat about four feet, missing the top plane by about 3 inches, and I was thrown as far as my belt would let me. If I hadn't been strapped in I'd have been thrown right out! It sent all the W/T instruments flying in the front seat. Acland and Dickson (who are with me) have both been promoted [to flight lieutenant] and the Sqn Com says I will probably be about March 31st. I'm a month junior to Dickson, but Acland is a good deal senior – a year or so, to either of us. Now I'm the senior sub – and the only one as the other one is I believe going away from us. I'm *almost* certain to get it in March. I was rather disappointed at the time, but at any rate I would have been very lucky if I had got it then as I've under a year's seniority

MONDAY, 7 JANUARY

Went to Donibristle in BE2e to bring back Sqn Com or Acland who had gone in Pups. Flew back with the former. Very bumpy up and very cold in front seat as there was no front wind screen. Was wiping my nose – not a word, on my gloves, which immediately became covered with ice at 3500! Gallehawk returned from a joy (!) trip in a 2C, in a very heavy snowstorm in the dark.

TUESDAY, 8 JANUARY

No flying owing to strong wind and bitterly cold weather. Unloaded some more 1½ Strutters from trucks. Only junior officer of F Squadron at station as Acland and Dickson stayed in the digs owing to colds.

WEDNESDAY, 9 JANUARY

Went for two trips of about 25 to 35 minutes between snow storms. 38 knot wind on the ground! After taxiing nearly up to the shed, into the wind all the time, the bus was blown right over on her nose and then on her back. Got a small end of her prop. Machine badly knocked about, but self not hurt. Wrote a long letter to Meta.

THURSDAY, 10 JANUARY

Went up in a Pup for about 25 minutes; got on OK, though I've not been up in one since October last. Made jolly good landing. Machine had no windscreen so was just about frozen. Went to pictures in the evening with Dickson; quite a good show.

FRIDAY, 11 JANUARY

Was not up at all and came away by 2.36 train. Had tea with Lieutenant Smith at the Bingo.

SATURDAY, 12 JANUARY

Came away from drome by 2.36 train and went to digs. Acland and Dickson went to Roxburgh and played billiards, after which I met them and we went and had tea at the Bingo and then I went off to Smith at the pension. He sings very good songs to his own accompaniment making up the song as he goes along.

SUNDAY, 13 JANUARY

Bitterly cold day. Went to Church and had a wretched sort · of a lecture on food economy. All about the bally army and she didn't seem to know who got her the food, or who it was that kept Fritz from her doors. These sort of people annoy me intensely.

MONDAY, 14 JANUARY

Very cold day and I didn't go up at all. Went and had 1½ hours skating on a pond with Miller and Dickson. Ice about four inches thick. Got on all right for me! Nothing much doing. F/S-L Price nearly knocked his innards out in a crash in a Pup, by being thrown against Vickers cocking handle. 30 degrees of frost tonight! The three of us went to Smith's tonight and had a jolly good time playing bagatelle and the piano. Also Smith telling yarns of the Stock Exchange.

TUESDAY, 15 JANUARY

Another very cold day. Hung about most of the morning till I got a BE2c and did 28 minutes. Went up for 45 minutes in a 1½ Strutter bomber. First trip since I was at Cranwell. Set incidence, folded my arms and went up to 7000 feet. Very cold, but machine priceless. I made a very good landing.

The Sopwith 1½ Strutter (or the Admiralty Type 9400 as was its official designation) would now be Jack's main aircraft type for the rest of the war. It was the first of the famous Sopwith line to achieve fame as a fighting aeroplane in 1916 with the RNAS at Luxeuil in France. It was also the first British aircraft to enter service fitted with interrupter gear to prevent the pilot's fixed Vickers machine gun firing when the revolving blades of the propeller were in the way; the observer in the rear cockpit had a Lewis gun on a moveable mounting, so it was a true two-seat fighter and in its day was very effective in this role. Strutters were also used by the RNAS as single-seat bombers. Jack would fly the aircraft in a third role, ship-borne reconnaissance. It was just as pleasant an aircraft to fly as the Pup and was very well liked by all who flew the type.

Jack's view, in his letter at the end of the week, was as follows:

I've been flying Sopwith 1½ Strutters this last week for the first time since Cranwell. You may remember I got lost in a fog in one and landed at Spittlegate. As we hope to put the wind up the Huns in them soon, we get in as much time as possible now. They're a most priceless machine to fly – and land. I had an old one up to just over 10,000 feet last week, which wasn't bad, as she had seen over six months service in France. My observer, Petty Officer Paddy Hayes (who is a very good man, lightweight boxing champion of the Fleet and very keen to get any excitement and was at school with Jimmy McGrath of Portaferry) who was doing wireless, was as lively as an icicle when we got down.

WEDNESDAY, 16 JANUARY
Very cold and misty day and so I hung about all day but did not get up. Went with Dickson to Smith's and we played bagatelle and the piano for some time. Letters from Mother, P and K.

THURSDAY, 17 JANUARY
Priceless day. Was up three times in 1½ Strutter doing photography and W/T. Went up to 10,000 last time and coming down lost all my pressure, but got in all right. Flight Lieut Clifford crashed a mono Bristol. Saw Grand Fleet out, evidently on PZ.

FRIDAY, 18 JANUARY

Too wet for any flying. Lectures all day (perhaps). Gallehawk came here for supper and we then went round to Smith's and had a row. Then we saw him off for town by the 10.40 train. Letter from Jack Smith.

SATURDAY, 19 JANUARY

No flying as it was too wet. Came away by the 2.36 train. Tea at the Bingo.

SUNDAY, 20 JANUARY

Was at Rutland's for lunch and then a six-mile walk. Then WO Adams for tea and when I got back Smith was at our digs for supper. Very nice afternoon. Very big convoy went out today.

MONDAY, 21 JANUARY

Nice in the afternoon. Put in about 30 minutes on BE2c. Flew up and down Dunbar High Street about three times low down and zoomed over the Church spire also flew along sands at about two feet up and chased Tommies drilling. News of Naval action outside Dardanelles. *Breslau* put down and *Goeben* beached. Two of our Monitors put down.

The light cruiser SMS *Breslau* and the battle cruiser SMS *Goeben* (which for diplomatic reasons had been transferred to the Turkish Navy in 1914, though still retaining their German crews) sailed from the Dardanelles on 10 January 1918 and encountered British ships near the island of Imbros. Unfortunately for the British, the two ships capable of countering *Goeben* – the pre-*Dreadnought* battleships *Agamemnon* and *Lord Nelson* – were absent, and the remainder of the force, consisting of destroyers and monitors, was outgunned. In the battle which followed the monitors *M28* and *Raglan* were sunk. However, the enemy ships ran into a minefield. *Breslau* hit five mines and sank immediately with the loss of 330 lives. But *Goeben*, which had struck three mines and been badly holed and was also attacked by Short 184s from the seaplane carrier *Empress* and other British aircraft, ran aground on the Nagara Bank and was unable to get free. She remained stranded until 26 January when she was towed off and taken to Constantinople. The mine damage was not repaired until after the war.

TUESDAY, 22 JANUARY

No flying as it was far too wet. Consequently we had lectures all day. I went to Edinburgh after lunch to see 'Our Naval Air Power' at the picture house; v g show. Flying off deck shown and airships, Cranwell etc, etc. Letter from Uncle John.

Jack gave a few more details of the film's contents in his letter home:

We were allowed to go as it shows us going off the deck and flying round. It shows Cranwell, East Fortune (airships and two of us stunting around one) and some fine ones of Handley Pages in formation over Westgate. Also the *Furious* from a height of 7000 feet (really taken at about 1500 feet). It just says 'how a battleship looks from that height' and doesn't give the name. It also shows some very fine H.12s (flying boats). Altogether it's very well worth seeing if you get a chance – even if you haven't a Middy [midshipman] at home to get the tea ready!

This twenty-five minute film was made by the newsreel cameraman Frederick W Engholm who joined the Royal Navy in 1917 and was appointed by Vice Admiral Sir Douglas Brownrigg as the official cinematographer to the Admiralty.

WEDNESDAY, 23 JANUARY

Very thick fog all day so no flying. Nothing special happened at all today. Letter from Mother.

THURSDAY, 24 JANUARY

Fine day but too windy for flying – Flight Commander Smith went up in a Pup and was blown over landing. Machine right on its back, centre section collapsed and left wing and empennage. Pilot had only about two inches clearance for his head; luckily he got off practically unhurt.

Got a photo of it. Letter from Tony enclosing prints. Firing on Bethanen [sic] sands in afternoon.

FRIDAY, 25 JANUARY
Too windy for flying and so went to lectures. Came down to sands for firing practice.

SATURDAY, 26 JANUARY
Too windy for any flying. Came back by 2.36 train having done nothing all day. Went for a stroll round the Comer promenade in the evening.

SUNDAY, 27 JANUARY
Very nice day but much too windy for any flying. Went to Church in morning and a long walk in afternoon. Had tea with Micky Smith. After dinner went to see Rev Mr Kirk; stayed there till about 12; house all locked when I got back, so had to break one of the window catches with my stick to get in.

Mr Kirk proved to have much in common with Jack, as he knew Ireland well, including the Ards Peninsula and the villages of Donaghadee, Portaferry and Ballywalter, with which the McCleery family were very familiar.

He remembers Mr Boyd and Mr Glass and has photos of the church. I think he said he was there in 1891. He's a very nice chap and has nearly three years in France, and is going again in about a week or so, to stay for the duration. He has also the MC [Military Cross] and was near the Ulster Division for some time.

MONDAY, 28 JANUARY
Fine day, but very windy. Submarine reported and Acland was to have gone out to try and bomb it, but engine oiled up and konked out. I went firing on the sands with a Lewis.

TUESDAY, 29 JANUARY
Got in 10 minutes on a 1½ Strutter; nearly had a bad crash getting off as one wing bumped down and I couldn't get it

up again. I was only about 15 feet up. Then the oil pulsator glass blew up in the air and deluged me with oil and glass. Got quite a fright at first as I didn't know what it was. Very windy and flying washed out after lunch.

WEDNESDAY, 30 JANUARY

Very windy. Took Adams up for 30 minutes in 1½ Strutter (A6) [the code number and letter of this particular aircraft marked as such on the fuselage] to do W/T over Dunbar. Got to 7000 feet. F/S-L Brierley practically killed by spinning a Camel into the ground. Gun grip went nearly through his head and one foot off. Machine an awful wreck, but at present the pilot's still alive. It would be almost more merciful if he died. He was quite young, a nice sort and married. Pilot died during the night.

The Camel was the outstanding dogfighter of the war but because it was under-ruddered it responded with lightning speed to the right hand torque of its rotary engine. In the hands of a novice pilot, if all but the gentlest touch of right rudder was applied in a turn to the right the result was often a fatal spin into the ground. Once mastered, there was no fighter that was more responsive or manoeuvrable.

THURSDAY, 31 JANUARY

Very nice day. Went up to 11,000 feet in 1½ Strutter (A6) and when coming down my carburettor fine adjustment lever rod came loose in the 'off' position. Spiralled down. Got into the aerodrome on a bad bit of ground and both my wheels crumpled up (not the undercarriage). Machine went over with a rush and I hurt my right leg, but was luckily strapped in. My observer wasn't, but he managed to keep in somehow. She went over very hard. Weird feeling, hanging upside down; released my belt and scrambled out. Got photo of bus. Also about 5 other crashes today. Two other machines being wrecked, and the others – minor ones. Went round to Dr MacDonald's for supper. Smith arrived later.

FRIDAY, 1 FEBRUARY

Was up for about 10 minutes today. Weather not very good today; one folder Pup crashed today, but the pilot was not hurt. Zepp [the British Rigid Airship R24 was based at East Fortune] went up and NS4 [as also was this North Sea Class non-rigid airship] also a Coastal [another non-rigid airship type] whose engines konked out. She landed at Dundee.

Flight Commander Moore has a particular memory of this period at East Fortune. One day as he was flying around he saw that there were no airships in the giant shed and that both sets of doors at either end were open, so he flew right through. As he admitted, it was a foolhardy stunt but an enjoyable one.

SATURDAY, 2 FEBRUARY

Very nice morning. Up for about 20 minutes. The funeral was today in Edinburgh. [Presumably of F/S-L Brierley.] Came away by the 2.36 train and had tea by myself for a change. Went round to Smith's after supper, had four WOs to dinner and we had a very musical evening. Smith was screamingly funny doing 'Grand Operas'! Got back at 12.15.

He supplied some more details about a typical evening with Lieutenant Smith in his latest letter:

I was round at Lt Smith's last night, with about four other officers and three ladies and we'd a 'musical evening'. He's quite the funniest chap I've ever come across and we're pretty chummy. He's like a very super Percy French in some ways. He can make up songs, comic or otherwise, on the spot and sing them to his own accompaniment. He does what he calls 'Grand Operas' by himself. We were in tears most of the evening.

Percy French (1854–1920) was one of Ireland's foremost song-writers and entertainers in his day. Among his most famous songs are the comic 'Abdul Abulbul Amir', 'Are Ye Right There Michael' and the nostalgic ballads 'Come Back Paddy Reilly to

Ballyjamesduff' and 'The Mountains of Mourne'. The modern Irish tenor, Brendan O'Dowda, was a great student and exponent of Percy French songs.

SUNDAY, 3 FEBRUARY

Very nice day indeed. Got up at 9.50 and went to Church. Quite good sermon. Went for a walk in afternoon. Very mild out and the air full of flies, just like spring.

MONDAY, 4 FEBRUARY

Priceless day, but rather windy and so had only one flight. Doing wireless with Miller. Rather unpleasantly bumpy up topsides.

TUESDAY, 5 FEBRUARY

Very good day, odd showers and windy, but managed to get in about 2¼ hours on a BE2e and 1½ Strutters. Very gusty near the ground, the latter machines ballooning up when they'd nearly stopped. Pictures in the evening.

WEDNESDAY, 6 FEBRUARY

Too windy and uncertain for flying. Went to see our rehearsal for Smith's concert and then came away by the 2.36. Nothing doing at all.

THURSDAY, 7 FEBRUARY

Very nice day, so took Adams up in a BE2e and we flew up and down Dunbar High Street, chased fishing boats and old Micky Smith who was firing guns on the sands. Priceless trip, only inches over the telegraph wires.

FRIDAY, 8 FEBRUARY

No flying except 35 minutes on a BE2e. Fearfully bumpy day and very hard to land right end up but I did manage it. Played rugger against the men after lunch and beat 'em by 16–13. Hurt my left knee a bit.

SATURDAY, 9 FEBRUARY

No flying so came away by the 2.36. We all went round the shops and ragged the girls in them. Had tea at the Bingo with the others. After lunch went to Smith's for a rag. Quite fun only we were all a bit stiff and tired but very full out.

SUNDAY, 10 FEBRUARY

Church morning and evening. Said goodbye to Mr Kirk who goes to France tonight. One of the chaps I knew at school has been killed in France and his mother was staying in Dunbar, so I had supper there.

MONDAY, 11 FEBRUARY

Flew over Dunbar again low down, but as I got a very bad headache I came away early. Letter from Hunter.

There are no diary entries for the next two weeks but Jack wrote home on Tuesday:

We had a most extraordinary accident here today. I was going up for a joy trip in a 1½ Strutter and was strapped in when suddenly I saw a Pup coming straight for us at about 80 knots. I was behind as passenger and undid my belt and got ready to jump. Then it swerved clear and went straight for the shed doors. I saw visions of a little splash on the door like when you kill a fly on the wall with a slipper! However he flew through the doors into the shed with about four feet on either side clearance. Then a most appalling crash. He was quite unhurt but smashed three machines. Some escape!

His next letter, a few days later, relates:

We've been having pretty rotten weather here lately, and except for one day, Thursday, when I was up five times, I've done very little flying. The ship is practically ready now and we will be at sea almost certainly within a month. We expect to join her about the 2nd or 4th. We may or may not get a week's leave first.

Mr McCleery must have tried to arrange to come over to Edinburgh or Dunbar to see Jack as he wrote a letter to his father only on 21 February:

I received your wire [telegram] last night when I came back from the aerodrome. I am afraid however I would hardly like to arrange anything just now as I am expecting to go to Cranwell the first fine day we get. I was to have gone today but the weather is very stormy and, as it is a very long flight, I wasn't allowed to go and am just waiting for better weather. If I go, I will probably have to stay for at least four days, and then, if the weather is not good enough to fly back, I may have to stay even longer. We are expecting though to get four or five days leave just before joining the ship. The squadron as a whole will not leave here till after the 2nd, but some of the men will be on the ship earlier and will require officers. Also we have been told that we will have to go to Grain for a week for practice in an experimental work. This week I am afraid it [his father's visit] would be quite out of the running for me, and the only other thing would be to cross on Monday night (letting me know what time you would arrive in Edinburgh) and I would try and meet you some time in Edinburgh on Tuesday afternoon [26th]. But the question for me is will I be here then? My own idea would be this. Wait till we are on the ship. Our Squadron Commander says we'll be stationed 'here'. We've taken over Turnhouse from the RFC for our own use. It's in easy reach of town. Then if you could get over you could see me the first day at Turnhouse and I could probably get special leave to Edinburgh. Please let me know what you think, as really my candid idea at present is that it's 100 to 1 that I'll not be here if you come just now and that it would be advisable to wait.

The airfield at Turnhouse had opened in 1915; it was only seven miles out of the centre of Edinburgh and indeed would become the city's civil airport in 1947.

It is obvious that Jack was keen to see his father but did not want him to have a wasted journey, nor did he wish to offend by putting him off without a very full explanation. In the event he made a very wise decision as he was granted leave from Monday morning.

MONDAY, 25 FEBRUARY
Left Dunbar by 8.30 train for East Fortune. Caught 11.20 to Edinburgh; the 1 o'clock to Glasgow and the 4.10 to Stranraer. Slept on a couch at the King's Arms – quite a nice old place. Caught boat at 7 pm. Very rough crossing indeed and hawser parted when we got across to Larne and were being made fast to the pier. Got to town [Belfast] at about 1.30 and home.

TUESDAY, 26 FEBRUARY
Saw Mrs Herriot and went to the Mill. Saw Meta in the afternoon and also Bunty. Rang up Kathleen in the usual way. Hunter returned last night to Lee after leave. Rotten luck. Bike going awfully well, considering.

WEDNESDAY, 27 FEBRUARY
Blinded down to Whitehouse and spent the morning with Kathleen. Also saw Ina for a few minutes. Rex expecting to be home for Easter.

THURSDAY, 28 FEBRUARY
Went for a joy ride out to the tar patch with Tony and we did some priceless blinding or 'stouring' as poor old George would have called it. Took many photos. Developed a film after tea with Tony's help. Saw Bunty again.

FRIDAY, 1 MARCH
Went to Bunty's for dinner. Annah Jones, Kathleen and Eillen [sic] and Frank there. Tony went with me. Had a very good time, learning to 'dance' etc; also played the banjoline for some time.

SATURDAY, 2 MARCH
Went to Dunmurry in morning: no-one there, so chased after pigeons with the gun, but couldn't get near them. After dinner went to Whitehouse with Tony in the carrier. Went a walk through many muddy fields and took photos without number. Had tea there and came home. Managed to 'rev' up Grey's Lane in bottom with Tony up. Jolly good

show indeed for the old bus. Had tea again with Uncle H and Aunt Amy after which I showed them all my new photos. Then a walk down the road with Father and Tony.

SUNDAY, 3 MARCH

Walked to Church both times with Mother. Good services and a new organist who was very good indeed, I thought. Usual 'how do' with Miss Wright in Church, nice old lady.

MONDAY, 4 MARCH

Said goodbye to Bunty and Kathleen just after brekker as they, or rather Bunty goes to the Tech and K— was going back to Whitehouse. Went off by 5.20 pm. Bunty and Kathleen were on the station as I went past so blew them kisses which were of course returned. Back to the war and more worse luck, and Grain at that.

TUESDAY, 5 MARCH

Got into a 1st class carriage and slept most of the way down to Euston; breakfast at Euston. Left luggage at Charing Cross, had lunch there and met Acland after. Caught 5.20 and arrived in this unmentionable hole at 7.30 pm. Supper. Have small cubicle to myself, which is *fairly* comfortable.

WEDNESDAY, 6 MARCH

Did about 20 minutes in an old Curtiss and enjoyed it awfully, as I'd not seen one since Eastchurch days.

THURSDAY, 7 MARCH

Up in a skid Pup and tried landing between flags. Bust some wires though landing was quite good. Wakened up at about 11 o'clock by heavy gunfire, air raid going on, could hear machines and bombs but too sleepy to bother much; they got up to London – two aircraft; killed 11 and injured 46.

Jack's understanding of the raid is confirmed by a report in that week's *Flight* magazine:

Last night's air raid appears to have been carried out by seven or eight enemy aeroplanes, of which two reached and bombed London. The first two raiders approached the Isle of Thanet about 10.55 pm and proceeded up the Thames Estuary. Both were turned back before reaching London. Meanwhile a third raider came across the Essex coast at 11.20 pm and steered west. At 11.45 pm it was reported over East London, and a few minutes later dropped bombs in the South-Western and North-Western districts. At 11.50 pm, a fourth aeroplane, which had also come in across Essex dropped bombs to the north of London, and then proceeded south across the capital, dropping its remaining bombs in the northern district between 12.20 and 12.30 am. The remaining enemy machines, all of which came in across the Essex coast, were turned before they reached London. A certain amount of damage was caused to residential property in London, several houses having been demolished. Latest police reports state that 11 persons were killed and 46 injured in last night's aeroplane raid.

While they were at East Fortune, Jack and the other pilots from *Furious* had practised landings on a marked-off space on the airfield to simulate the accuracy they would need when attempting landings on the re-fitted aircraft carrier. Meanwhile, the technical staff at the Isle of Grain had been working to devise an arresting gear that would keep the aircraft in a straight line and enable it to land without hazarding a plunge off the side of the deck into the sea. It consisted of a series of parallel wires, running fore and aft, raised a few inches above deck level by blocks of wood, rather like the strings on the neck of a guitar. Hooks were fixed on the undercarriage of aircraft designed for carrier operations, with the aim that these would engage the wires and so slow down the machine. A dummy wooden deck was also constructed. Some aircraft retained their wheeled undercarriage; others were fitted experimentally with wooden landing skids. Taking off from the grass airfield on skids was accomplished by rocking the machine back and forth until it gathered way. The date 7 March was also significant in that it saw the first successful take-off of a Ship Strutter (N5644) from Q turret of the battle cruiser HMAS *Australia* by Flight Commander DG Donald RNAS.

FRIDAY, 8 MARCH

Up in a wheel Pup for about 30 minutes. Good landing and then up in a dear old 1½ for about 10 minutes; good landing also. Boxing tournament in the evening and some quite good sport.

SATURDAY, 9 MARCH

Nice day, but no machines – great relief; sat on beach most of the morning and watched big flying boats. Attempted air raid in the afternoon; heard the firing and machines, but couldn't see anything.

SUNDAY, 10 MARCH

No flying as there was a heavy fog. Spent quiet day in my cubicle. Letters from Mother and Kenneth.

FRIDAY, 15 MARCH

My birthday. Letters from home – and Bunty and Kathleen. Former sent me very nice little saccharine case and the latter a farthing identity disc – awfully neat. Very nice ginger bread from home. Also shamrock – with lots of four-leafed ones. B & K sent me a five-leafed one tied with a bit of silk.

The work on *Furious* had been completed in record time, the original estimate of six months being reduced to four and on this day, still under the command of Captain Nicholson, *Furious* re-commissioned and hoisted the flag of Rear Admiral Phillimore. She left the floating dock at Newcastle and sailed for Rosyth on St Patrick's Day, 17 March.

In his last letter written from Grain, Jack described something of the experience of being in the path of the German raiders on their way, more or less successfully, to London:

I'm trying to hurry up with this letter as it's a priceless night for a raid and we may have one. It's not easy to write by candle – especially if one's outside watching the sport. We'd one a few nights ago – at least we were in darkness waiting for one but we'd no luck. Complete darkness is our first warning [as the air raid precautions would trigger any electric lights being extinguished] and then the barrage [from anti-aircraft guns which fired more in hope than in expectation] and various sized chunks of metal clattering off the roofs of the huts [expended ammunition shrapnel which had failed to connect with a German aeroplane]. If a large picture arrives for me would you please keep it, and sometime when you've time get it framed in a dark frame for me please? It's called the Sea Hawk and is of a Short seaplane on patrol. It's quite a good picture and is done by an RNAS man, and I couldn't resist it, as I've done the job myself before now.

MONDAY, 18 MARCH

Flying as usual. Wing Com Busteed told me tonight that I've to report to ship Wednesday pm. Very decent day, and spent a good deal of time in 1½ Strutter. Acland, Dickson and I told that evening to report on board *Furious* on Wednesday. So an awful job packing.

TUESDAY, 19 MARCH

Left Grain by 1.10 pm. Spent afternoon in town with Acland and Dickson. Naval train full up so went by 10.30 pm, King's Cross. Acland, whose uncle is the RTO [Rail Transport Officer] there got a 1st class compartment reserved for us. Slept most of the night, till we got to Berwick and from there to Dunbar of happy memories!

CHAPTER NINE

HMS *Furious* – Reborn and Very Active

WEDNESDAY, 20 MARCH

> Wing Comm Busteed on same train so couldn't go into Edinburgh as planned. Reported on board am. Got on board with ship under way. Left gear on picket boat and scrambled up the underside of the gangplank as it was being hoisted. Rutland landed on deck at 11.03 am – very bumpy indeed; machine practically out of control. Busteed did it with ship at anchor. Landed much too fast, deleted machine and cut his nose badly. Cheery start off.

No doubt Jack was impressed by the altered profile of *Furious*, now with flat decks fore and aft, with the central superstructure and funnel in between. The officers would have been delighted by the spacious new wardroom formed from the circular barbette where once had been the aft 18-inch gun. He would also have been startled by the remarkable transformation of her paint scheme. The uniform coating of battleship grey had been replaced by vivid streaks of blue, light green, light grey and extra dark grey. Since the beginning of the war the Admiralty had experimented with different ways and means of camouflaging ships to make them less visible to the enemy at sea. However, even if the camouflage looked effective in harbour, to the U-boat captain low down on the water it was a different matter. He could always see the outline of the ship silhouetted against the sky. An artist, Norman Wilkinson, proposed a radically different approach – the enemy would be deceived by ships being painted so conspicuously that they would confuse the onlooker by creating an optical illusion which would mislead the U-boat's lookouts as they tried to calculate the course, size and speed of its prey. This became known as dazzle-painting. Large flat areas of contrasting colours on the hull and superstructure acted to break up the accepted form and outline of the ship and made the normal reference points for an attacking U-boat more difficult to establish. Design of the dazzle patterns was carried out at the Royal Academy in Piccadilly and trained dazzle officers supervised the painting of the ships in port. There is no proof that dazzle-painting worked but there is some evidence that it did indeed confuse an observer's eye. For example, the skipper of a convoy escort recalled:

> The sixth in the line was 'dazzle-painted' and it appeared to me to be steering at least eight points different to the other ships in the line. So remarkable was this optical illusion that I sent for all my officers and asked for their opinion as to the course of the ship. Not one officer agreed within four points. This optical illusion continued until the ship in question was past our beam when it was seen that she was steering the same course as the others.

Geoffrey Moore later made the interesting comment that the pilots had not been consulted about the alterations to *Furious* and that they looked at the ship with a critical and lively eye. Squadron Commander Rutland was the first to try landing on the new deck aft on a skid-equipped Pup. He was not very keen on the skid undercarriages as they were unsprung and due to their rigidity were liable to break on contact with the deck, no matter how smooth a landing had been effected. Their only advantages were that it was easier to fits hooks than to a wheeled undercarriage and the skids did not roll away as the aircraft scraped to a halt. *Furious* was steaming at 28 knots in order to generate sufficient wind over the deck, as there was a light wind and a calm sea. If there had been more wind on the bows then *Furious* could have reduced speed and this would have caused much less disturbance over the stern as the exhaust gases would also have been considerably reduced. In the event Rutland encountered heavy turbulence and as he slowed to just above stalling speed, his aircraft wallowed and pitched alarmingly. He landed safely but heavily, breaking an undercarriage strut in the process when it touched one of the baulks of wood under the arrester wires. Rutland had already voiced his unease as he believed that the eddies formed by the passage of any large body (such as *Furious*) through the surrounding air was certain to be complicated by additional obstructions such as the superstructure and funnel amidships. He could be flying alongside the ship and the air would be quite smooth and uniform but the worst effects were always going to be just where an approaching pilot needed to line his aircraft up for landing, about 150–180 feet abaft of the funnel.

As Jack noted in his diary above, Wing Commander Busteed, an equally proficient and experienced pilot, fared even worse. As the ship was at anchor he did not have to worry about the turbulence created by funnel exhaust gases but as he had no wind over the deck to allow him to remain flying at the slowest possible speed above a stall, he came in too fast and ended up crashing into the safety net with the painful result indicated. Rutland and the other pilots, while sympathetic, were also wryly amused; firstly because Busteed's Pup, N6438, bore the rather appropriate name *Excuse Me* and secondly because he had boasted beforehand that it was 'too easy'.

The strategic aims of the Royal Navy in 1918, when *Furious* rejoined the Fleet may be summed up in the words of the C-in-C:

> The correct strategy of the Grand Fleet is no longer to endeavour to bring the enemy to action at any cost, but rather to contain him in his bases until the general situation becomes more favourable to us. This does not mean that action should be avoided if conditions favour us, or that our role should be passive and purely defensive.

The Admiralty and the War Cabinet agreed with Admiral Beatty's point of view, taking to heart the observation of a New York newspaper that at Jutland the German Fleet had 'assaulted its jailor but was still in jail' nearly two years later. By the spring

1918 the worst of the U-boat war was nearly over; the Royal Navy, together with the US Navy, had succeeded in reducing the monthly loss of merchant shipping to a sustainable level – more merchant tonnage was being built in British and American shipyards than was being sunk. Moreover, U-boat losses continued to mount and a steady rate of attrition was maintained. The blockade of German sea-borne commerce continued and the High Seas Fleet remained for the most part impotent and inactive. It was confidently believed that the steady flow of men and supplies across the Atlantic would tip the balance on the Western Front in the Allies' favour. *Furious* would be firstly devoted to the tasks of working up and experimental landings on the new deck; thereafter the main objectives of her operational sweeps would be reconnaissance of enemy minefields, protection of British ships from airborne attack and surveillance, a daring strike on an enemy base and with an underlying motive of trying to draw out the enemy fleet to its doom.

THURSDAY, 21 MARCH
Went ashore to Turnhouse in morning. Flew round ship in Pup. Awfully bad up. Walked to Barnton with FSLs Thomas Thyne and Joseph Langton and then to Queensferry. Very tired as it was a warm day and I'd a coat on. Wrote to Bunty and sent a wire home.

FRIDAY, 22 MARCH
Very warm nice day. Spent day doing nothing most of the time in the gunroom. Admiral Phillimore arrived on board.

SATURDAY, 23 MARCH
Duty Officer, so spent day on board cleaning up hangars etc. Nothing much doing. German big push started today I think.

The German offensive had begun with Operation *Michael*, on the Somme-Arras sector, one of a rolling series of attacks which would become known as the *Kaiserschlacht*. This was General Erich von Ludendorff's great gamble, to strike on the Western Front and defeat the British and French armies before the Americans could arrive in strength and change the balance of forces decisively

SUNDAY, 24 MARCH

Usual Sunday routine; Church as usual. Spent most of afternoon down in the gunroom.

MONDAY, 25 MARCH

Lovely day. Jackson landed on deck – horrible sight, but Thyne trying it put the wind up me terribly – and most other people. I didn't feel right for nearly one hour after it. He just missed death by about six inches several times and then was stopped trying it, and flew back. It's by far the most risky job I've come against. It's obvious it's a wash out but I suppose they'll go on till someone's killed before they stop it.

TUESDAY, 26 MARCH

Have got an awfully severe cold in my chest and a slight catarrh, whatever that may happen to be. Spent day very quietly and wrote letters.

This was Jack's first letter home since he had arrived once more on the ship and he began by apologising for not having been in touch before:

I'm sorry for not having written before this, but we are so busy at present trying to get things straight on board, that there's very little time to spare. I've been slinging a hammock up till now, but I am going into quite a decent cabin tonight, nearly amidships, so I'm quite pleased. I could hardly find my way about the ship when I arrived, it was so changed but that's all I can say about the ship.

THURSDAY, 28 MARCH

Acland, Dickson and Rutland went ashore to fly on to deck. Rutland landed, and was blown up against the combing down the deck. The deck party rushed out to catch him, but machine blown over the side about a second too quick for them. I saw pilot dropping out and the machine going after him. Terrible sight and shook me properly. Luckily machine caught in tubes below – upside down and didn't fall on him. He was in the ditch for about 20 minutes. That washed it out for the day thank heavens. It put the wind properly up a lot of visitors from the carriers.

Rutland's mishap happened because the lift cables from the hangar had stretched and the top of the lift was a couple of inches below the deck level. His Pup drifted sideways and the undercarriage caught against the edge of the deck and went up on one wing tip. At the same moment the engine fired briefly and the propeller also touched the ridge in the deck which was enough to tip it over the side of the ship. Making a snap decision that probably saved his life, he jumped clear. He later wrote:

> When it did roll over I was ready, pushed out with my feet and took the biggest tumble of my life. I was travelling sideways at 28 knots and fell 55 feet. On striking the water I immediately swam down, though the impetus of my fall had already taken me to a great depth. From my experience as a diver I reckon that I must have gone down 30 to 40 feet, for it had begun to get dark, as it does when one reaches that depth in a diving dress. But I was anxious to be deep enough to clear the ship's propellers. When I struck out for the surface, I seemed an unconscionable time reaching it. I then swam around waiting for the lifeboat. Finding a cushion that had fallen out of the aircraft, I used that to assist myself to remain afloat, instead of trying to swim to a Kelvin life-buoy a few hundred yards away. *Furious* had put her helm over and completed a circle before she dropped the lifeboat. It was twenty minutes from the time I entered the water until I was picked up but this was much the quickest method with a ship steaming at high speed and was a smart piece of work. I climbed into the boat without assistance and the only injury of which I was conscious at the moment was two lovely black eyes, though later I found that I had twisted my knee and loosened a bit of cartilage, which gave me some trouble.

Jack's particular friend, Dickson, well remembered the black eyes with which Rutland came back aboard and subsequently described his account as vividly correct. The aircraft did not in fact fall clear of the ship into the water. It turned upside down and became wedged on the twin torpedo tubes which were fitted on either side of *Furious*, two decks below the flying deck. They projected out over the side and a sparking-plug in the engine caught in a counter-sunk rivet-hole. Had Rutland not jumped from the aircraft it is likely his head would have been smashed onto the ship's side or the torpedo tubes. He in all probability saved his life with not more than a second or two to spare by his quick thinking.

FRIDAY, 29 MARCH

Sunday routine, so divisions and church in morning. Very cold up on cable deck during service, and I don't think it will have improved my cold a great deal.

SATURDAY, 30 MARCH

Did not go ashore to fly on account of my cold. Got a wind-shield for my observer's cockpit in our 1½ Strutter. Turned out a very wet afternoon indeed, so spent most of my time in the cabin. Wrote to Cox's and arranged about my pay.

MONDAY, 1 APRIL

RNAS and RFC join together to form the RAF, worse luck. Whole RNAS fed to the teeth, and a good many resignations going in. Will do so myself if they try to interfere with my job.

Before it was disestablished the RNAS had reached a strength of 55,000 personnel, nearly 3000 aeroplanes and over 100 airships. Jack wrote home on the following day; it was undoubtedly the unhappiest and indeed angriest letter of all those he penned:

I'm afraid I've missed my promotion again this time, as no Admiralty list has been published this quarter for the RNAS. Of course, at present I'm supposed to be a Lieutenant RAF, but I hope and we all do that the whole thing will fall through. I personally am going to refuse to transfer to the RAF because (1) it's only the RFC under another name and is therefore Army all through, and (2) we transfer for the duration, or 4 years, *whichever is the longest.* So you may see me home again and in civvies in another 3 months if all's well. Of course, as I come from Ireland I can't be conscripted, but even then a great many RNAS people are going to refuse to transfer, as they'd rather for one thing (to say nothing of other reasons) be a Tommy for the duration rather than an RAF officer for 4 years from the date of transfer. I'm sure a good many of the RFC will raise the same moan too. If I do come out of it, I'll try and get a commission in the RNVR, which is a bit of a come down but not so bad as the RAF, and get on the Dover patrol. I never want to spend a week like the last one again. I can't tell you why, but it shook me to the core, and also most of the others. This is a very scrappy letter, but my news is all mixed up in my head and consequently on the paper too. So far I've only been ashore once since I came on board, mostly due though to my cold. One of our pilots took up a commander for a joy ride yesterday (his first flight). Had an engine seizure, and a forced landing in a ploughed field and turned over. As his passenger wasn't even strapped in and bashed his nose in, I should think he'd have more appreciation for the risks a pilot runs in future! Well, I must close know, hoping to be paid some day (I've not had any for two months owing to moving about) though I have a cheque book, and hoping you are all well.

The Dover Patrol was one of the most important Royal Navy commands of the First World War and consisted of many different types of warship from cruisers, monitors, destroyers, submarines, armed trawlers and drifters to paddle mine-sweepers, armed yachts, motor launches and coastal motor boats; as well as seaplanes, aeroplanes and airships. It performed a number of duties in the lower half of the North Sea and the Dover Straits: anti-submarine patrols; escorting merchant vessels, hospital and troop ships; laying mines and constructing mine barrages; sweeping up German mines; bombarding German military positions on the Belgian coast; and sinking or trying to sink U-boats. Its flag officer in 1918 was the charismatic Vice Admiral Roger Keyes, whose drive and tactical acumen had considerably improved the Dover Patrol's kill rate of German submarines since he assumed command at the end of

1917. It is not surprising that an enterprising young officer such as Jack would wish to serve there, even though it would still be second best to the RNAS.

THURSDAY, 4 APRIL

Went ashore to fly. Had a forced landing in a Pup and pulled it off OK. Then did an hour over the ship and the drome. Quite a good day, so walked back to Dalmeny.

SATURDAY, 6 APRIL

Very poor weather, so did not go ashore to fly. Two 1½ Strutters with Gallehawk and Jackson flew off at anchor. Very sticky sight as there was no wind at all and they just missed the ditch by about two feet each.

SUNDAY, 7 APRIL

Usual Sunday routine; Captain quite pleased with our machine all painted.

It would seem that Jack was also very pleased with his handiwork, as he wrote:

I wish you could see my bus – I've the cowl [the engine cowling] all painted – and I did it myself mostly, in about eight inch horizontal stripes of bright navy blue and a sort of red lead colour. It looks quite well, so do the others.

No doubt the pilots were pleased at being able to customise their aircraft but there was also a practical point to this – if as it would have appeared the plan for aircraft to take off from and land back on *Furious* now had to be modified in the light of the highly dangerous landing experiments, then it would be of considerable help in spotting an aircraft ditching in the North Sea when returning from a mission, if it was to be painted in bright colours.

Jack's parents, being canny and careful Ulster Scots, must have expressed concern over his financial situation and he replied:

You need not send me any money, thank you, as I don't intend to pay any mess bills till I get paid.

Monday, 8 April

Minelayer and about 14 TBDs went out, followed by six light cruisers and the 1st Battle Cruiser Squadron (BCS). Went ashore to fly but didn't go up. Walked back. F/S-L Davis killed in a BE2e while passenger with F/S-L Bird. The latter got off very badly and then stalled the bus at Donibristle. Pilot seriously injured. [NP Davis and GA Bird in B4556.]

Tuesday, 9 April

Went to Edinburgh with Rattray and Acland. Did some shopping and much walking. Had a very good tea at Mackie's.

Wednesday, 10 April

Was to have flown off the deck this morning but weather very dud so washed out. Spent most of morning at guns and afternoon in cabin. Wrote to Bunty and Tony.

Thursday, 11 April

No flying owing to very nasty weather. Went from four to one hour's notice at 7.30 pm. Of course was DO and just getting down to dinner when I was told I had to call out Duty Watch to lash down for sea. Very rough prospects. Busy till 10 o'clock and then turned in. Went out at 11 o'clock; seems a big affair. Huns seem to be getting near Calais and have got Armentières, so German Fleet may come out. Hope so – in some ways.

During the course of 1918 an engagement between the Grand Fleet and the High Seas Fleet was keenly anticipated on the British side. As regards events in France, the *Michael* offensive had passed its zenith and had come to a halt within ten miles of Amiens. The Germans had gained territory but at a heavy cost, the British and French were battered but undefeated – the line had held. On 9 April, the German Operation *Georgette* began in Flanders. Field Marshal Haig, the British C-in-C, issued his famous 'backs to the wall' command in his Order of the Day on 11 April. Again the defenders heroically held the line.

Friday, 12 April
Up at 5.30 am. Two 1½ Strutters on deck and lashed down. Acland and Jackson duty pilots. Heavy mist all over. Grand Fleet out also, counted 36 warships. What's the game as we are patrolling N and S 80 miles out from Rosyth? Beautiful calm sea – still two mechanics very ill. Stores officer never left his cabin! On our way back again! Wonder will we still hold Calais when we have got back to port.

Saturday, 13 April
At 1½ hours' notice again. Went to ½ an hour for a short time, causing intense satisfaction and excitement.

Sunday, 14 April
Usual Sunday routine; went for a walk over Burntisland golf links till 3.45 pm and then returned to ship.

It would seem that Jack was slightly more reconciled to the RAF (but only slightly) as he wrote:

About Tony joining up, unless he cared to try for RNVR snotty – midshipman, which is a pretty rough job in many ways, though he'd soon be on a ship of some sort, I'd suggest the RAF and apply at the beginning to a school for a seaplane job. I shouldn't really advise land machines. I don't think there's any chance of Probationary Sub-Lieutenant in the RNVR now, but of course, he might not have objections to the RAF like we do who have been with the fleet some time.

Monday, 15 April
Went out into Forth pretty early and Gallehawk and Dickson landed on the deck very successfully with an eight knot air speed. I was to have gone next, but we had to return to our new buoy, G5, I think it is. Two Yanks in. Deuce of a scrap in after flat tonight; Dickson and I were trapped and lashed and he was put in a bath – I missed that

part, but got half killed all the same. Didn't finish till
1.30 am!

Apparently Dickson was invited to dinner by Admiral
Phillimore to celebrate his successful landing; presumably
Gallehawk was included also, though his name is not mentioned
in this connection.

TUESDAY, 16 APRIL

I flew 1½ Strutter off deck at anchor in the afternoon. Ship
not into wind, so I put the wind up most of the spectators
by turning into it across the deck. Lovely bus. Went to EF
and had my compasses swung and then back to
Donibristle. Most of the way at 6500 feet. Bitterly cold. Ship
at 2½ hours' notice.

THURSDAY, 18 APRIL

Suddenly went from four hours to 1½ along with the battle
cruisers and light cruisers. Only for about an hour and then
reverted. Nobody knows why.

FRIDAY, 19 APRIL

Sir Eric Geddes and some Admiral came on board by
destroyer to watch Gallehawk and Acland land. Former
landed right at end of dock with engine choked. Very lucky
he didn't go over like Rutland. Acland made a fine one
right at top of the ramp. Full calibre firing, and also at night.

The First Lord of the Admiralty, Sir Eric Geddes, was a heavily
built Scotsman and former general manager of the North-
Eastern Railway. He was one of the 'men of push and go'
brought into government service by the then Minister of
Munitions and now Prime Minister, David Lloyd George, in
1915. He created something of a stir within the Admiralty by his
predilection for medals and titles – including elevation to the
unmerited rank of vice admiral in May 1917. He further
compounded the sin by wearing his Royal Navy officer's cap
pulled down at a jaunty angle in imitation of Sir David Beatty.

SATURDAY, 20 APRIL

> Snow on the ground in the morning; I stayed on board all day. We went to 2½ hours; notice at about 4 o'clock and to one hour's at 7.30. Turned out there was a fight with the Harwich forces and Hun light cruisers this morning but no details so far. Very bad toothache. Have again been recommended for promotion (3rd time!). Cinematograph pictures in the wardroom at 8.30 pm; quite good show.

A large number of destroyers, flotilla leaders and light cruisers were centred at Harwich, under the command of Commodore Reginald Tyrwhitt. These light, fast ships were intended to provide effective scouting and reconnaissance, whilst still being able to engage German light forces, and to frustrate the enemy's attempts at minelaying in the English Channel. It was planned that the Harwich Force would operate when possible in conjunction with the Dover Patrol, and the Admiralty intended that the Harwich Force would also be available to support the Grand Fleet if it moved into the area. Tyrwhitt was also expected to carry out reconnaissance of German naval activities in the southern parts of the North Sea, and to escort ships sailing between the Thames and Holland.

That evening Jack wrote home and was able to supply his parents with some details of his domestic arrangements:

> I was in Edingrad, as of course it's called now [presumably the young officers were making an ironic comment on St Petersburg/Petrograd] on Tuesday I think it was and purchased two cushions and a bed cover. The other chap in the cabin did ditto and so we have quite a comfortable cabin now, especially with my deck chair. The worst drawback is that we never get any but electric light in it and it gets very fuggy at night, with the natural results in the morning when our servant attempts to get one up! Did I tell you we had a terrific rough house a few nights ago! The cabins raided the after flat (slinging). We were hopelessly outnumbered and finally got locked in a cabin. We were all 'steaming' and in our pyjamas but about six of us clambered out of a scuttle [porthole] up the side of the ship and onto the quarterdeck. Then we rushed them – at least

two of us did under the impression we were being backed up. We weren't though, and got collared – seven on each of us. We were both tied up – I still have cuts on my legs from the lashings and one of us, not me, got a cold bath. It lasted from 11.30 till 1.30 and for three days after I could hardly walk! It was one of the best rags we've ever had on the ship.

Monday, 22 April

Big Naval raid on Ostend and Zeebrugge. Ports were blocked by sinking old cruisers and a submarine. 700 marines landed – most of them from the Grand Fleet. Only 300 were left, so the scrap was pretty fierce. 1st BCs and LCs etc out. Went ashore to fly and put in two hours on Pups and 1½ Strutters. Went up to 6000 feet. Judging from smoke, Fleet getting ready to weigh. Engine cut out two times when zooming round Yank ships.

This was, perhaps, the Dover Patrol's finest hour. The plan was to impede the enemy's access to the sea from its destroyer and submarine base at Bruges by blocking the canal mouth at Zeebrugge with sunken warships. In the end it was less than wholly successful but was indeed valiant as the subsequent award of 'eleven VCs before breakfast', as well as twenty-one DSOs and twenty-nine DSCs, testified.

Tuesday, 23 April

Proceeded to get under way at 3 o'clock am, from four hours' notice. Then reverted to 2½; evidently on account of last night's raid on the coast. We are having quite exciting and mysterious times nowadays.

Jack was certainly right in his assessment as coincidentally, Admiral Scheer had decided on a bold strike for his High Seas Fleet. A strong force, commanded by Admiral Hipper, acting as bait, would attack a Scandinavian convoy off the coast of Norway, while German battleships were stationed to the south in the hope that there would be a substantial (but not over-whelmingly powerful) British response. If all went according to plan, Scheer hoped to inflict heavy losses on the Grand Fleet. A strict wireless silence, except for only the most essential messages, was maintained, in order to limit interception of signals by the Admiralty. Fog in the North Sea cloaked the German ships but also hampered any reconnaissance by Zeppelins. Hipper was unable to find the convoy – it had not in fact sailed that day. However, the Grand Fleet had been alerted. In order to be closer to the enemy, it had been based at Rosyth since the middle of April. Through a thick blanket of fog it set out: thirty-one battleships, four battle cruisers, two cruisers, twenty-four light cruisers, and eighty-five destroyers. It was the last time during the war that the full might of the Grand Fleet was set in motion, but Beatty's luck was out. The High Seas Fleet was once more out of reach and heading for home.

WEDNESDAY, 24 APRIL

At 1½ hrs notice. When Fleet went out negative us [minus *Furious*] as our condensers were wrong. We followed on at 2.15 pm and caught 'em up at about 7 o'clock – *Repulse*, *Renown*, *Princess Royal*, *Lion* and *Tiger* to starboard. Thick fog for a long time and then we got out of it.

THURSDAY, 25 APRIL

Duty pilot. Went over to Little Fisher Bank. Up at 4 o'clock am. Airship sighted at about 5 o'clock, by *Birmingham*. At about 6 o'clock signal came: four German battle cruisers, four light cruisers and TBDs steaming 55W about 30 miles off. Prepared to fly off but didn't go worse luck. Beautiful weather. Nearly bumped a mine, or rather two of 'em. I saw one about 15 yards off us; we went through a field of 'em! TBD F0l nearly rammed us and we in turn – the *Courageous*! Priceless weather.

FRIDAY, 26 APRIL

Arrived back at about 7.30 am. Before getting in, Thyne flew off in a Pup and crashed it on the deck. Bumped his head a bit. Gallehawk intends flying on in a 1½ Strutter this evening. Battle Fleet at 2½ hours' notice. Cruisers and selves at 1½. Hope we go out again.

Saturday, 27 April

Nothing doing as it was very misty early morning; spent day on ship. Had a meeting of the 'Gut Club' in our cabin after the pictures tonight. Still at 1½ hours notice.

Jack had received a food parcel from his mother and the Gut Club comprised five young and hungry officers who made a valiant attempt to eat all the contents.

Sunday, 28 April

Usual Sunday routine. Wrote home. Very nice day indeed but a good deal of wind.

Monday, 29 April

Very nice day, but a good deal of wind; 1½ hrs notice. Observer Lieut. Miller and F/S-L Mears killed at Donibristle in a 1½ Strutter crash. Mears was one of the best chaps imaginable and Miller a very fine maths and theoretical man. Both a great loss to the Squadron. Arranged a rough house in the gunroom after dinner to try and buck up the younger pilots and observers. It seemed rather callous but was the best thing to do in my opinion.

Lieutenant HF Mears and Captain GH Miller were killed when the 1½ Strutter, A5986, flown by Mears, crashed when it lost speed turning sharply in a gusty wind.

Tuesday, 30 April

Very windy day. Reverted to four hours' notice about 11 o'clock. Had to go to RN Hospital, South Queensferry, in the afternoon in staff motor boat, calling and delivering telegrams at HMS *Lion*. Had to get all details re procedure for funerals. They were both fearfully smashed up. Caused by stalling on a climbing turn to left. Machine hit ground from 200 feet on her nose with full engine. It must have been awful to have to get them out. Mears was such a fine young chap.

Wednesday, 1 May

Went ashore at 7.30 to fly but no machine ready.

Thursday, 2 May
Went ashore with funeral party to Dunfermline. Acted as pall bearer. Miller only was buried up here; Mears went home. After lunch ship got under way and did full calibre firing – shooting poor.

Friday, 3 May
Went ashore to fly. Put in some time in a Pup. Took a 1½ Strutter (W/T) up to Linlithgow and Stirling. At latter place had to turn owing to engine vibration. On return, found nose piece, cam box and back plate all loose. Lucky I got back, as engine might have come out.

Sunday, 5 May
Church as usual. Brilliant morning but very poor afternoon with wind and mist.

Monday, 6 May
Went ashore to fly again. No bus ready till 4 o'clock and then when I did get up the petrol began to pour over my feet so came down and washed out. Bristol monoplane with Captain Woodhouse landed.

The Bristol M.1C monoplane was a notable curiosity and also one of the most underrated single-seat fighters of the war. Due to official distrust of monoplanes its operational fighting service was limited to a handful of machines in Macedonia and Mesopotamia. It is likely that the Bristol which Jack saw came from the training establishment at Turnberry or Ayr.

Tuesday, 7 May
Went ashore with Acland and ordered khaki from Andersons and a blue mess dress from Gieves. Met a very nice American ensign from US Battleship *Florida* and had tea with him.

This would have been his new Royal Air Force uniform, ordinary military khaki with rank distinctions denoted in blue braid on the cuffs, so it would appear that Jack and his colleagues had decided to remain with the RAF and not seek re-employment with the Dover Patrol. The light blue mess dress with gold braid rank stripes was much more spectacular and had allegedly been chosen by the actress Gladys Cooper or alternatively had been left over from material ordered by the Tsar prior to the Bolshevik Revolution. It was indeed somewhat theatrical in appearance and was replaced by the familiar RAF blue-grey in September 1919.

Wednesday, 8 May

Duty Officer and very busy too unloading and loading lighters. In the afternoon Jackson landed a 1½ Strutter on the deck. He ought to have seriously hurt himself, but was pulled up by some horns engaging the sand bags, that were designed not to!

Jackson's fortunate landing on the deck is the last such on *Furious* recorded by Jack in his diary. His account tallies with the official record that some thirteen landings were made, only three of which involved no damage to the machine. The aft deck-landing experiment was therefore a failure but *Furious* was still to be of great use even though her pilots would now have to plan either to make a landfall or ditch their aeroplane in the sea.

Jack's next letter was dated 9 May. He must have been a little confused over dates because, despite the fact that he had written only a few days before, he began with:

I'm very sorry for not writing sooner, but I have been unable to as I've been kept pretty busy lately. I've been ashore at 7 am for about five out of the last eight days and didn't get back till 7.30 again. Flying, of course. Two of our chaps, you will be sorry to hear, were killed last week, but you don't need to worry about me, as it was pure bad flying on the pilot's part. He was a very nice young chap, too. I had to act as pall bearer with some others – and a sword. When I was over Stirling the other day I had to turn back with engine vibration. When I did land I found that the engine was all loose and another half hour would have seen it out and me having an exciting time trying to land without it! I went ashore on Monday and purchased khaki and a blue mess uniform. We are to be allowed £25 for it, but it hasn't arrived so far and neither has this month's pay from Cox's. We can wear our blue [RNAS uniform] on board or at the aerodrome, but must go ashore in khaki, worse luck.

Also on 9 May it was noted in the log that Lieutenant Colonel Bell Davies, VC, DSO, RAF joined the ship from *Campania*, to become the new senior flying officer. He was one of only two RNAS pilots to be awarded the Victoria Cross (the other being Flight Sub-Lieutenant Rex Warneford, who shot down the Zeppelin LZ37 over Ostend on 7 June 1915). Bell Davies had won his VC over Bulgaria, where following a bombing mission he landed his single-seater Nieuport under enemy fire to rescue a fellow pilot, Flight Sub-Lieutenant GF Smiley, whose Farman had been shot down. Later Bell Davies had commanded No. 3 Wing, equipped with Sopwith 1½ Strutter bombers and fighters, on active service in France. He would always regard the Strutter as one of his favourite aircraft. Next, as we know, he was senior flying officer of the seaplane carrier HMS *Campania*; while serving in Scapa Flow he experimented with making the 1½ Strutter more readily stowable and operable at sea by making its wings detachable. He was very popular with his pilots who, according to Geoffrey Moore:

Hero-worshipped him and would have done anything for him. He had a fresh, rather pink complexion and looked extraordinarily youthful for his years.

WEDNESDAY, 15 MAY
Went ashore for a week to Turnhouse with A Flight at 7.30. Rotten day so I did not fly as I'd a very bad head. Cleared up in evening and went for a walk. Rotten blankets to sleep in; filthy.

There were no diary entries between 8 and 15 May so Jack's letter fills in the gap:

I'm sorry for again being late with my letter and also for the use of pencil. I have come here [Turnhouse] to do some special work along with some others and I forgot to bring ink among my gear and my pen has got to the blotting stage. I have done a good deal of flying lately, yesterday I put in 3½ hours and had two forced landings, luckily both in aerodrome. A few days ago I flew over the school in a Pup and zoomed at some of them in the cricket field at about 100 knots. I scattered one or two of them quite successfully. Kenneth may have seen me and written to you about it. I'm getting my khaki uniform fitted tomorrow – worse luck. Have you seen it yet? [khaki uniform] It's the weirdest sight we could hope for – absolutely the edge. Yesterday afternoon I was flying in ice clouds at only 6000 feet so you can guess what it was like in a draughty bus without any flying gear except helmet, muffler, goggles and thin kid gloves! Acland and I had an offer of a job at a seaplane station at Newlyn in Cornwall, but we are not taking it, as we both applied to go east to the Mediterranean or anywhere out there. We expect, all of us, to go to France for a few months and then back to the Fleet again. No one, however, really knows what is to be yet. I should like to go for a month or two as it would improve one's flying and quickness a lot. I'm fearfully ham handed at present. Today is very windy and the bumps the worst species imaginable. One machine was blown over on the ground. I hope to be back in the ship again soon, as it's better than this.

He had his wish the very next afternoon. This was the start of a period of intensive work for *Furious* over the next few weeks, accompanying units of the Fleet in a variety of operations, primarily to provide air cover and, hopefully, drive off or shoot down enemy Zeppelins or seaplanes.

THURSDAY, 16 MAY

Semaphore in morning owing to rain. Pulled in a tug-of-war against the station but got beaten. At lunch, signal came to return to ship, which we did. Got under way at 6.30 with 1st and 3rd LCS. Minelaying stunt, the layers being on ahead.

FRIDAY, 17 MAY

Up at 3 o'clock. Had some tea and dry bread. Submarine sighted at about 9.45 by light cruiser *Phaeton* on ahead; our

TBDs dropped two depth charges on it and fairly shook this ship up. Zepp reported by directional W/T. Lovely weather, sea like a pond. 4-funneled cruiser *Amphitrite* and the *Angora* are the minelayers. Within 30 miles of Denmark at 7 o'clock. Left MLs for a short while. Saw some most remarkable cases of mirage. LCs and TBDs assuming all sorts of shapes and our own reflection about 5 miles away! Saw a large mine go by our starboard quarter. Did 6–8 am watch in the foretop for submarine lookout. Thought we saw two tracks of mouldies [torpedoes] across our bows. At about 8 o'clock MLs returned according to orders saying they had been sighted by large Hun seaplane; so began to return. Hun ships supposed to be after us as we are only a very small force, *Glorious* with Admiral Napier's flag and ourselves and LCs and TBDs. Inside the Jutland Bank! Did the 10–12 watch on the bridge. Turned in on three chairs till 3 o'clock. Then turned in my cabin at 4 and slept like a log till 10.45 am! When on watch saw flashes of lightning which we finally got into as a thunderstorm. Lovely; also heard gunfire astern. Seven hours sleep in 48 hours! Got back about 6.30 pm. One light cruiser Camel pilot killed landing at Donibristle. [FS-L MHW Trendall in N6766.]

SUNDAY, 19 MAY
Beautiful day and no wind; RA Tyrwhitt up here for a conference today. P'raps something doing. Three more Camels this evening on board. What's up? Great buzzes about a bombing raid on Cuxhaven. Hope it's true.

Writing home that evening Jack made a particular request which says a lot about his sense of honour, his relationship with his parents and also the strain which he must have been enduring – losing friends and colleagues in flying accidents, watching for mines and torpedoes, taking responsibility in a warship on active service in the roughest of seas.

Just before I close I want to ask you if I can have your permission to smoke, as sometimes nowadays I wish I could; I know you don't like it, but, well I don't know what to say, but I've wanted to for some time and never liked to ask you because you might not like it. I feel that I want to when we're at sea very often and doing watches all alone.

Monday, 20 May

Was to have gone to Turnhouse today, but we may be going out to sea again. Lovely day, very warm. Got under way at 3.30 together with 3rd LCs and 13th Flotilla destroyers – seven in number. Glorious evening. On watch in foretop 6–8. Stunt is called F1 and is an attempt to get some Zepps or seaplanes.

Tuesday, 21 May

GQs at 3.15 am and sent up three Camels on deck. Glorious morning, hardly a ripple on the sea. Several mines seen and two submarines. Watch 8–10 and spent most of it firing rifles at mines. Next watch: 10–12 midnight. Altogether about six Zepps reported by directional W/T. Alarm went in morning, but it was our own destroyer *Abdiel*. TBDs out minelaying. At 10.30 *Abdiel* reported 13 planes flying due W (towards us) but we didn't see 'em. Slept in gunroom on three chairs. Rattray flew off in 1½ Strutter on a recce and two hours later landed by TBD *Verulam*. [Flight Sub-Lieutenant MH Rattray and observer Ross were given £10 each in case they had to land in neutral territory.] Put up two smoke screens to attract any hostile forces that may be about.

The use of smoke screens to attract attention is interesting as normally smoke was made to conceal warships from the enemy's guns.

Wednesday, 22 May

GQs at 3 o'clock. Beautiful blood red sunrise. 6–8 watch and sent down to flying deck (after) to fire Lewis guns at mines. Saw about 11 before breakfast. Spent most of the day doing this. Zepp sighted by light cruisers and two Camels sent off with no result. More subs sighted 4–6 watch – more mines. Hit several but they did not go off; some within 30 yards of us. Turned in 9 o'clock; just dozing when alarm went up and put on clothes any old how – no socks or collar etc. Turned out to be TBD firing at mines with a 6-inch on the horizon. Turned in again. Eyes very painful with use of glasses most of day, and felt ready to drop – actually.

Thursday, 23 May

Up at 3.30 for 4–6 watch on bridge; just getting in sight of May Island. Had a priceless cup of cocoa before going on – like thick cream! Made fast to buoy at 6.30 am. Turned in at 7 and was wakened up at 8.15. Used some bad language – all I could summon up on the spur of the moment, turned over and slept till wakened at 11.15. If I'd not been called, I'd have slept till 3 or 4 pm. A flight supposed to land, but owing to the fact we may go to sea again, nothing has happened yet – 2.30. Hope it's sea again! Channel has been mined for us outside May Island by some priceless Hun submarine since we went out!

Friday, 24 May

Landed for Turnhouse at about 10.30. Sports day, so Acland, Thyne and I went to Grad [Edinburgh]. Was fitted on for my Khaki. Very good fit; my light blue not ready yet. Had tea at Mackies and went to the pictures. Very good concert in evening by station.

Saturday, 25 May

Put in over three hours flying BEs, Pups and Strutters. Lovely day for flying. Flew in formation with Acland and Thyne to EF in the afternoon. Visited Dunbar and North Berwick. Had to fly round a thunderstorm on way back, and landed in rain.

Jack spent the evening writing a long letter on notepaper headed 'Royal Flying Corps, Turnhouse, Midlothian', which gave a very good description of life at sea with the Fleet:

Here I am again at this place, presumably for a week, but so I was last time and it only lasted one day. We went to sea that day we were recalled. It was glorious weather, the sea not quite glassy but next door to it. Hun submarines were knocking around and lots of mines but that was about all the excitement, except the mirages which were simply weird. Say we had some short funnelled light cruisers or destroyers a mile or two away from us. One moment all would look quite normal and then suddenly the funnels would grow longer and longer like a very ancient cruiser's, and then perhaps the whole caboodle rise up about 500 or 600 feet! The first one I saw, I could have sworn it was a light cruiser with a big battle practice target alongside it. Or they would look like comic seaplane carriers. This is the sort of idea I mean: [Here, Jack inserted a rough sketch.]

These rough sketches are about the same size in proportion to the first one, as the actual mirages were; only as I've said, some of them rose into the air! All of them were pretty black in colour though it was a perfect night. We weren't on a joy trip either. Well, we got back, and the next day but one went out again. Again we had most priceless weather. I took watches – foretop (submarine lookout) during the day and bridge at night, two hours on. It's rather a strain as it's a pretty responsible job, the former especially as you can imagine, and also a great strain on one's eyes. Mine are just all right today again. Most of the day watch is spent trying to blow up mines with a rifle and when not on watch we had two Lewis guns rigged up which we used. I hit several but they did not go off – perhaps just as well! We passed at one time ten mines in eleven minutes, close up within 30 yards of us and great, big, horned blighters they were! So you can see the foretop watch entails some responsibility! Submarines are about too! The first two nights I had two hours odd sleep each from 12–2 or 2.30 am with all my clothes on and lying on three chairs. Oh it's a lovely war! [From the song written by JP Long and Maurice Scott in 1917 and which was part of the repertoire of the contemporary music hall star and male impersonator Ella Shields.] The next night I turned in at 8.30 pm as I'd no watch till 4 o'c next morning. I was just getting off to sleep (in my bunk and pyjamas) at 9.30 when the alarm went outside my door. On clothes any old how – no socks, collar etc and rushed up top to find it a wash out. I was annoyed too! I

finally turned in at 6.30 am and was wakened at 11.15 am.
Yes I did get up, but I slept all afternoon!

He then went on to describe events at Turnhouse, including the
somewhat dangerous practice of teasing senior officers:

Today (Saturday) was fine and I put in just over three
hours, mostly joy riding and W/T. I gave a Sub (RN) his
first trip – in a BE2c and nearly made him sick. I just put
him on the line between a spin and a spiral and that shook
him to the core! In the afternoon three of us flew to East
Fortune in formation, low down and had a glorious trip. On
the way back we ran against a thunderstorm and had to go
round it in a heavy mist. Acland was flying one of the two-
seaters with our Flag Commander as passenger and he
seemed to be slightly nervous (he didn't turn his head
around at all!) I flew round just in front of the machine
about 30 feet away and got him into my slipstream and
very nearly upset the machine, which shook him considerably, as he shook his fist at me, in order to keep me off. I
took this to be a friendly greeting (I didn't as a matter of
fact, I know what it was meant to be) and did it again much
to his discomfort! Acland, of course, knew what I was up to,
so that he intensified the competition as much as he could.
The FC is quite a good chap, but thinks he knows a lot
about flying – and he doesn't! It was lovely above the
clouds.

He concluded the letter in his usual way with love to all but
added somewhat mysteriously:

You can trust me never to break my pledge.

SUNDAY, 26 MAY

Only 20 minutes in forenoon as I had to wait for compasses
on a 1½ to be swung prior to going to Donibristle. Flew in
afternoon in BE and Pup, doing spins and cartwheels. Made
myself very nearly sick and in the BE; my passenger too.
Lovely day.

MONDAY, 27 MAY

Signal from Admiral Commanding Aircraft that Acland and I are to learn to fly DH4s. Machine not ready. Just going off in BE to stunt when recall came: got under way – with three TBDs at 2 o'clock. Did 2–4 watch. Going down to South Dogger Bank, some cheek! Fairly good weather, and calm.

The plan for Acland and Jack to learn to fly DH4s was interesting. According to Richard Bell Davies in his autobiography, thought was being given to using *Furious* and her aircraft to attack the Zeppelins at their bases. Sopwith 1½ Strutters could have been used in the bombing role but as they were no longer being manufactured, a decision was made to conserve the limited numbers of these available and use their long range and endurance for reconnaissance missions. The Airco DH4 was the best and most reliable British day bomber of its time but had not been flown off a ship. The other alternative would be to use the single-seat Sopwith Camels with which *Furious* was now equipped – however the bomb load which a Camel could carry and the distance it could fly with it was less than the capability of the DH4. In the event Camels were used and the war was over before the carrier-borne DH4 was developed.

It is slightly surprising that Jack did not mention in his diary a most unusual event which took place on board *Furious* on 27 May. A successful experiment was carried out in landing the three-man, non-rigid airship SSZ 59 on her after deck while the carrier was moored at the G8 buoy in the Firth of Forth. However, as the ship's log noted the landing time as 09.50, the first flight off at 10.30 and the final departure at 10.50, it is likely that Jack was still ashore at Donibristle and missed the event.

TUESDAY, 28 MAY

Up at 2.15 am, and had some Ship's cocoa and dry bread. General Quarters at 2.45. Went on watch at 4 till 6. Saw five sailing ships – probably full up with Huns and W/T. Just missed a mine by about five yards! Saw another some 100 yards off. A good many Zepps reported by directional W/T, but too far away for us to go after 'em as we're in the middle of big minefields. Did 6–8 watch in evening; getting pretty rough. We have been a long way South; about 78 miles N of Terschelling. Are now steaming NE.

WEDNESDAY, 29 MAY

Within 10 miles of Denmark at 2.30 this morning. Up at 2.15; GQs at 3.30–4.15; usual buckets of cocoa. 8–10 watch. Submarines sighted. Also three boats picked up by our escort from Danish ship torpedoed last night; crews saved. Slept from 11 am till 4 pm; GQs again. Pretty heavy sea running. Did 10–12 watch. We arrived in (having been recalled) at 11.45; at 2½ hrs notice when we got in. Big Hun push on again in France, so we may be out again soon. Had an alarm at 6.30, but it turned out to be 20th Flotilla.

Ludendorff had continued with the pattern of waves of offensives on the Western Front, attacking towards Amiens at the end of April and on the Aisne on 27 May – initial success being followed by stiffening resistance and the restoration of the familiar stalemate. Ground was gained at a punitively heavy cost but the desired breakthrough was never achieved.

THURSDAY, 30 MAY

Did relieve decks: 7.30–8.30 in morning. At 1½ hours notice and probably going out tonight. Rest of fleet at 2½ hours. Big number of TBDs went out at breakfast time. Reverted to usual notice at lunch time and B flight to land. When they got to the gangway, they were told no pilots to land. 'Nother buzz! Heard tonight we are going out again in the morning! Some sea time!

FRIDAY, 31 MAY

Got underway at 6 o'clock. Rather misty day, but awfully hot. 6th LCS in front of us. Three TBDs with us and the 1st BCs behind us. It's a sweep this time, I think. We are to be within 10 miles of Danish coast at 3 am tomorrow – Borung, I think, the place is called. Had to get flash and gas gear this morning; cheery omens! My action station is the forward 5.5-inch ammunition supply in the mess decks. Hot place in action, too. 4–6 watch; about six mines; very calm and still. Harwich forces and 1st and 2nd BCs out, but not with us.

2nd anniversary of Jutland – we drank a toast 'Sweethearts and wives – may they never meet!' [A very traditional naval toast which is still, of course, in regular use by the Service in the twenty-first century.]

SATURDAY, 1 JUNE

Up at 1.45 am; sea very rough; within sight of Danish lights. Report of four Hun battle cruisers about 10 miles N of our position, so we altered course to due S and then W. Also several reports of Zepps during my watch 6–8 am. Left the 6th LCs to Southward at 5 o'clock this morning; getting calmer or rather less rough. Usual GQs at 3; only had to stand to till 4.30. I slept on chairs in the gunroom. Two *Kaiser* Class battleships reported S of us at 6.40 am. Two seaplanes dropped bombs on *Lion* and straddled her escort, but did not hit anyone! Sharwood brought one down in a Camel. Two TBDs (Harwich force) got mined this afternoon, but I think they are getting back to port.

Captain AC Sharwood RAF took off from the revolving platform fitted to the light cruiser HMAS *Sydney* in his Sopwith 2F.1 Camel, N6783, on the morning of 1 June. He was joined by Captain LB Gibson in his Camel, N6756, launched from HMAS *Melbourne*. Sharwood intercepted the two German seaplanes which had been spotted, chasing them for sixty miles and shooting one down. His Lewis gun then jammed so he broke off to search for his ship. He instead found a destroyer, HMS *Sharpshooter*, from the Harwich Force and ditched nearby, being catapulted from his cockpit into the sea some 500 yards from the ship. He was picked up and the Camel was retrieved by the cruiser, HMS *Canterbury*. His claim of one aircraft forced down was not confirmed and his gallantry went unrewarded but he had proved that by driving away the unwanted intruders from the vicinity of the 2nd Light Cruiser Squadron, the concept of fighters on board major warships was a valid one.

SUNDAY, 2 JUNE

Got in about 5 am. Usual Sunday routine, but not rounds of ship. Went a walk from Braefoot to Aberdour and back in afternoon with Thyne. Awfully hot. Photograph of George in *Sporting & Dramatic* in Old Man Curtiss. It was funny as he had been in my thoughts all afternoon. B flight landed. Awful fug in my cabin. Padre gave a very short sermon on account of us all being so tired; rather nice of him as the men are nearly done. Special prayers of thanks for the safety of this ship during the past days.

On Sunday Jack wrote home again and covered a variety of topics in the order that they came into his head:

I've just got the first mail I've had for a long time, so I've consequently got too many letters to answer to be able to write a long letter! Please thank Kitty for her very nice little letter and the card she sent me. She seems to be getting on very well with her writing nowadays. I had a letter from K and he says he saw me [flying over the school]. Today is the King's birthday so all the ships are having a make and mend. Your parcel has just arrived this moment. [The letter stops and then resumes in a darker shade of ink.] Thank you very much for the chocolate and the cake and also the fugs [underpants] of course. Thank you for washing the latter. They seem to be getting it rough in France nowadays, the whole Grand Fleet is longing for the Huns to come out, but from my own experience they don't come out very often. What do you think of the Billing case? It's like reading a book and it seems we have got a good many German dupes at our head. I don't think I ever really took any interest in a trial before, but PB seems to be all there at present and to know a good deal about Asquith and Darling not to their favour.

Noel Pemberton Billing, 1880–1948, was the son of a Birmingham iron founder. He left school and home at the age of fourteen and flourished in many fields as a yacht salesman, gun-runner, inventor, aeroplane designer (some of which Jack remarked upon at Eastchurch), RNVR officer, right-wing Member of Parliament, editor, publisher, law graduate and entrepreneur. His aircraft included some of the earliest successful flying boats. His company was bought by Hubert Scott-Paine, which became the Supermarine Company, later taken over in turn by

Vickers. It is believed that he coined the term Fokker Fodder when speaking out in the House of Commons about the inferior performance of British combat aircraft in 1916. Pemberton Billing was prosecuted as the result of an article he had published in his *Imperialist* (sometimes known as *Vigilante*) magazine in January 1918, in which he alleged that the Germans had compiled a Black Book containing the names of 47,000 British subjects who, because of their sexual preferences, were being blackmailed into undermining the British war effort. He publicly attacked Margot Asquith, wife of the former Liberal prime minister, hinting that she was entangled in this. The trial was presided over by Mr Justice Darling and began on 29 May 1918. It lasted only six days with Pemberton Billing representing himself. Following long and confusing instructions from the judge, the jury returned a verdict in Pemberton Billing's favour.

MONDAY, 3 JUNE
    Relieve decks 7.30–8.30; nice morning, really warm. At divisions, we had 'Eternal Father strong to save' and it was rather touching, I thought, after the work we have been doing. Skipper gave talk to the men about leave breaking and finally said that as we had the most dangerous job in the Fleet and were most often at sea, it looked very like cold feet-sensation! A lot of the ship's company down sick with flu.

TUESDAY, 4 JUNE
    Flew off at about 11.30 and did runs over forward deck with skid 1½ Strutter. Did very well in spite of vertical breeze. Bust skid which took eight inches off prop. Flew back low and slow and turned on my nose in drome: Admiral very bucked. Nice looking waiting ambulance and doctor not needed! Langton and Haywood had a bad crash – machine, a BE2e, burnt right out. Both chaps 'all right'.

While deck landings had ceased, Jack undertook some equally hazardous 'touch and go' approaches. It is a measure of his skill and confidence as a pilot that he was able to recover to Turnhouse and make a survivable crash-landing, given the damage sustained to his machine.

WEDNESDAY, 5 JUNE
Relieve decks 7.30–8.30; lovely day; no wind and very warm. Wind rose in afternoon, so flew 1½ Strutter off [noted in ship's log at exactly 2.39 pm] and did runs over forward deck. Touched each time; believe it was quite good. Then flew back at 7000 feet; priceless up topsides.

It is equally a measure of his cool bravery and belief in himself as a pilot that he continued with the experiment successfully the following day.

SATURDAY, 8 JUNE
Went out firing in the afternoon, and also tried our fogscreen – a priceless thing, which works splendidly. Was at my action station most of the afternoon – forward 5.5-inch supply.

SUNDAY, 9 JUNE
Whole of the Battle Fleet went out this afternoon: one of the most wonderful and inspiring sights I have ever had the good luck to see. They are probably bound for Scapa. We are at 1½ hrs notice and the usual buzzes are going round.

Jack (and no doubt the rest of the crew of *Furious*) was enjoying the break from time at sea:

We have been having a rest for a short time and it's just about due, too. On Thursday or Friday (I can't say which) I went up to the school and saw Kenneth. He seems very well and cheery, so I told him that it would be nearly impossible to satisfactorily arrange a day out at Turnhouse and explained why. I've been wearing my khaki lately and I don't object to it as much as I expected – though I'm not fond of it by a long way. I have been doing a little more flying this week and was fortunate in making myself rather popular with the Admiral, though I only heard this after and did not have to speak to him. I had to have a talk to the skipper by myself, along with two others.

My cabin has been fearfully hot lately, as I think I told you there is no scuttle attached and all the air is just blown straight in (ready tinned) through a pipe and there's no real method of ventilating it. Nowadays the ventilator is off pretty often and then it's the limit and one wakes up with a fearful head in the morning and a throat lined with cement and sandpaper. I and some of the officers have been recommended (again!) for promotion to captain. The list is expected to be in the papers about July 1st, but the odds are on all the promotions being RFC and not RNAS or RAF. I've given up trying to count the number of times this has been done.

Monday, 10 June

Several new pilots came on board today for a few days while ours are ashore. We are going out at 1.50 in the morning, and I'm to be Duty Pilot.

Tuesday, 11 June

When I got up at 8 o'clock we were most of 130 miles across the North Sea; a little chop on but not very bad. Am to fly off at 7.30 tomorrow to within 27 miles of Sylt; then to Blaargaun Point [sic] and back. [Blåvandshuk lighthouse was situated at Denmark's westernmost point and was a landmark for the whole area.] Bell Davies says it's too close in for a 1½ Strutter but I'm full out as it's some special information that is required. Turned in at 9 o'clock. Norwegian coast round the Lister light sighted at 11.30 tonight quite plainly.

Wednesday, 12 June

Up at 1.40 am and to GQs. Weather very rough indeed. Fine sight watching the destroyers, but lots of sympathy for the poor men in them. Saw Danish coast (Borbing) [sic] quite plainly at 4.45; could see houses, trees, lighthouses and chimneys with naked eye. Looks peaceful. Weather too rough for flying; was to have gone at 4.30 again but too rough and also at 5.30. Fed up to the teeth. Turned back at 11.30 pm.

THURSDAY, 13 JUNE
Up at 2.15 am and GQs. On our way home and should be back about 7 o'clock pm. Will probably be out again soon for a good stunt. Got in at 7.30 pm; very rough inside. No mails tonight owing to weather. Sing-song in wardroom.

FRIDAY, 14 JUNE
Did relieve decks 7.30–8.30. Mails arrived: a very big one for us; I got four letters of sorts.

Virtually all the letters which have survived were written to his parents but the one which Jack wrote to his brother Tony that Friday has been preserved. It would appear that Tony had sent some photographs of a subject that was dear to Jack's heart.

That's a ripping exhaust pipe you have put on the bike – it might make a better row without the silencer blocked. It would make her run better and faster as there would be a good deal less back pressure. What on earth made the handlebars go? I hope you didn't get hurt when they konked out.

He continued with matters technical for a while and then turned to life in *Furious*.

The North Sea is no picnic this weather and the cold is rather uncomfortable when on watch in the foretop or bridge. I see in some paper today, which arrived with the mail, that some imaginative Hun says that there will be a big naval battle soon which will finish us off. Well, the sooner the better, and they won't have to go to much trouble to find us and when they do – – ! I'm getting quite used to getting up at 1.30 am now and going on deck dressed any old how. It is very rough in harbour now and unsafe for any boats to be out. I saw the finest sight of my life last Sunday and have got some photos to remember it by. [This was the whole of the Grand Fleet putting to sea.] I have also seen strange lands and things. I think we are out of quarantine [for influenza] now, but I'm not sure, at any rate I've not had it so far and am very fit but also extremely mouldy!

He concluded with some advice concerning Tony's desire to follow in his footsteps:

> If you've got to go to London, be sure and impress your examiners or whoever it is that you want to be with the Fleet and say you've a brother there. If possible try and get a promise from them that you will get the job. I'll try and pull some strings up here later on. Tons of red tape. I wish you could see me all rigged up in my anti-gas and anti-flash gear. It's a priceless sight. I've got my banjoline rigged up with a banjo bridge now and it has a far better tone except on the top string.

He signed off with:

> Well, must close now, if you get time write again soon and let me know how you're getting on etc. With best love to all, I remain, Your loving brother,

Sunday, 16 June

Usual Sunday routine. Turned out a wet day. 5th Battle Squadron returned this morning early. Minelayers, *Princess Margaret*, *Angora*, *London* and *Amphitrite* went out this evening, with a big flotilla of TBDs and light cruisers. 1st BCS went out later to support them.

Austrian offensive against the Italians.

This was the Austrian big push to try and knock Italy out of the war. As with the German advances in Belgium and France, it succeeded initially, the high tide of the Austro-Hungarian advance being stopped at the River Piave on 15 June where the line held.

Monday, 17 June

Relieve decks. Divisions etc as usual 5–10 am. One of the 1st BS returned – *Revenge* I think. Not quite so cold, but dull. We are going to a new berth this afternoon nearer the bridge. Father and Mother married 21 years ago today. Many Happy Returns. Got steam up at 3 o'clock and got under way with 1st Light Cruiser Squadron and seven TBDs at 8.30.

TUESDAY, 18 JUNE

Didn't get up till 9 o'clock as we were not far out; fine clear weather. Did usual sub lookouts in foretops. Sighted Norway at 5 o'clock and went in within 10 miles; lovely bit of coast. Just off Lister light and could see houses. W/T from Dutch Mail steamer saying she's being chased by Hun TBDs; also light cruisers reported by sub. Stayed there and stood by twice for flying till 8.30. Then South East. Turned in 9.30–10 but no sleep till 12.30.

The next morning would be notable for the first kill made by an aircraft launched from *Furious*, graphically described by Jack in his diary and in his subsequent letter home:

WEDNESDAY, 19 JUNE

Up 1.45 am. GQs. Brekker 6.30 and stood by to fly 6.40. At 7.00 two German seaplanes flew up. Gave recognition signal (wrong of course); one came to within 2000 feet of us at 1000 feet up. Port one cleared off at first shot, starboard one stayed and dropped two bombs (small ones) which lit near TBD escort. Could see Iron Crosses plainly and observer up taking photos. Daley and Basden went up in Camels and engaged them, but they got away. Aircraft and pilots picked up by TBDs *Wolfhound* and *Valentine*. Enemy aircraft looked fast and like Schneiders, Camel from *Galatea* flew off and now missing. Starboard Hun deserves Iron Cross for his pluck. Dirty weather coming on. Turned in with a headache at 9 o'clock. Two more Huns over at 12.15. One dropped its bombs – big ones from 3000 feet and they all lit within 30 yards of our starboard side. F/S-L Heath – from Cranwell, went up and brought one down intact with a shot in his radiator. Lovely machine. We passed within 20 yards of it. Passengers picked up by TBD *Valentine* in which Heath was. Other Hun escaped OK. Machine had to be sunk by gunfire owing to us receiving a signal to retire North as fast as possible. We made good 24 knots all after-noon. Crowds of mines sculling about.

A Camel was kept ranged at readiness on the fore deck of *Furious*. The German seaplane which was shot down by Lieutenant Grahame Heath was the Friedrichshafen FF49c, 1796, flown by *Leutnant der Reserve* Wenke and *Flugzuegmaat* [NCO Aeroplane Mate] Schirra. The FF49c was an advanced variant of this highly useful and widely used patrol aircraft. Lieutenant Colonel Bell Davies (now with his RAF rank) tried in vain to persuade Captain Nicholson to heave to and hoist the seaplane on board *Furious* to take back to port as a trophy. Mindful of the fact that if there were U-boats about, the stationary carrier would provide a once-in-a-lifetime target, Nicholson wisely decided not to tarry and ordered that it should instead be sunk by gunfire. This was accomplished with rather more success than the anti-aircraft fire sent up by the 4-inch high-angle guns belonging to *Furious* when the seaplanes were first spotted. All that it succeeded in shooting down was the carrier's own galley funnel. These were always known in the RN as Charley Nobles, after a captain of that name who kept his galley funnel brightly polished. To enable cooking in the galley to continue and the men to be fed, a temporary replacement was fitted, on which some wag chalked surreptitiously, 'Sacred to the memory of Charley Noble. RIP.'

It is not surprising that Captain Nicholson was very wary of the danger posed by torpedoes as he had been the captain of the old armoured cruiser, *Hogue*, which along with her sister ships *Aboukir* and *Cressy*, was sunk by the *U-9* on 22 September 1914 in the Broad Fourteens off the Dutch coast with the loss of more than 1400 lives.

Jack admired Nicholson for his dash and charm and noted that he had learned a hard lesson when he had stopped *Hogue* in the water to rescue survivors from the *Aboukir*.

After the war it was discovered that the German seaplane's pilot had been the secretary of the sports committee at List seaplane station and that his failure to return caused considerable inconvenience and annoyance as he was unable to organise a previously arranged sports day!

THURSDAY, 20 JUNE
Returned to Rosyth – *Lion*'s buoy at 3.30. Yesterday F/S-L Smith went into ditch over after deck by being released by mistake! Did 12–2 and 8–10 this morning; very tired.

FRIDAY, 21 JUNE
Went to Edinburgh with 2nd Lieutenant Thompson and saw a very good show at picture house opposite North British Hotel. My light blue mess kit arrived last night and I wore it tonight for the first time; some stuff. I was the first to wear it on board. Sent for by Wing Com and got cheered in the wardroom by about 50 officers and felt very embarrassed. We will probably have light blue for service wear by the end of the year.

That week's letter must have created a heightened level of interest at the McCleery senior breakfast table:

I'm writing early this week in order to try and be sure I get it off and also to ask you have you seen the papers about our scrap in the North Sea? It was priceless, the best show I've seen and the Huns were fine and did their job splendidly, though we weren't hit at all. The 19th was a busy day as we got strafed twice. The first one was early in the morning and he attacked us from low down – we were all standing watching him up on the deck and could see the bombs dropping one by one. The afternoon show was more exciting as they dropped their eggs within 30 yards of us – plonk, plonk, plonk – about seven of them one after the other. You will see we got one of 'em down – I got photos of him in the ditch, a beautiful bus and the two of the crew standing up waiting to be picked up. Strange though it may seem we all revelled in it and nearly burst our jackets laughing at their cheek! I'll have some priceless yarns to tell you when we get into dock again – probably about the end of the year.

SATURDAY, 22 JUNE
Went ashore to Aberdour and had tea; very warm afternoon and one shower. Walked back to Braefoot Pier and met the motor boat. May be going out tonight.

SUNDAY, 23 JUNE
Weekday routine owing to the large amount of work in hand. Sailed ashore in whaler, and had tea. Very rough coming back and ran on a reef!

MONDAY, 24 JUNE
Went ashore to Edinburgh.

WEDNESDAY, 26 JUNE
Been on the ship *12 months today*. Expected to go out tonight but didn't for some reason or other. Stayed on board all day.

THURSDAY, 27 JUNE
Wet, miserable day; stayed on board. Went to 2½ hrs notice at about 6 pm. Got under way at about 10.30 with 1st LCS and eight destroyers. About eight more pilots came on board for the stunt.

SATURDAY, 29 JUNE
Calm weather, but pretty cloudy and poor visibility. Up at about 12.45 after about ¾ of an hour's sleep; dark and very cold. Could see the lighthouses on the Danish coast quite clearly. Turned back at 2 o'clock owing to dud weather. Sighted 5th BS and 1st BCS about 10 o'clock. Flew off deck at 7.40 in 1½ Strutter. Got back to Turnhouse at 10 o'clock. Slept in my shirt – ugh.

SUNDAY, 30 JUNE
Up at 3.15 am. Saw the Panther – a frightful looking machine and two DH9s. Also the N50 and the Griffin. Returned to ship by 11.15 am boat. About six letters for me.

The aircraft which Jack saw at Turnhouse included a Parnall Panther, N92, one of the first British aeroplanes designed specifically for operation from aircraft carriers. It was a stubby, two-seat biplane with a fuselage that hinged aft to allow more compact stowage at sea. Access to the cockpit was odd in that it was by means of a hole in the upper wing. Two other design features were floatation bags on either side of the undercarriage and a hydrovane attached to prevent the aircraft nosing over if it had to land in the sea. It served in the front line from the aircraft carriers *Argus* and *Hermes* from 1919 until 1926. The Airco DH9 was designed as a replacement for the excellent DH4. It suffered in comparison due to engine unreliability but nevertheless saw widespread service. Its performance was radically improved by the installation of the American Liberty engine and the subsequent re-design produced the DH9A which served with the RAF until 1931. N50 was the unique Sopwith B.1 Tractor biplane, which served as a prototype for the Grain Griffin, only half a dozen of which were built. It is likely that these aircraft were at Turnhouse for trials purposes.

MONDAY, 1 JULY
Went ashore to Turnhouse for a week. Went up to Edinburgh in the afternoon with some others. Feeling rather dud.

TUESDAY, 2 JULY
Got violent pains all over me. So did not fly; perfect weather. Had a hot bath in the evening and felt rather better.

WEDNESDAY, 3 JULY
Pains all gone, but eyes very sore and very bad cold so did not fly. Glorious weather. Temperature 101.

THURSDAY, 4 JULY
Went sick this morning and felt pretty bad, but temp now 99.

FRIDAY, 5 JULY
Still in bed, but feeling better and pulse and temp about normal. Get up tomorrow I expect.

SATURDAY, 6 JULY
Got up at about 11 o'clock; lovely day. Recall came just as I was on my way to station in Edinburgh. Two chaps killed in a 1½ Strutter. Saw them get off, but not crash; awful mess I believe. [Lieutenant DJJ De Villiers and CPO WM Garner in A5257.] Got on ship about 7 o'clock and under way almost at once; it's only a PZ though. Also Adam killed in a 1½ Strutter on the *Glorious*; went off turret and crashed on to deck – poor old chap.

Lieutenant HW Adam was killed on 5 July when flying Sopwith 1½ Strutter A5990; the aircraft failed to gain flying speed, hit the deck and fell into the sea.

Sunday, 7 July

Lovely day, but a bit cold. Did 8–10 in the morning and 6–8 in the evening. Sea air doing me good. Whole fleet out, over 100 ships large and small, some fine sights and smoke screens. Wish the Huns could see us! On our way back I was the first to spot enemy and also a seaplane of theirs.

Monday, 8 July

Did the 4–5 watch, beginning at 4.40! Got in about 8.45; whole fleet down here now. Fine day. No leave ashore though as King and Queen of Belgium came round the fleet in the destroyer *Oak*. She stopped alongside us and we flew off a Camel which did some stunts for them. King and Queen of Belgium came on board. Jackson and Thyne in Camels and self in 1½ Strutter flew off and gave an exhibition of a sort for them. He is a fine big man while she is small and somewhat insignificant but was very busy taking pictures with a small camera. They seemed very interested and pleased by our show. Very bad thunderstorm in afternoon; two Kite Balloons struck by lightning. However it cleared up and ship got into wind just in time for our effort.

Jack had received a letter from home with disappointing news:

I was sorry to hear the Tony had been turned down [for flying training]. I would strongly advise him to try and get into the RNVR, either as a temporary snotty or sub on the Dover Patrol or coastal motor boats, and probably later on a destroyer. They are always glad of people who understand internal combustion engines for that job. I would advise Tony to write to the Secretary of the Admiralty, saying he wants a job with the RN in some form or other.

I've half a mind to chuck this lot and do so, as the Air Board hasn't passed any fleet promotions again this time and tons of [former] RFC have had it. Also 'War Office RFC Military Wing' which is supposed to be washed out now. I have an idea the Admiral, who is rather fed up about the general run of things, as everyone is, is going to try and get the Admiralty to put them through like the RFC are doing. I hope so, as if anyone's does I expect mine will, as I was recommended there before. I'm rather fed up about this promotion business as only for the RAF I'd have had two rings up four or five months ago. I've only done some 21½ hours flying during the past three months! It's the limit!

He was also somewhat exercised in his mind about matters sartorial:

Three chaps I knew, one very well, were killed on Saturday. It was very sad. I wish Mother wouldn't worry about me, though, as I'm all right, and it's not comforting to know the light blue mess kit sounds like hospital blue! The light blue uniform is now being made official wear, but it will not come into force for some months yet, as we have to wear out the khaki. Whether we get an allowance for it we don't yet know. I haven't yet got my £25 for the khaki. My gear seems to have swollen somewhat and my servant has to ask me each day whether I'll wear my khaki, or my No. 1, 2 or 3 blue or my light blue, whether I'll wear boots or black shoes or brown shoes – in fact I get quite mixed up and usually have everything out before I decide which to wear! Next time I come home you'd better look out for a pretty brown gent in pretty light blue and gold! By the way a penny stamp does for your letters to me while I'm in the ship and mine from the ship go free of postage.

WEDNESDAY, 10 JULY
Dull day and a good deal of rain. Went up to Edinburgh with a clerk and to the pictures; quite a good show.

THURSDAY, 11 JULY
Fine day. No shore leave as ship got under way for sub-calibre firing; shooting very good. [Sub-calibre practices involved exercising the larger guns with smaller charges.] Also repel aircraft! My two machine guns are on the

landing deck and have a good snap. Sent up two balloons, but couldn't tell if we hit them.

FRIDAY, 12 JULY
Nice morning. GQs just after divisions and then refuel aircraft. Nothing special doing.

SATURDAY, 13 JULY
Nice day. Nothing special doing. Spent afternoon on board. Concert on USS *Wyoming* at 8.30; wouldn't have missed it for anything. Very comfortable ship.

The USS *Wyoming* was one of four capital ships of Battleship Division 9 of the US Atlantic Fleet (the others being *New York*, *Florida* and *Delaware*) which had sailed from Hampton Roads to Scapa Flow in November 1917. They were coal burning and were not the most up to date battleships in the American fleet because Britain could not guarantee to supply sufficient oil fuel which was used by the most modern vessels. However, they were still impressive. The *Wyoming*, which was completed in 1912, displaced 26,000 tons and was armed with twelve 12-inch guns and twenty-one 5-inch guns. The four ships arrived at Scapa early in December and were re-designated as the 6th Battle Squadron of the Grand Fleet. In February the 6th Battle Squadron had escorted its first Norwegian convoy. The US Navy ships were under the command of Admiral Hugh Rodman, the 'Kentucky Admiral', who very sensibly decided to listen and learn as the Royal Navy 'had had three years of actual warfare and knew the game from the ground-floor up.'
Jack's impression was as follows:

I was on board the USS *Wyoming* for a concert and it was a priceless show, I wouldn't have missed it for anything. The ships are very fine inside, evidently built more for comfort than work, especially when compared to this [*Furious*] or any other of our own modern ships, which are built for work first and comfort afterwards.

In contrast US sailors when asked to give their opinion of His Majesty's ships stated that they were too cold for anyone brought up in an American home and were also poorly ventilated. The absence of such labour-saving devices as laundries, motor-driven dough-mixers and potato peelers was deprecated. The availability of hard liquor (rum for the men and pink gin in the wardroom) was, however, appreciated as the US ships were 'dry'.

SUNDAY, 14 JULY
Very nice day, but very warm. Church as usual in the morning. Went ashore with Rattray in the afternoon to Aberdeen; met two girls he knew.

MONDAY, 15 JULY
Fine day. Did not go ashore as I had to release Wing Com Davies in a Camel. [Jack must have found it hard to think of this hero of the RNAS as a Lieutenant Colonel in the upstart RAF.] He swerved off – little wind and that astern and crashed into the ditch. Practically unhurt. Another German push started again. First gain 5 miles on big front.

Bell Davies had been experimenting with a modification he caused to be made to the Camel's wheels. He had noticed that the pilots of Camels which had to ditch usually came back on board with a bloody nose or a pair of black eyes. This was because the Camel tended to pitch down rapidly on ditching, causing the prominent breech of the Vickers gun to come into violent collision with the pilot's face. Padding around the danger area was tried but still left the possibility that a pilot could be knocked unconscious and be in danger of drowning. It was thought that if the high water resistance of the wheels could be reduced then the pitching movement could be similarly alleviated. To this end Bell Davies reversed a Camel's wheels on its axle so that the convex hubs pointed inwards. He further devised a quick-release gear to dispense with them entirely. He was, as he admitted, impatient to try it out and attempted a take-off in harbour with little or no wind over the deck to give the aircraft lift. As he accelerated down the foredeck, his aircraft took a sharp right hand turn and he went straight downwards. He came back on deck with the same superficial facial injuries he had been seeking to prevent. Later trials proved the practicality of the concept.

The big German push resulted in the Second Battle of the Marne and the last throw of the dice for the Kaiser's generals. Thereafter the Allies began their counter-attack, which would go from strength to strength.

Tuesday, 16 July

Watches again: my first day on: 8.30–12.30, 4–6, 8.30–10. Strafe it! Not much of a day as it rained most of the morning. Went to short notice at 8.30 and got under way at about 12 o'clock.

CHAPTER TEN

From the Tondern Raid to the Armistice

The world's first true carrier-borne strike on an enemy air base came from a desire to hit the German Zeppelins hard by destroying them at their base rather than in the air. The RN had tried this several times since the Cuxhaven Raid in 1914 but with very mixed results. The previous attack on Tondern by the Sopwith Babies of *Engadine* and *Vindex* in 1916 had caused the Grand Fleet's C-in-C, Admiral Jellicoe, to remark:

> The weather conditions were very favourable – light southerly winds and calm sea. I should have thought them ideal for seaplane operations and the failure of the machines to rise (an experience which has been so frequent on previous occasions) confirms my opinion that our efforts should be devoted to providing arrangements for starting aircraft from the deck of a ship.

Furious was just such a ship and Bell Davies was very keen to use her in just such a role. As previously noted it was decided to use the Camels rather than the 1½ Strutters as the latter were in short supply and were too valuable and irreplaceable for reconnaissance work to be expended in this way – as indeed were the aircrews trained for this duty. Intensive training at Turnhouse had taken place – in the words of Bell Davies it was a rush job. Camels had attacked and dropped practice bombs at low level on outlines marked out on the ground of the giant Zeppelin sheds at Tondern (which was then part of the German province of Schleswig but is now Tønder and in modern day Denmark) and also live bombs on targets in the Firth of Forth.

Operational Orders were drafted and issued by Rear Admiral Phillimore as follows:

1. The two flights for attacking Tondern will leave at as short intervals as possible after 03.00, or as soon after that time as light permits of formation being picked up and kept. On account of limited fuel endurance, it is important that time should not be wasted picking up formation.
2. The attack should be made at low altitude, after which machines of each flight should endeavour to meet at a pre-arranged rendezvous before returning, but only a few minutes can be allowed for this.
3. Aeroplanes should pass to seaward of Blaavand Point, and neutral territory [Denmark] should not be infringed.
4. If a Zeppelin is encountered on the outward journey, it should be attacked, bombs being dropped beforehand. If encountered on homeward journey it should be attacked irrespective of fuel remaining, machine landing in Denmark or Germany afterwards if necessary.
5. Fighting with enemy aircraft other than Zeppelins should be avoided.
6. If visibility on return is so low that inshore destroyer cannot be sighted, pilots should endeavour to pick up Fleet by taking their departure and steering North 45 degrees West Magnetic from Lynvig Lighthouse.
7. Pilots are to be instructed in the position and movement of ships between the hours 03.00 and 06.30. On return of machines, destroyers when ready to pick up aeroplanes will hoist an affirmative flag. Pilots should land about two cables ahead of a destroyer, selecting the one nearest *Furious* which has this flag flying. The inshore destroyer will not be used for picking up.
8. If, on return, ships are seen to be steaming away from coast and destroyers are not flying affirmative flag, pilots should

close *Furious* and read deck signals on her alighting deck before alighting in sea.

9. Pilots should be guided by the amount of fuel remaining when deciding to carry out orders in paras 6 and 8.

The first attempt, Operation *F5*, planned for 20 June, was abandoned, presumably because of the encounter with the seaplanes the previous day. *F6* was intended for 27 June. Jack had noted that eight more pilots had come on board 'for the stunt'. But it too was called off due to very adverse weather and high winds. F7 would now consist of seven aircraft, not the eight as planned, due to the fact that Major Moore had been posted to command RAF Turnhouse and it was too late to train a replacement. The pilots designated for the mission were Captain WF Dickson, Captain TK Thyne, Captain WD Jackson, Captain BA Smart, Lieutenant WA Yeulett, Lieutenant S Dawson and Lieutenant NE Williams. All seven had passed muster with Bell Davies with regard to the necessary flying, bomb-dropping and navigational skills. The fact that neither Jack nor his friend Acland was selected is no reflection on their ability – they were 1½ Strutter pilots and were being retained for specialised reconnaissance duties – of which more later.

WEDNESDAY, 17 JULY

Did the 6–8 am watch in foretop; saw a submarine and one of our escorts dropped depth charges on it. Saw the conning tower after the first one, but nothing after the next. Misty weather but pretty calm though a windy sky. Turned in at 8.30 as we are to be up again at 2 o'clock. Old Hay is on board from the *Campania* for the trip; was very glad to see him again.

THURSDAY, 18 JULY

Up at 2 o'clock and got deck signals ready. Very warm morning. Bomb flight did not leave as dirty weather was coming on. Heavy thunderstorm broke and it was pretty dirty for a while. We are waiting till tomorrow to see if the weather clears. Sighted the 1st Division of 1st BS – *Revenge* etc also the 7th LCs who are with them. We have the 1st and 8th Flotilla TBDs who are getting it pretty rough.

all attempts to land on *Furious* were an entire success, as was the case with this 1½ Strutter.

Jack getting airborne in a 1½ Strutter and climbing away from *Furious*.

The King and Queen of the
Belgians visiting HMS *Furious*
in July 1918.

Jack aboard HMS *Furious* in June
1918 in the new light blue uniform
of the RAF.

Jack with the Observers of
B Flight in 1918.

'Yours from back seat' –
Pilot Officer Paddy Hayes.

The following three photographs are of the two dangerous and successful reconnaissance missions flown by Jack and Paddy Hayes in September and October 1918.

Waiting for *Umpire*.

Recovering the Strutter
to TBD *Wessex*.

Paddy and Jack with the Strutter
aboard TBD *Wessex*.

Jack in a DH9 at Turnhouse.

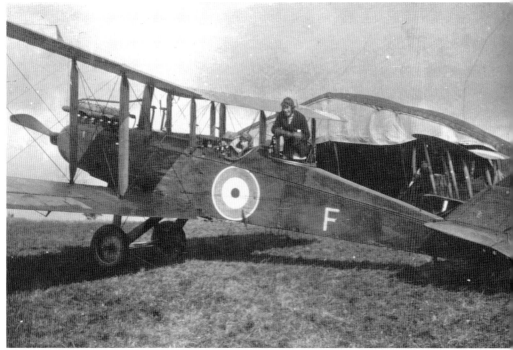

aerial view of HMS *Furious* in 1918.

S *Furious* from astern.

King George V aboard HMS *Oak* sailing past *Furious* in 1918.

...ng to meet the surrendering German High Seas Fleet on 21 November 1918.

The scene on the bridge of *Furious* as she searches for the surrendering German Fleet.

The High Seas Fleet in the Firth of Forth.

German warships in Scapa Flow.

The British Grand Fleet in the Forth.

Lighthouse Lane [off the coast of Denmark] as usual this morning. A lot of Danish fishing smacks about. Turned in 8.30.

Furious had been accompanied from Rosyth by the 1st Light Cruiser Squadron (*Caledon, Galatea, Royalist, Phaeton* and *Inconstant*) and her destroyer escort. These comprised Force A. They were joined by a powerful covering force, the 1st Battle Squadron (the oil-burning, 15-inch-armed, modern battleships *Revenge, Royal Sovereign, Ramilles, Royal Oak* and *Resolution*), the 7th Light Cruiser Squadron (*Carysfort, Aurora, Penelope* and *Undaunted*) and their destroyers, making up Force B.

As regards the decision to launch the Camels from *Furious*, this was down to Bell Davies as the senior RAF officer on board. He needed to be certain that the weather conditions would not only allow for the mission to reach the Tondern sheds but also that the predicted wind strength and direction would permit a good chance of returning to where British ships would be waiting to pick them up or, in the worst case, flying on into neutral Denmark to land with the prospect of being interned. Admiral Phillimore said to him, 'It's for you to decide and I shan't influence you. But I expect you know what I hope.'

FRIDAY, 19 JULY
Up at 2.30. Bombing flight left at 3.30 to bomb Tondern. At about 6.30 Thyne was picked up by destroyer *Viceroy* with engine trouble. Dickson and Smart got back OK. Result very successful as three Zepps were destroyed and probably three sheds. Jackson, Dawson, Williams and Yeullett missing. Weather very thick. There were at least 3 direct hits on the biggest shed and Dickson said flames went over 700 feet. Going back now at 22 kts. German seaplane attacked *Valiant* but was driven off; their W/T very busy!

The attack was launched with *Furious* some twelve miles off the coast of Denmark and eighty miles from Tondern. The first flight was composed of Jackson, Dickson and Williams; they were quickly followed by the second flight, Smart, Thyne, Dawson and Yeullett. The two formations headed south-eastwards while *Furious* withdrew to the west to the pre-arranged rendezvous and recovery position. Thyne suffered engine trouble and was picked up by the destroyer *Viceroy*. The six remaining Camels crossed the coast at a height of 5000 feet and passed over the northern end of the Isle of Sylt. They picked up the line of the road to Tondern and followed it to their target. Tondern had been a major base for the Imperial German Navy's Airship Division since 1915. The key targets were the three massive Zeppelin sheds named *Toni*, *Tobias* and *Toska*. Bombing commenced from a height of 700 feet. Surprise was complete and great damage was effected, with two Zeppelins, L54 (LZ99) and L60 (LZ108), being totally destroyed inside the blazing sheds. The gas plant for the production of hydrogen was also severely damaged. Tondern was effectively out of the war. The Camels had scattered after making their attacks and all that remained was for the individual pilots and their aircraft to return safely. After an hour's anxious flying Dickson was recovered by the destroyer *Violent*, as also was Smart. Jackson and Williams landed in Denmark in the vicinity of Esbjerg and were joined at the Palads Hotellet by Dawson, where all three were held under guard by the Danish police. Sadly, Yeullett did not return from the mission and it can only be assumed that he ran out of fuel, ditched in the sea or fjord and drowned. His aircraft was washed ashore near Havrvig on 24 July and his body was washed up on a beach near Holmsland (on the shores of Ringkøbing Fjord) on 28 July. He was buried in Havrvig Churchyard.

SATURDAY, 20 JULY

Got back about 4 o'clock. Very good news about missing pilots. All but Yeullett are in Denmark; nothing is known of him and he may have crashed as a wheel came off his bus when leaving the deck. Papers report three Zepps destroyed and only the walls remaining of the big shed. Pictures in the evening. Only one letter! French advance of five miles on Western Front.

SUNDAY, 21 JULY

Very wet day indeed. Church as usual. Probably going ashore tomorrow for a week. Had a very bad headache. News came through that Dawson got petrol and oil and came out to look for us. Some cheek. Also an ammunition dump was sent up.

Monday, 22 July

Spent most of morning practising for the King going round the Fleet. He came round in the *Oak* about 10.30 am and we cheered ship. Unfortunately he is coming on board tomorrow afternoon. Most of the day has been very wet. Went to wardroom and dragged Smart, Dickson and Thyne down to gunroom for usual show. Smart and Dickson both get the DSO this morning; am very sorry for Thyne whose engine konked on the way. Great reports in the paper, but no news of Yeullett.

Lieutenant Dawson reached Britain again first, followed by Jackson and Williams in August (via Sweden). Smart's DSO was, of course, his second, as he had previously received the award for shooting down the Zeppelin L23. DFCs went to Jackson, Thyne, Williams and Dawson, with a posthumous award to Yeullett.

Tuesday, 23 July

Dull morning, but no rain. King comes on board at 3 pm for half an hour. Managed to get out of flying 1½ Strutter off deck luckily, but am officer of No. 1 division. Turned out very wet so we were not inspected by the King.

Wednesday, 24 July

Went ashore to Turnhouse for a week. Flew a BE2c round by Linlithgow Palace, Borestone, Stirling, the Wallace Monument and back. Walked out to Kirkliston after dinner with Haywood (Observer).

Thursday, 25 July

Did not fly at all. Went to Edinburgh and up to the school to see K. but he had gone yesterday. Rode out to Linlithgow on push bike with Haywood after dinner and was shown all over palace for the second time. Had a look in Visitor's Book but couldn't find our names from our visit in 1913. But saw gun where we had photo taken.

FRIDAY, 26 JULY

Did a spin on a BE2c for the first time. Then flew in a 1½ Strutter through a hole in the clouds to 9000 feet. Clouds like the North Pole beneath me – flat expanse of dazzling white, like ice with ice bergs peaking up through it. Spiralled down with the engine off, a fine sensation in a nice flying bus – just the shriek of the wind.

The reference to doing a spin is of interest. In the early years of the war when pilots were being trained they were cautioned to regard the spin as a manoeuvre that should be avoided. A great many lives were lost as pilots were not therefore trained in spin recovery. It was not until August 1916 that the test pilot at Farnborough, Major Frank Gooden, wrote down the correct procedure to be followed upon entering a spin: switch off motor, control stick put central and pushed forward, rudder put in centre. The aircraft would enter a nose dive and once the speed had built up, could easily be pulled out with the control stick being eased back slightly. Trainee pilots following the scheme devised by Major Robert Smith Barry were in future taught how to enter a spin and how to recover from it safely, so developing their confidence and airmanship. As he said, 'The object is not to prevent fliers from getting into difficulties or dangers but to show them how to get out of it satisfactorily.' Pilots like Jack who now wanted to try this for themselves found that it was a perfectly safe and indeed enjoyable manoeuvre – provided they allowed themselves plenty of height starting a spin.

SATURDAY, 27 JULY

Flew to Glasgow and back in a BE; Gallehawk brought me back in it and we had a pretty sticky get-off owing to a dud engine and small drome.

WEDNESDAY, 31 JULY

Rejoined ship again and also three new subs.

THURSDAY, 1 AUGUST

Pilots all back from Turnhouse as we are going out. Paddy Hayes joined ship, now a 2nd Lieut. Weather is not too good on this side. Got under way at 10 o'clock pm.

FRIDAY, 2 AUGUST

Weather cleared up and a flat calm everywhere. Excitement started after lunch when in the Skagerrak. Saw one Hun submarine lying awash quite plainly, about 10 depth charges on her after she dived. Then later a torpedo just missed the *Royalist* (LC). And another a TBD. The latter submarine probably sunk. Two mouldies also fired at us, but missed us. Am standing by to fly off at 6.45 in the morning to investigate Sylt with Acland.

SATURDAY, 3 AUGUST

Wakened at 4.55 and told I was to fly off at 5.30. Bolted my breakfast and got on deck; Acland already there; then washed out as wind was getting up. Other machine got back about 8.15 with 1¼ gallons of petrol left! Nothing to report. His airbags would not blow up and his Rotherham pump broke! At lunch time, the alarm went and we went to 30 knots. It was one of our own light cruisers which did not answer the challenge but bolted into the mist! On our way back; no more mouldies or mines seen.

SUNDAY, 4 AUGUST

4th Anniversary of War. Did 8–10 watch, but got in at 8.30, so had not much work. Pretty tired and weary! Dawson came back tonight, having escaped from Denmark. Got some stories to tell, too!

In the letter which he wrote home on Monday Jack was able to tell his parents that he had been recommended for promotion again.

TUESDAY, 6 AUGUST

Went to two hours' notice, but washed out; think it was owing to a Zepp raid. Later found out it was due to this. Pilots came off and went back again to Turnhouse.

WEDNESDAY, 7 AUGUST

Went to immediate notice for first time this year: speed for 22 knots. Went out at 3.30. The biggest convoy I have so far seen was lying off Burntisland; also the minelayers. Fairly rough weather. I did the 6–8 watch in foretop. This is the 13th trip this year. Oh, horrible thought!

THURSDAY, 8 AUGUST

Machines on deck at 3.30; action stations at 4–5.30. Very poor weather: pretty rough and no visibility at all. We are down round the South Dogger light and sighted it; we went past it about 70 yards off and I expect we shook them somewhat. Hun aircraft near us (by W/T) but we could see nothing. Turned back at 3.30. Did 10–12 pm watch on bridge. Getting rough and a 45 knot air speed on the bridge. Seas coming down the boat deck continuously. Absolutely tired out tonight; I could fall asleep standing up I believe.

FRIDAY, 9 AUGUST

Got back about 6.30 so did not have to turn out. I am very tired indeed and my eyes sore. Two Camels and a 1½ Strutter flown off to Turnhouse.

That weekend Jack received two parcels from home, one of which may have been the result of a fruit-picking expedition in rural Portaferry, where he learned from his mother that electric lights had just been installed.

First of all I must thank you for the two parcels. The first one was in fine condition and couldn't have been more welcome. The second one, however, puzzled some of us at first, as it smelled somewhat and when held in an inverted position, a long stream of a yellowish, pink liquid poured forth. And we gazed spellbound, for verily the smell of it was enough and it stank in our nostrils! However, thank you and Aunt Eliza very much for sending the gooseberries, for if they had been all right we'd have enjoyed them very much. But it did put the wind up some of us when the parcel began to leak!

I'm enclosing four snaps taken with my camera at about 4000 feet. They give you a very good idea of what another bus looks like in the air near one's own machine. The 'man in black' is myself. The weather here has been awfully hot;

my cabin has been simply unbearable the last few nights. You see I've an iron deck above – no wooden one on this ship at all. We've had some dirty rough weather lately, but I'm glad to say I revel in rough weather now and so far have not felt any results! Of course the destroyers get it very badly. I think I'd rather be in the front line in France than in a TBD in some of the weather we get.

TUESDAY, 13 AUGUST
Went to sea with 1st BCS. Off to North Dogger Bank as the Huns are sweeping a minefield there and we may or may not get them. They may have aircraft up too, though it's a long way from land. Nice evening but a bit rough.

One of the three light cruisers accompanying *Furious* was HMS *Caroline*, which since 1924 was moored in Belfast as the headquarters ship of the Ulster Division RNVR and subsequently RNR. She is the last known surviving vessel to have been present at the Battle of Jutland.

WEDNESDAY, 14 AUGUST
Getting pretty rough in the morning and towards evening far too rough for any flying. Seas coming over (even) after flying deck and a 50 knot wind at the foretop ladder. We are going to turn back tonight sometime.

THURSDAY, 15 AUGUST
Got back OK and three machines flew off in the Firth. Probably go ashore tomorrow to fly.

FRIDAY, 16 AUGUST
Went ashore for a week. Did no flying today so went to Edinburgh with Thyne by 3.41 train. Dinner at North British Hotel.

The ship's log noted that Captain WD Jackson rejoined *Furious* that day, having 'escaped from Denmark.'

MONDAY, 19 AUGUST

Lieutenant Heath killed today in a Camel. Up at 5000 feet for two hours this morning in my summer clothes. Pretty cold up there. Flew the Griffin; don't care for it much though it's fast.

Lieutenant G Heath was killed making a forced landing after an engine failure near Turnhouse in Camel E4414.

TUESDAY, 20 AUGUST

Up at 10,000 feet for 1¾ hours in my old 1½ Strutter. Not so frightfully cold today. Engine not very good.

Jack's letter that afternoon mentioned the Grain Griffin:

I was up for the first time in a new two-seater we have. It was very fast and climbed well but it was rather awkward getting off and landing, partly because it's hard to see out of and also lack of control. I nearly crashed it – undercarriage I mean, when landing, but managed to pull it off – not the undercarriage this time!

WEDNESDAY, 21 AUGUST

Forced landing in the drome in my 1½ Strutter as the ignition wires came adrift. Pulled landing off all right.

THURSDAY, 22 AUGUST

Recalled at 8.15 am. Got underway about 2.30 with the whole fleet; weather rough; going on a PZ.

FRIDAY, 23 AUGUST

Wakened up this morning by New Testament hitting me on the face; things flying everywhere. Very rough indeed: our piano thrown across the wardroom floor. Awful job having breakfast. Seas coming all over our decks, quarterdeck going right under and several of the officers sick. I felt nasty at breakfast – I'd been up to fly since 5 am, but got OK. Lost sight of TBDs in some of the waves. This cabin flat full of water, up to three inches, and several cabins flooded out. Rolling 20 degrees.

It would appear that Jack's throwaway line about revelling in bad weather at sea had been a little premature – as he was quick to admit:

I'm back on the ship once again and have had some awful weather lately. I never want to be at sea again in stuff like we have had recently. It fairly shook us up. You could have no idea of the size of the waves and unfortunately photos do not show them up decently, but we were chucked about all over the place. I wasn't sick but was very uncomfortable twice. Several of the officers were pretty sick and a good many of the ship's company. Sometimes the waves would rise up and we would be on top of them, then there would be a shiver as if we'd struck a submarine or something, and then the horrible plunge – ugh! I did enjoy it on deck but down below it was beastly. I staggered to a settee in the wardroom and slept till about 7 am. Then the stewards tried to lay the table – unsuccessfully. Finally we had our utensils handed to us as we sat down. One officer spent about 15 minutes trying to catch a big hunk of corned beef which had come in through the pantry window – it was a priceless sight! Also to watch the stewards trying to reach us with porridge and tea! I spent the afternoon on top. You have an idea of the height of our top hamper [upper decks], well from there you could see destroyers and light cruisers disappearing from view altogether in the trough of the waves. How any human being can stand a TBD for several days in a sea like this I don't know. Out of the wardroom scuttles, which were mostly underwater, you could not see any other ships at all for the waves. I'd like to send some of the people at home and elsewhere who could have but didn't join up on a TBD for a week! [Then Jack mentions by name some of his contemporaries whom he would select for this experience.] They'd just about die off – but it would do them good I expect. I must say that I enjoyed the experience, though I'm not hankering for another dose! It's a sight well worth seeing and not easily forgotten.

SATURDAY, 24 AUGUST
Got in about 5.30 with everything calm again. Carley rafts badly twisted and smoke screen gear washed over the side.

WEDNESDAY, 28 AUGUST
Suddenly went to immediate notice and went to sea at about 3.30 am. Five German battle cruisers reported steering NW. However, at about 10.30 am we got the signal to return to base and it turned out that the ships were USN minesweepers so nuthin' doing! Rotten luck.

THURSDAY, 29 AUGUST
Went to immediate notice – Grand Fleet at 2½ hours. Reverted shortly afterwards.

FRIDAY, 30 AUGUST
Went to short notice – 2½ hours in the morning, then to 1½ and finally, 4 o'clock we were at immediate notice. Pilots came on board and we were expecting to go to sea any time. Still at immediate notice when I turned in. 2nd BCS and 6th LCS went out at midnight tonight.

SATURDAY, 31 AUGUST
Still at immediate notice; at about 1 pm we went to 1½ hours again. Buzz going about that a landing on the Belgian coast is to be attempted behind the German lines.

An amphibious operation on the Flanders coast had indeed been on the cards in the autumn of 1917 but had been cancelled. In truth the war on the Western Front had already turned in favour of the Allies. The Australian and Canadian Corps of Fourth Army, guarded on either flank by British and French troops, had inflicted heavy losses on the enemy near Amiens on 8 August – 'the black day of the German army in the history of the war', according to Ludendorff. He offered his resignation to the Kaiser, which was refused, but both could see that the war must be brought to a conclusion and one which would not favour Germany. Further Allied assaults followed near Albert and Arras. By the end of August the Germans were pulling back all along the front line.

Sunday, 1 September

Still at short notice! Went to usual notice by signal at about 11.30 – 'Revert to usual notice till 6.30, then Grand Fleet at 2½'. Wonder what it all means as that means we are at 1½ then? Some big stunt on of some description. 6th LCS came in alone at 4.15 this afternoon. Where are the 2nd BCS?

Jack wrote home of an interesting job offer, made while he was ashore, on Monday:

I was in rather a fix this week as I was offered a job at East Fortune as Flight Commander, promotion as soon as I got there and in a job that really suited me – low flying. Well there was a lot to say for it and I couldn't make up my mind. I didn't want to leave this ship and all the chaps I've been with in her for the last 14 months, and I didn't want to leave the Fleet at all. The other job would have taken me probably somewhere out east, of course I was very keen to go there, but when I thought everything through I decided to stay with the ship.

Tuesday, 3 September

Recalled to ship, and at short notice for a while. Then reverted and A flight went ashore.

It would appear that the experience with the gooseberries had not discouraged Jack's mother as he wrote:

If you have not yet sent the tomatoes I have my doubts about them, as they might be kept lying ashore some days if we were to go out to sea. Though thank you very much for them all the same.

Saturday, 7 September

Returned to Turnhouse again. Took up BE with a mechanic and spun and cartwheeled it. He hadn't been up before and wasn't sure he liked it. Also took up a snotty and frightened him.

MONDAY, 9 SEPTEMBER

Went up in DH9 to 13,000 feet with Mackenzie. Not awfully struck by it. Fearfully cold coming down. Apparently you can see the Irish coast from 18,000 feet on a clear day! East Fortune has applied for me but I told them I still don't want to go. Went to Edinburgh and pictures in the evening.

SATURDAY, 14 SEPTEMBER

Ship under way for firing. Flew off deck and proceeded to May Island; then steered 56 degrees doing a reconnaissance on 70 degrees line allowing for wind. Sighted 1st BS about 15–20 miles to southward; worked round them and kept in touch, out of sight in clouds. Got into a hail squall and also a heavy rain storm. In the air three hours and frozen stiff.

Jack's mother pressed on regardless and was determined that her son should have some home-grown tomatoes, so he was able to write on 16 September:

First of all I must thank you for the tomatoes which arrived with one exception in perfect condition. They *were* beauties and were greatly appreciated. I should love to have some more but please don't send any till I ask you as they might be lying around some time before I got them. I'll return the box in a day or two.

A few days ago I had a three-hour trip out of sight of land and it was no joke. The cold was intense and a rain storm did not help, but when I got into the thick of a hail squall at 5000 feet, my engine stopped twice for about ten seconds each time – no ships or land in sight and this in a land machine [a 1½ Strutter], it put the wind up me properly. Still I got back [to Turnhouse] and we had done pretty well. It wasn't active service [not in contact with the enemy or over enemy-held territory] but it was active enough part of the time! Especially in the hail, as I got nearly out of control and my face felt as if it was being torn to ribbons and the bumps – ugh! The clouds were like sooty smoke, too.

This was to be excellent preparation for a sortie which Jack and Paddy Hayes would undertake the following week, which definitely was active service.

MONDAY, 23 SEPTEMBER
Was to have gone on leave today but was recalled and we went to sea. PZ. Am to fly off in the morning.

TUESDAY, 24 SEPTEMBER
Flew off with Paddy Hayes and did a 3½ hour reconnaissance. Did the job very well I believe. Awful visibility – nil. Landed in ditch beside the *Umpire* and was picked up; sea getting up considerably. Was sick after lunch and in the evening. Next TBD had her bridge carried away in the storm.

This was an excellent feat of flying and navigation, undertaking reconnaissance mission F26 in poor visibility and returning to be picked up by *Umpire*, which was a Modified R Class destroyer of 1085 tons; when the alternatives would have been heading for internment in Denmark or being lost at sea. The standard drill on arriving in the vicinity of a friendly destroyer was to make a low pass to attract the crew's attention, switch off the engine and glide in to land in the sea about 500 yards ahead of the ship, inflate the airbags with compressed air and await the arrival of the sea boat. His forthcoming leave was well-deserved.

WEDNESDAY, 25 SEPTEMBER
Went through a minefield as we had lost our bearings in the storm when escorting other ships. Got in at 4.30 pm. Awfully cold and wet and tired.

THURSDAY, 26 SEPTEMBER
Crossed by Glasgow and Ardrossan for a week's leave. Arrived in about 7 o'clock and met Tony. Went up to the Mill for my bike and rode home while they were at breakfast. Gave them some surprise. Train left Caledonian at 8.15 and got to Ardrossan about 11.55. Long time since I crossed that way. All the civvies had wind up about subs! Quite a good day. Went round and saw Mabel Hunter after dinner. Saw Mr and Mrs H also.

SATURDAY, 28 SEPTEMBER

Buzzing about on the bike most of the day; rain off and on. Jack Britton came round after dinner.

SUNDAY, 29 SEPTEMBER

Walked down to Church with Mother twice. Came up with May McArthur. Raining hard most of the time.

MONDAY, 30 SEPTEMBER

Rode over to the Mill in the morning. Saw Meta in the afternoon; also met Eric Pinkerton and John Mayne. Former is now an RNVR snotty on the *Sawfly* at Grimsby. Fleet went out to chase German High Seas Fleet, but came in again as they had got near Heligoland and were too far away. Still they have been out.

TUESDAY, 1 OCTOBER

Jack Smith and Jack Britton came for tea; former looking pretty fit. Walked over to Mrs Herriot's with him for a while. Hope to meet him in town tomorrow at 1 o'clock, opposite Foster & Dowses and ride over for lunch with him.

Events in Germany were moving at a rapid pace. On this day the Kaiser asked his cousin, Prince Max, the heir to the Grand Duchy of Baden, to become chancellor and with a mandate to seek an armistice as soon as it could be arranged. Ludendorff had suffered a breakdown and recommended speedy action to save the German Army from destruction – the toll on its resources had been almost unbearable with over one million casualties since the beginning of his offensives in the spring. The Kaiser retorted that he should have considered this earlier and that he, Wilhelm, was not a magician.

WEDNESDAY, 2 OCTOBER

Met Jack downtown and had a fine ride – a bit skiddy as he came off in front of a dog. Got there in good time. Saw 'em all, looking well and fit. Previously saw Meta for some time; went a walk round by the Bridge and Castle Park after tea with Meta. Then a walk with Father.

Thursday, 3 October
> Down town on the bike in the morning. Spent some time at Meta's and got a photo. Saw Miss Craig. Left by Ardrossan boat at 9.30 pm. Good crossing with a bit of a rock on but managed to sleep.

Jack therefore missed the temporary secondment of Lieutenant Colonel Bell Davies to HMS *Argus*, the first stem to stern flush deck aircraft carrier, which had been converted from the requisitioned Italian liner *Conte Rosso*. Leaving Acland in command, he joined *Argus* in the Firth of Forth. He had decided that he could not take any of the other pilots from *Furious* as they were needed on board, so he recruited another pilot from Turnhouse, Captain LH Cockey RAF. Wooden ramps were laid on the flight deck with fore and aft wires stretched in between, while a pair of 1½ Strutters were fitted with overlapping hooks on their axles. Between 24 and 26 September and on 1 October, they made a series of take-offs from and landings on the 567 feet long deck – a major milestone in the development of carrier-borne aviation.

Jack did mention going to the cinema in Edinburgh on his way back to *Furious* and that he enjoyed a film titled 'Twelve Good Lives and True', which starred one of his favourite actors, the popular American, Sidney Drew. He also noted in his letter of 6 October:

> The Huns have asked for an Armistice – I hope they get it.

Saturday, 12 October
> Pulled a dinghy in to Aberdour and back with Cole. Fine day and good exercise; got back just at dusk. *Nairana* returned from the German coast where she did fine work. Had most of 'em on board and a cheery evening. Germany said to have accepted the peace terms!

Prince Max had sent a diplomatic note to President Wilson of the USA, indicating that Wilson's Fourteen Points would form an acceptable basis for negotiation. (The Fourteen Points were first outlined in a speech Wilson gave to the American Congress in January 1918. They became the basis for the terms of the German surrender, as negotiated at the Paris Peace Conference in 1919.

The Fourteen Points speech was the only explicit statement of war aims by any of the nations fighting in World War One.) A few days later came the reply that the Allies demanded that German forces must evacuate all occupied territory in France and Belgium. Meanwhile, the Allied armies rolled on remorselessly with a co-ordinated series of offensives.

Sunday, 13 October

Went ashore in charge of B flight at 1.10 pm. Lorry konked out several times on the way. Walked to Cramond with Kirkland. Turned in at 9 o'clock and at 10.25 pm was wakened and told we were recalled: got all the officers on board OK by about 1 o'clock; four men left ashore. Got turned in about 2.15 am! Three German battle cruisers out steering NW full speed. 1st BCS went out at about 3 o'clock.

He had written home that morning in some haste as he was packing to go ashore:

I expect my second ring to come at any time now within the next fortnight, so I'm feeling pretty pleased with things in general. There was great excitement in the mess last night, as the *Dundee Telegraph* said the Hun reply was going to the USA last night and that they were *accepting* Wilson's terms; also that some Hun troops raised the Red Flag and threatened to march on Berlin! There has been no news since, so we are all wondering what the W/T will have to say.

Monday, 14 October

Douai supposed to have been taken. Germans trying to get time to square up their line by 'accepting' peace terms. Battle cruisers came back this evening.

The war at sea was far from over. On 4 October, the Japanese passenger ship *Hirano Maru* en route from Liverpool to Yokohama, had been torpedoed off the Irish coast by the *UB-91* with the loss of 292 lives. This was followed on 10 October by the sinking of the Irish mail steamer on its way from Dublin to Holyhead, the RMS *Leinster*; a particularly ruthless act, as she was torpedoed once by *UB-123* and then a second time while sinking. Some 176 were drowned, including many women and children. By an ironic and just twist of fate *UB-123* did not make it home safely. She hit a mine in the North Sea and sank. On 14 October President Wilson issued a demand for the end of the U-boat campaign and made this conditional as regards the acceptance of terms for an armistice.

Tuesday, 15 October

Went to short notice this morning and went out at about 12.15 pm. Some more extra pilots on board. Going to try to do the same old, often attempted, reconnaissance. I'm down for first machine with Paddy Hayes; we're down to leave at 6 o'clock. Good weather this evening but it looks like rain. Turned in at 9 o' clock.

Wednesday, 16 October

Up at 4.45 and had breakfast at 5 am. Weather awful for flying, clouds at 800 feet and pretty heavy rain. Operation delayed and finally abandoned at about 1.30 pm. We had a very close call with a mine but the Officer of the Watch managed to clear it. 5th BS out with us. Weather continued bad all day and at about midnight I was wakened up by being chucked about my bunk. It had got pretty rough but only lasted a couple of hours. Glad I wasn't in a TBD though.

The chief of the German Naval Staff and former commander of the High Seas Fleet, Admiral Scheer, who had removed his headquarters from Berlin to Spa in Belgium, rejected the demands for the cessation of unrestricted U-boat warfare and demanded a wholly unrealistic new building programme instead, declaring that the Navy did not need an armistice.

Thursday, 17 October

Weather clearing up somewhat but a good deal of wind. Got in about 12.30. Had a good wash and shave, and felt clean again. There's nothing like being a pig at sea! News came through in the evening that we had captured Lille and Courtrai. Also the RN and RAF had entered Ostend – it must have been empty.

In Berlin Ludendorff had changed his mind and had stated that Germany could fight on.

FRIDAY, 18 OCTOBER

Went ashore to Turnhouse again. Am OC [Officer Commanding] flight! Weather very wet indeed so no flying. Had dinner in Edinburgh with some of the boys.

SATURDAY, 19 OCTOBER

No flying as it was wet all day. Took a short walk with Kirkland.

SUNDAY, 20 OCTOBER

Divisions as usual. Tested a BE2c in afternoon and engine failed. Acland came up and told me I'd been promoted. Good news – Captain McCleery.

The Kaiser declared an end to the U-boat campaign against merchant vessels but an angry Admiral Scheer issued orders recalling all submarines to base with a view to placing them at the disposal of Admiral Hipper, the C-in-C of the High Seas Fleet, for action against Allied warships.

MONDAY, 21 OCTOBER

Got my appointment as Captain, dated back to 8th August!! Not so bad, if it's not a mistake. Recalled at 6.30 and came on ship at 9.30 am. Going out again at 12 o'clock I believe for another F stunt. Suppose I'll finish up in a TBD if the weather's good! – or Denmark. Got under way about noon; weather not very good. Am standing by to do the oft attempted Sylt reconnaissance. Hope we manage OK.

Jack wrote home that morning with the good news of his overdue promotion:

Just another short note as I'm in an awful hurry to get it posted and I won't have a chance of writing again for a day or two. [He had been briefed regarding the likely mission and was well aware of the danger it involved.] Yesterday afternoon I was up testing a machine and as usual my engine konked out. I got back and landed on the drome and was feeling anything but cheery when Acland turned up from the ship and told me my promotion had come through. I didn't feel quite so mouldy after that! Well I'm Captain and Flight Commander now, dated back to *Aug 8th* this year! So I've a good deal of pay to come in if this is right. And best of all, I'm remaining on board, so you can imagine how braced I am with life! Captain McCleery – Phew, sounds all right, doesn't it? I can hardly write I'm so excited now, it was worth the wait and what's more several people higher up were good enough to say I'd well earned it! Well I must close now, hoping you will excuse this scribble, with best love to all.

TUESDAY, 22 OCTOBER

Weather very dud. Stood by to fly off at 6.15 am; washed out till 8.30; weather still very bad, but sent me off. Sighted six enemy sweepers and TBD; they did not fire, though we were only 1000 feet up over centre ship. 20 minutes later two seaplanes left the water, with a big sea running, and gave chase. Shook them off in clouds and altered course. Sighted Blaarand Huk – eight miles; followed the coast up past Lyndrig Light to Borhung Light and landed there beside HMS *Wessex*; tail broke up in sea. Our undercarriage stove in the whaler and when we got to ship we had to jump for the life lines as she was just sinking. Had a dry change and lunch; then slept till dinner at 8 o'clock. Stayed on deck till 11 o'clock; not very rough.

Wessex was a modern W Class destroyer of 1100 tons. This was Jack's second challenging and hazardous mission of this nature, designated F13, which he completed with total success. It was by no means beyond possibility that he and his observer would be in line for a gallantry award.

Meanwhile, at Wilhelmshaven on the same day a confidential message was brought from Admiral Scheer to Admiral Hipper. He was instructed to prepare the High Seas Fleet to attack the Grand Fleet at the earliest possible opportunity. The German Government was not informed. The admirals appeared to have taken leave of reality; they wished to inflict as much damage as possible, not to win the war but to restore the reputation of the Imperial German Navy in 'an honourable battle by the fleet – even if it should be a fight to the death – will sow the seed for a new German fleet of the future.'

WEDNESDAY, 23 OCTOBER

Had a good breakfast and we got in about noon; got back to *Furious*. Admiral very pleased with our show and says Beatty will be too. Am awfully tired after it all. Danish coast is a fine straight sand beach, but inland the country is very bad – low and very gorsy, with also a great deal of water. Saw one military station, and some small villages – wooden huts very much scattered about. One priceless old windmill at work. During the stunt, flew in clouds at 1000–1500 feet most of the time and also encountered a heavy rain squall. In all I saw four seaplanes, only two of which gave chase; also three Hun submarines.

THURSDAY, 24 OCTOBER

At one hour's notice early this morning, but reverted to two hours. BCS is out with light cruisers. P'raps they intend catching 'my' sweepers. Misty morning.

Admiral Hipper had issued his orders to the High Seas Fleet. Eighteen battleships, five battle cruisers, twelve light cruisers and seventy-two destroyers would proceed to sea and attempt to draw the Grand Fleet over waiting minefields and lurking U-boats. Raiding flotillas of cruisers and destroyers would launch provocative bombardments on the Belgian and English coasts.

Bell Davies had returned to the *Argus* towards the end of October as the ship had been fitted with a dummy island structure on the starboard side of the flight deck, in which could be contained the funnel, bridge, chartroom etc. Further landing trials were made but this time in a Sopwith Pup as the island took up enough width to make attempting landings with the larger wingspan 1½ Strutter inadvisable. These were successful and resulted in the post-war carriers *Hermes* and *Eagle* being completed with islands in 1923 and 1924 respectively.

Friday, 25 October
Went ashore again to Turnhouse.

Saturday, 26 October
Played a round of 14 holes of golf on the course. Put in some time flying.

Sunday, 27 October
Recalled to the ship by mistake and returned on board. Then went back to Turnhouse.

Hipper's plan was approved by Scheer and the operation was planned for three days' hence.

Monday, 28 October
Flying as usual; W/T etc. Did a lot of short BE trips and spun her. Went up in the DH9 but it was too misty for her.

Tuesday, 29 October
Flying as usual.

The German admirals had not made allowance for the war-weariness of their sailors and their very reasonable desire not to die in a lost cause. Morale was low, food rations were poor, discipline was harsh and there was little in the way of sport or entertainment. In addition, the sailors were distrustful and harboured bitter feelings towards their officers. That evening the desertions and mutinies began. As it spread, Hipper realised that the 'honourable death for the glory of the fleet' which he had envisaged held little appeal for the majority, nor did they want to see the peace negotiations sabotaged. The operation was cancelled and the fleet was dispersed to Kiel, Cuxhaven and Wilhelmshaven.

Wednesday, 30 October
Up in a 1½ Strutter to 9000 feet for W/T and later in the day took up Lieutenant Leslie Russell (E) of the *Umpire* for a joy ride; took him up to 8000 feet. Recalled at 9 o'clock and got on board about 10.15 pm. Great flap, but nothing seems to be doing.

It had been some ten days since Jack's last letter home, a fairly lengthy gap, for which he apologised:

> I'm sorry for being so late this time, but it couldn't be helped, as I've been kept pretty busy ashore at Turnhouse till last night. Since I last wrote I've had another trip in a destroyer though it wasn't as bad as the first one. I wasn't sick and only felt bad for an hour after I got on board as I was so very tired. Remind me to tell of it when I see you again, it was rather amusing. Well, I was chased and had to run from four Huns, but I got away in a cloud and shook them off. I believe it was a very good show and the admiral and the other staff people were very pleased indeed. As a matter of fact (confidentially) I was told it nearly went further than that. Anyway it was a pretty interesting show and I was very glad it turned out well. I've just heard today that I may have to go to the *Queen Elizabeth* permanently, but not if I can help it! There's too much gold lace there for my simple tastes and even if she is the fleet flagship, I've no desire to swing around on a buoy for the rest of the war.

As with other capital ships in the Grand Fleet, Admiral Beatty's flagship, the battleship *Queen Elizabeth*, had been fitted with turret ramps fore and aft for a Camel and a 1½ Strutter. It may well have been that serving in her would have been more restrictive for a young officer and that there would have been rather more protocol observed. There was also a certain amount of one-upmanship with regard to the amount of action seen since Jutland by those not spending the war 'swinging around on a buoy' in a battleship. However, in fairness it must be recognised that Beatty did an excellent job as C-in-C in maintaining the Grand Fleet's morale and confidence that it would 'administer to the High Seas Fleet an almighty drubbing' if battle were joined in 1917 or 1918.

Jack continued his letter:

> Thank you all very much for the congratulations on my step up. Did you know I had a letter from all the foremen at the Mill with all their signatures? I don't think I was ever so pleased as when I got it; it *was* nice of them to send it. I was

very glad I was able to do something to justify it in a small way so soon after.

The letter to which Jack referred was dated 25 October and was written on notepaper headed William Ross & Co. Ltd, Flax Spinners, Clonard Mills, Belfast and was addressed to Captain JM McCleery:

Dear Sir,
    We feel that we cannot allow this occasion to pass without congratulating you on your well merited promotion; we wish you a pleasant and successful career and a safe return. Sincerely yours,
    William J Henning, Thomas E Morrison, John McCann, Andrew Templeton, Thomas McCleane, Alexander Thompson.

Jack concluded his letter with some sporting news of a school rugby match and some social news of his own:

I had intended to see the match against Glenalmond on Saturday but was prevented. It seems to have been a good game and Merchiston won by 24 – nil. I had dinner with the Admiral again a few nights ago, so I'm getting on pretty well in the gold lace department at present.

Friday, 1 November
Turkey packs up with practically unconditional surrender. Austria will probably do the same, as they have lost 50,000 men and are retreating before the Italians, British and French very fast. Still at short notice. Duty Officer today and moved into a single cabin – OK.

Austria-Hungary had agreed to an armistice with Italy on 29 October and would extend this to the rest of the Allies on 2 November. Turkey signed an Armistice on 30 October.

Saturday, 2 November
Still at short notice. Out for sub-calibre firing in the morning. Revolution in Austria.

Sunday, 3 November

Usual Sunday routine except for a bit more work cleaning up for tomorrow.

Jack was able to report the following in his letter home:

I've been kept pretty well occupied by one thing and another during the past week, including moving into a new cabin – a single, in accordance with my dignity! It's very nice to have one alone and as it's a little farther forward in the ship it will be a bit better at sea. I wonder how long the war will last now with Turkey and Austria both out of it to all intents and purposes.

Monday, 4 November

Japanese Admiral Prince Yorihito and Prince Arthur of Connaught came on board this afternoon and a Camel and a 1½ Strutter were rigged for their benefit. Rained most of the day. 13,000 prisoners taken on Western Front by British and 200 guns. Italians have taken over 100,000 Austrians prisoner and Austria has packed up to General Diaz's terms.

In Kiel, Workers' and Sailors' Councils had been formed, which on this day took control of the port. The last major land engagement on the Western Front, the Battle of the Sambre, brought the death of the poet Lieutenant Wilfred Owen, but also at last convinced the German High Command that the game was indeed up.

Tuesday, 5 November

Wet most of today. Duty Officer, but very little to do. Still at short notice.

Wednesday, 6 November

It is 12 months today since George was killed; how short a time it seems! Still at short notice. British, French and Americans break through in France. *Campania* dragged her anchor tonight, broke adrift, struck the *Glorious* and sank in Burntisland Roads. No lives lost.

Campania was lying at anchor off Burntisland in the Firth of Forth. A sudden Force 10 squall caused the ship to drag anchor. She collided first with the bow of the nearby battleship *Royal Oak*, and then scraped along the side of the battle cruiser *Glorious*. *Campania*'s hull was breached by the initial collision with *Royal Oak*, flooding her engine room and losing all main electrical power. The ship then started to settle by the stern, sinking some five hours after breaking free. The ship's crew were all rescued by neighbouring vessels. A Naval Board of Enquiry into the incident held *Campania*'s watch officer largely responsible for her loss, citing specifically the failure to drop a second anchor once the ship started to drift.

THURSDAY, 7 NOVEMBER

Am Senior Flying Officer on board today. Lieutenant Holden crashed into ditch; not hurt at all, luckily. At 4 o'clock, signal from Vice-Admiral Battle Cruiser Fleet 'Hostilities ceased at 2 pm today (official)'. Some noise in the mess!

At 5 o'clock – signal from C-in-C 'Cancel signal re (above)!' So is it peace or not? Great excitement of course everywhere!

FRIDAY, 8 NOVEMBER

Still at 2½ hours' notice, so it's evidently going to remain so till the end of the war. No more news from France. Last night's peace rumours unfounded.

SATURDAY, 9 NOVEMBER

No special news till the evening when we heard definitely, the Hun delegates had arrived with Foch. Mutiny in the German Fleet. Kaiser and Crown Prince have abdicated. HMS *Britannia* torpedoed in Southern Seas; about 40 lost.

On this fateful day at the Imperial German High Command HQ at Spa, the Kaiser was informed by Ludendorff's replacement, General Wilhelm Groener:

Sire, you no longer have an army. The army will march home in peace and order under its leaders and commanding generals, but not under the command of Your Majesty, for it no longer stands behind Your Majesty.

The Red Flag had been hoisted on Admiral Hipper's flagship, *Baden*; seeing that resistance was futile, Hipper cleared his cabin and went ashore. He informed the Kaiser that he could no longer rely on the Navy; Wilhelm replied that he no longer had a navy. By that evening he had abdicated and the next morning travelled into exile in Holland.

A republic was proclaimed in Germany. Revolution was sweeping the country. Marshal Foch of France, representing the Allied armies, and the First Sea Lord, Admiral Wemyss, on behalf of the Allied navies, met the German delegation in a railway carriage in the forest of Compiègne and dictated their terms. When the German naval representative baulked at the demand for the internment of the Fleet, on the grounds that it had never been defeated, Wemyss replied that it was welcome to come out and test the assertion.

The battleship *Britannia* was on a voyage to Gibraltar when she was torpedoed off Cape Trafalgar by the German submarine *UB-50*. After the first explosion, the ship listed ten degrees to port. A few minutes later, a second explosion started a fire in a 9.2-inch magazine, which in turn caused a cordite explosion. Darkness below decks made it virtually impossible to find the flooding valves for the magazines, and those the crew did find were poorly located and therefore hard to turn, and the resulting failure to properly flood the burning magazine probably doomed the ship. *Britannia* held her 10-degree list for 2½ hours before sinking, allowing most of the rest of the crew to be taken off. Toxic smoke from the burning cordite killed most of the men who were lost in the sinking; fifty men died and eighty were injured.

SUNDAY, 10 NOVEMBER
No more news so far. Message from Beatty read by Skipper after church: saying that an armistice does not mean peace and that we will need to be ready in the fleet.

MONDAY, 11 NOVEMBER
PEACE

Got the official news of the armistice being signed early this morning. Not much work done! C-in-C ordered all our ships to 'Splice the main brace'. Great show in the evening of search lights, sirens, rockets etc. See letter for this date. We are back to Mons again, as the Canadians have captured it.

That evening Jack wrote of the historic events in a detailed, thoughtful and quite profound letter:

This is written just after one of the finest sights that I suppose has ever been seen in the world – the Silent Navy gone mad! We got the peace news, or rather the armistice news this morning and after dinner tonight the fun started. Firstly *all* the searchlights in the Grand Fleet began to give a show, Very lights and all description of rockets went up and burst into coloured lights, and the sirens were blowing till it was perfectly impossible to even hear each other yelling. After a while different ships began to paint their searchlights with fine effect.

Then suddenly a burst of cheering was heard from far up the line of battle cruisers and battleships; the cheering grew and finally an American launch, packed with men came past playing 'Tipperary' and 'Pack up your Troubles' etc, and at the bows, held up by some of the sailors were the Stars and Stripes and the White Ensign flying side by side. It was too thrilling for words and I feel it was worth five years' life to see it. The Silent Navy – Ye Gods! It has all died down now, but not till it had lasted I'm sure most of two hours (my watch had stopped and little wonder).

Still in a way there is in the Fleet a certain feeling of disappointment. Four years of strict preparation and at the end no scrap – though this past 14 days it has been expected day after day. Somehow, I know it's selfish, but we are all the same, I feel very disappointed that for us it has evidently finished so quietly. Till today I've not been off the ship for a fortnight. Today I went to Turnhouse to fly, but did not do much and was frozen at 8000 feet.

As to my getting out, I'll feel very sorry to leave the sea as it has a fascination for me, but at any rate I doubt if I'll be able to get out for at least six months. I hope to finish by flying over the Hun fleet when it is given over to us. Of course there's a chance that there will be some sort of scrap before it is given up. I hope there is and so do we all.

Edinburgh has gone mad I believe and I hear the girls have started to kiss the sailors and soldiers – sailors first in Edinburgh. Me for Edinburgh tomorrow! Well I'm glad and proud to be able to say, as I think I can safely, that I've been on the most active service ship in the fleet during the past 18 months and one with probably the most dangerous work of any of the big ships.

Still as Beatty has warned us all, it's only an armistice and we may have to enforce its terms and at any rate we must be more ready even than before. Good old navy. Tomorrow the work will go on as if we were six months back, no difference, just the ceaseless working up of efficiency – general quarters, action, fire and repel aircraft stations in preparation for perhaps the next war if there ever is one. I'll be here in the Fleet if there is one and I'm still fit, at any rate.

TUESDAY, 12 NOVEMBER

No more special news since yesterday. Was DO and had to show a Major Murrie and Old Rutland round the ship.

Chapter Eleven

The Surrender of the High Seas Fleet

WEDNESDAY, 13 NOVEMBER

Cold day and misty, but no wind. Went ashore after lunch with Hocking to shoot on a farm near Aberdour; he got a pigeon and a pheasant which I drove up to him. I hit a pheasant, but he got away into a wood and the dog couldn't find him, worse luck. Saw some grouse but couldn't get near them. Tea at the farmhouse, made very comfortable by old lady looking after 'her boys'! German Admiral to come across in the *Königsberg* on Friday, I think, to see about arrangements for their fleet; poor devils. German men shooting their own officers. Crown Prince has been shot by them; good job, too.

Grand Admiral Crown Prince Wilhelm actually went into exile in Holland but Prince Henry of Prussia, the Kaiser's brother and C-in-C of the Baltic Fleet, had a narrow escape, fleeing from Kiel in a lorry flying a red flag. Hipper's representative in the modern light cruiser *Königsberg* was Rear Admiral Hugo Meurer.

FRIDAY, 15 NOVEMBER

Königsberg arrived; we can not see her as she lies inside May Island. Beatty refused to make any plans with the Soldiers and Sailors Council and only with the Admiral. That's the stuff to give 'em!

Meurer's task was to work out the details with Admiral Beatty and his staff of what had been agreed during the Armistice negotiations. The original idea had been for the complete surrender of the German Navy but the Prime Minister, David Lloyd George, backed away from this out of concern that if the Germans were pushed too hard they might want to continue fighting. Instead it was decided that ten battleships, six battle cruisers, eight light cruisers, fifty destroyers and all the U-boats should be interned in a neutral harbour until the peace terms were settled. Neither the British nor the German admirals (for diametrically opposite reasons) were overly happy with this solution. Nor were any neutral countries, Norway and Spain in particular, being contacted. In the end it was decided that the U-boats should be surrendered to Admiral Tyrwhitt at Harwich and that the High Seas Fleet would sail to the Firth of Forth before being interned in Scapa Flow.

SATURDAY, 16 NOVEMBER

No more special news lately. Got my 2nd ring on my RNAS blue!

Jack speculated about the *Königsberg* in his letter that evening:

I wonder how often she was out chasing us? She is one of their very latest light cruisers and can do – on paper – 35 knots, so I expect she has been out after us more than once. I hope to see the Hun fleet on Thursday or there-abouts, but there's quite a possibility unfortunately of not allowing this ship to go out with the Fleet for obvious reasons. To date you see we remain a 'mystery ship' and they may take it into their heads not to show us. I believe they are going to cut down the RAF to a very small force, but it will be some considerable time yet before they start. Also I'm told that they are going to have an RNAS again soon in the Fleet. So that's my job for the next war!

By the middle of 1919 naval aviation would form a very small part of the RAF, which itself had been pared to the bone – there was a spotter reconnaissance squadron, a fighter flight, half a torpedo squadron, a seaplane flight and a flying-boat flight. The Admiralty was deeply unhappy with merely providing platforms to take RAF aircraft, their crews and maintenance personnel to sea (though pilots and observers of spotter aircraft mounted on battleships and cruisers remained RN). The major and recurring theme of the next twenty years was to be a slow but determined campaign to wrest back the control that had been lost with the demise of the RNAS. However, considerable damage was done by the loss of experienced naval airmen to the RAF. If it is taken as a rule of thumb that naval aviators should be sailors who fly rather than airmen who go to sea; a generation of naval officers would rise to senior posts who knew little about the use of air power at sea. It was later to be contended with some bitterness that between the wars the development and procurement of naval aircraft was badly neglected. In fairness it should be said that money for the armed forces was tight all round and that the RAF was preoccupied with establishing and preserving a role for itself as an independent service and in fighting off attempts for it to be reabsorbed into the Army and the RN. In April 1924 the Fleet Air Arm was created as a branch of the RAF. It was not, however, until 1937 that it was announced in the House of Commons that control of the Fleet Air Arm would be handed over to the Royal Navy within two years, all personnel would be naval and the Admiralty would have its own shore-based air stations. In late 1938 Rear Admiral Richard Bell Davies VC, DSO, one of the few RNAS airmen of stature to have opted to remain in the RN in 1918, was appointed Rear Admiral Naval Air Stations.

Jack's thoughts had also turned to much less nautical matters:

I'm sure I don't know how I'll be able to get all my gear home again when the good time comes, or how I'll ever settle down to peace for that matter! I've already started making plans for Tony, Hunter, Jack and I, when I get my bike! Portaferry and Ballywalter will have a time of it! But we'll always miss George. I wrote a note to Mrs H last week on the day he was killed last year and got a nice letter back from her, saying Hunter was coming home.

Sunday, 17 November
Bitterly cold day. Church as usual after which Skipper read out a message from the High Commissioners of the Admiralty.

Monday, 18 November
Königsberg went away again; no special news. Expect the Hun ships in on Thursday.

Tuesday, 19 November
Went ashore to Turnhouse. Thick fog so did not fly. Had tea at the Golf House and then to Grad with Acland and Kirkland. Dinner at the North British Hotel.

Wednesday, 20 November
Took Acland up in a BE and nearly made him sick – so he says, spinning him. We were recalled for the 5 o'clock boat. We are to go out at 3.00 in the morning to meet the German ships! Hurrah. King and Queen visited the Fleet today.

At Wilhelmshaven the Germans prepared for *Der Tag*. The ships which were to be interned were made ready and skeleton crews were earmarked. Hipper refused to lead his command and instead delegated the duty to Rear Admiral Ludwig von Reuter. They assembled at Schillig Roads and prepared to cross the North Sea for the final time. The U-boats had already begun to surrender.

Thursday, 21 November
Am writing this as we steam back to base with the Hun fleet about three miles on the starboard beam. To see such fine ships surrender so ignominiously is an extraordinary sight. We are abreast the rear Hun battleship – I think it is the *Kronprinz* – she is there at any rate. Behind us, out of sight as it is a foggy day, are the light cruisers and TBDs which are being given up. What a humiliation for the Officers – British officers would never have done it. One of their

TBDs, *V-70*, was sunk last night by bumping a mine – one of her own I expect. They are all flying the German ensign. It cannot help but remain the flag of shame for ever now, after today's show. I saw them first from the foretop at 8.25; *Bayern* leading.

On that morning some 370 Allied warships and 90,000 men put on a massive display of naval might. They steamed out line astern to meet the Germans some forty miles off the Scottish coast. There with white ensigns flying, as if going into battle, they formed into two long columns six miles apart to await the Kaiser's ships. The light cruiser *Cardiff* and the destroyer flotillas went on ahead to escort the seventy German vessels and lead them into internment. They steamed slowly between the British columns, which were at action stations and ready to fire but with turrets trained fore and aft, in case of any ill-advised hostile intent. The Grand Fleet reversed course and the huge array of warships made its way slowly into the Firth of Forth, where they anchored that afternoon. The C-in-C ordered the historic signal to be made:

The German Flag is to be hauled down at 3.57 today and is not to be hoisted again without permission.

Jack mentioned in his diary that he was in the foretop. Accompanying him at this excellent vantage point was *The Daily Chronicle*'s Special Correspondent, Harold Begbie. As he wrote later to his parents, the young officer mentioned by Begbie in his article as exchanging pleasantries with him was Jack. Begbie had dined in the wardroom the previous night and had been invited to hear the junior officers' jazz band perform. He duly paid a visit to wardroom No. 2 (presumably the gunroom); where he could hardly hear himself think due to the noise of the jazz band and could hardly see owing to the fug of tobacco smoke. He enjoyed their performance for its enthusiasm and energy. Perhaps one of the musicians was Jack? He noticed other officers playing bridge or dominoes and one sitting alone, oblivious to the cacophony. He refused many offers of liquid hospitality and retired to bed at 10.30 pm, while the revels continued throughout the ship.

In this manner one of the strangest ships in the Grand Fleet, a ship which runs to hundreds of yards in length, the vast unguarded deck of which is like walking on the roof of the world and can carry comfortably over 20 aeroplanes and on whose deck that gallant fellow Edwin Dunning landed the first aeroplane ever to come down in this fashion – thus, I say, did *Furious* celebrate one of the greatest nights in British history.

In the early hours of the morning Begbie was roused from sleep by the captain's coxswain and made his way to the bridge:

There was now no revelry. A misty moon struggling with thick clouds, shone down upon a leaden sea that was almost garish with thousands of twinkling lights, but quite solemn. The Grand Fleet was getting under weigh. Miles of great ships were beginning to move. The Royal Navy was steaming down the Forth to reap the fruits of its labours. *Furious* with her trembling bows sending up the first rustle of water to disturb the silence, steamed for the first of the sea gates. On one side of us were the lights of Burntisland, on the other the lights of Leith, and behind us, stretching away into the darkness, were the moving lights of the Grand Fleet. Nothing could exceed in awe and beauty and rightness this superb procession of ships to reap the tremendous harvest of their infinite toil. The revelry of Wardroom No. 2 expressed the glad boyishness of the men who man the Fleet but this silent procession of the great ships themselves through the misty night and the cold air of winter expressed the austerity of a Sea Power which has created, assured and protected the freedom of the seas.

At the end of his long and eloquent article Begbie left the final words to Captain Nicholson:

The shadows fell upon captors and captives, the sun sank into darkening clouds, and as *Furious* picked up her buoy the captain turned to me with a smile, which was not without regret, and said, 'Well, that's the end of the story.'

Much later that day Jack wrote to his mother and father:

I saw the Hun ships surrendering after all! I am not going to write a letter about it, but am just enclosing my 'impression' I wrote when we were out with them. So you can count that as part of my letter this week. I thought the mist coming down over the Huns at anchor was very fitting. It seemed to show Germany simply fading away from everything. Father can certainly try and get that rigmarole of mine published if he likes [Jack's account of the Fleet's celebration of peace] but no names to be given – an 'eye witness' or HMS _____ (that's fine!) will do. I don't think he'll manage unless the *Magnet* or *Comic Cuts* wants it! Well it's past 11 now and I'm very tired so will ring off.

The *Magnet* was the weekly paper for boys featuring the stories of Greyfriars School by Frank Richards. *Comic Cuts* was a weekly comic aimed at an older market which ran for more than sixty years. Jack was overly pessimistic, as the *Belfast Telegraph* of 25 November featured his words under the heading:

Fleet and the Armistice, RAF Officer's Graphic Story. A Belfast RAF officer on one of His Majesty's ships writes.

To go back to the surrender of the High Seas Fleet, this is what Jack wrote as his 'impression':

I am writing this as we round up what was once the German High Seas Fleet. At 9.20 am I saw the first of the Hun battle cruisers from the spotting top. It was followed by nine or so other big ships, among them the better known ones being *Derfflinger*, *Von der Tann*, *Seydlitz*, *Molkte*, *Kaiser*, *Kronprinz Wilhelm*, *Markgraf*, *Prinzregent Luitpold*. Five big ships, easily identified for the most part by their big midship derricks and stump masts if nothing else. At times they were hard to see owing to the mist and their being at about the limit of visibility. Astern of us we have the *Vindictive* (just down from Scapa and dock yesterday) and the *Minotaur*. We kept position about three miles on the last Hun ship's beam for some time, then altered course to round up the light cruisers. We saw seven or eight of these – bigger ships and bigger targets than ours, with three big funnels. Then we met the TBDs – hundreds of them, the Huns being in the middle of ours. I have never seen so many destroyers since I came to sea and as the sun had condescended to show itself, it was a most wonderful sight. As I write a line of at least 14 British TBDs are passing us with ensigns (mostly new ones for the occasion) flying at the masthead. Then on our way in, the grey forms of the 'KG Vs' and the 'Revenges' (1st BS) became visible through the fog which was coming down again. When we got closer in the German battle cruisers and battleships are seen to be at anchor with our battle squadrons formed into a square around them. What a sight! Several aeroplanes are flying around them. Tomorrow I hope to fly over them and see more plainly for myself, the ships which we in the old *Furious*, were so often sent out to try and lure to their destruction. But what a sight to remember, the pride of Germany's navy at anchor in the Forth with a wall of steel surrounding them and as Admiral Beatty ordered, 'Turrets and guns are to be kept in the securing positions, but free. Guns are to be empty with cages up and loaded ready for ramming home. Directors and armoured towers are to be trained on. Correct range and deflection are to be kept set continuously on the sights.' It is almost unbelievable, but – it is true.

The interned ships were searched for ammunition before being moved up to Scapa Flow in smaller groups over the course of the following week, where a total of seventy-four German ships would anchor. It was noted by Assistant Paymaster Leslie Graham that *Furious* had covered a total distance of 23,477 miles since she had commissioned in 1917 until that November day.

FRIDAY, 22 NOVEMBER
Back to Turnhouse. Borrowed two shotguns and went with Acland round some of the fields. He got two pheasants and I got a hare – as usual! Got back about 4.30 pm.

SATURDAY, 23 NOVEMBER
Spent both morning and afternoon shooting with Acland as it was too misty for any flying. Got two ducks in the aerodrome; pickled a hare but didn't get him. Turned in early.

SUNDAY, 24 NOVEMBER
Weather cleared up so put in some flying. Went over German fleet in 1½ Strutter with Acland; ships simply filthy and men ditto and in every sort of rig-out. All rust and coal dust. Destroyers just getting under way for Scapa – very similar to the ones I flew over on my reconnaissance mission in the Bight. Took some photographs. Managed to lose my prop coming down for the first time in a 1½ Strutter.

MONDAY, 25 NOVEMBER
Too misty for flying. German fleet sailed for Scapa after dinner. Went to Grad and ordered a gun! Got a permit from Forth Garrison.

CHAPTER TWELVE

Jack's Last Weeks in the Service

TUESDAY, 26 NOVEMBER
Too misty for flying. Came on board for a really splendid concert; got some programmes to send home.

WEDNESDAY, 27 NOVEMBER
Smart and Wing Com both left ship, so am CO for a few days. Flew off nine machines – no crashes by a miracle! Got to get ready for an American entertainment on board, tomorrow afternoon.

THURSDAY, 28 NOVEMBER
CO again. All remaining machines on deck and hangars cleared for dancing and concert. Went ashore and bought my gun in afternoon. Some gun and case.

FRIDAY, 29 NOVEMBER
CO again. Nothing special doing today. Pictures in evening. *Daily Mail* has photo of the famous 'hush' ship, the floating aerodrome, the 'mystery ship' – *Furious* – on back page.

An anonymous article appeared on page four of the same issue. It is of interest to read and contains elements of accuracy but also quite a few rather misleading statements:

Deck Flying By One Who Does It.

For the last two and a half years the 'Deck Flying' branch of the Royal Air Force has 'carried on' secretly but with untiring energy and pluck. The general public are still practically ignorant of its work, which, however, has been indicated by the recent publication of photographs of some of the famous 'Hush! Hush!' ships from which much of this flying is done.

From being a mere experimental 'stunt' it has developed into one of the most vital and important weapons of Britain's sure shield, the Navy. Everyone has read glowing tributes to our splendid airmen in France and occasionally a word of praise for the seaplane men but hitherto the newspapers have not been able to print a word about the pilots who have flown ordinary land machines from the decks of ship – aye, not only from decks but also from small platforms constructed on the tops of gun turrets. Not only are there special ships carrying fast scouts, but also every light cruiser and battle-cruiser has one or more on board.

It may sound almost incredible to the layman that aeroplanes should be flown from platforms not more than 30 or 40 feet long. Yet it has been done every day of the week.

But the 'flying off' is only one of the wonders of this branch of the Service; the getting down or 'landing' is equally difficult and dangerous. Only the scout pilot himself can fully realise the difficulty of 'landing' a 'Camel' on the deck of a ship. But it has had to be done, the alternative being to land in the sea, which is next door to suicide, as the machine is merely an ordinary land aeroplane with nothing to keep it afloat.

It was this branch of the RAF that finally put 'paid' to all Germany's hopes of ever achieving a naval victory. The Huns had put all sorts of hopes in their Zeppelins, and indeed during the first naval engagements it seemed that these hopes were not entirely without foundation. Whenever our ships were at sea and wherever they were if the weather was favourable, they were watched the whole time by Zeppelins, and their movements were accurately reported to Berlin by wireless.

But with the advent of the 'Deck Scout' this arm of the

Imperial High Seas Fleet soon became paralysed. After a few very unsuccessful encounters with these fast scouts the 'Zepps' remained at home. They had always been safe against attack from the heavy, slow-climbing British seaplanes, but to be tackled in mid-ocean by one of the latest fighting scouts was more than they could stand. Thus the Zeppelin menace ceased to be a menace.

Also, it was the deck-fliers that caught and strafed the London bombers on their return journey; that escorted the seaplanes on countless raids on the Bruges docks; that destroyed Zeppelin sheds at Tondern; and that proved a terrible thorn in the side of Hun seaplanes.

SATURDAY, 30 NOVEMBER

CO again, but got ashore at 10 am with guns to shoot. Walked all day and got nothing at all. Only one chance – a pigeon which I missed of course.

SUNDAY, 1 DECEMBER

CO again. Usual Sunday routine. Helped to entertain some ladies who came aboard; one very nice girl.

MONDAY, 2 DECEMBER

Had to assist showing some Jap mission round the ship: explaining all sorts of things to them – that weren't important!

He wrote home that evening with various comments and items of news:

I would like several copies of the *Daily Chronicle* if you could get them and keep them. Begbie was all right but too much hot air... Another good bit of news. We – the whole Fleet are getting leave in two watches. I can't say yet which I'll get, but it is 10 days we are getting – what ho!.... We had a Japanese Naval Mission on board today and I was chosen with some others to show them round the ship. They didn't give me the Order of the Rising Sun though!.... I've been told – *confidentially this* – that my last stunt in the Bight was worth a DSO, but I've not been recommended for it as far as

I know and though it was one of the staff commanders said so, I don't think it was worth as much as that at any rate. Not from a pilot's point of view at any rate. The CO is back now so I'm as usual. I had to pay the men today – over £700 of cash to be counted à la mill. You can tell David that and say we were only 1/- out and we found it in about 10 minutes!.... The US ships, the 6th BS, left yesterday for good. Very comfortable but ugly looking – no lines at all. As they left we cheered them from the Grand Fleet and all the bands played Auld Lang Syne. It was quite impressive as they did ditto and had huge paying off pennants at their maintops. There's a buzz going around that we are for New York. I don't think it's likely at present.

TUESDAY, 3 DECEMBER
CO again till the evening. Wrote home to Kathleen.

WEDNESDAY, 4 DECEMBER
CO again as Bell Davies is on the *Argus*, experimenting. Am to go on leave on the 18th if all's well for 10 days. Got my photos – enlargements, and they are very good indeed. Hope to have them framed when I get home again. They look very fine indeed.
    FINIS

Bell Davies' experiments concerned modifications to the arresting or retaining wires, which had been proving problematical.
    It was on 4 December that Assistant Paymaster Graham sought Admiral Phillimore's permission, which was granted, to assemble information with a view to producing a book:

To form a souvenir for those of us who served during the 'war of wars' in the first of the great aircraft carriers – to be printed on board and bound ashore in leather or a good cloth binding with the crest in gilt. About 300 copies for officers, also about 1000 copies on paper or cartridge paper for the ship's company.

Sadly it would appear that this idea was not carried through and all that remain are Leslie Graham's draft rough notes.

There are no more entries in Jack's diary but he would continue writing a few more letters home. His next letter is dated 10 December and he anticipates coming home on leave in a week's time. The only external news item he imparts concerns the light cruiser *Cassandra*, which had been sent into the Baltic to operate against the Bolsheviks. On 5 December she ran into an uncharted German minefield, struck a mine and sank in the Gulf of Finland.

> She used to come out with us a lot and I had a friend on board her, he's all right, I saw him yesterday nothing the worse. He says the Baltic is full of mines, but as he hasn't been in the North Sea very much, I don't expect that it is any worse than this side of Denmark.

However he did have some important personal information to convey:

> I have put in an application to leave [the Service], which I'm posting you a copy of and I would like you to write to The Secretary, Air Ministry (Demobilisation), Hotel Cecil, Strand, London WC and see what you could do on much the same lines as I have written. There is an order out now against us putting in these chits but mine was in before this was revealed unto us, so it may go through.

His letter was addressed to the Commanding Officer, RAF Unit, HMS *Furious*, with a copy to the Commanding Officer HMS *Furious* and was dated 9 December 1918.

> Submitted:-
> In view of the impending demobilisation of the Service, I desire to apply for my release from the RAF for the following reasons:-
>
> (1) Immediately prior to joining the Service I was under instruction in my Father's business – Flax Spinning – as apprentice manager, which I renounced after having served only eighteen months.
> (2) The period necessary for an individual to become proficient in this business is usually five years.

(3) I am anxious to return to civil life in order that I may again resume the instruction in flax spinning in order to equip myself for the future.

(4) Being the elder son, my Father specially desires that I should be with him in the business at as early a date as possible, and is, I understand, requesting the Air Ministry to release me.

Flax spinning being the leading industry in the North of Ireland, and my Father's business being one of importance, it is specially requested that due consideration may be given to this my application to return to civil life, and that the necessity for my presence here is no longer a matter of urgency.

I have the honour to be, Sir,
Your obedient Servant,

JM McCleery Capt RAF

Jack did indeed get his leave and was so able to spend Christmas at home for the first time since 1915 and what a joyful occasion it must have been. He was back on board *Furious* on the last day of the year, having crossed on the ferry the night before. He didn't mention it so he may have just missed the visit to the ship by Admiral of the Fleet Lord Fisher that morning. The old admiral was shown around by Commander HR Buckle and on seeing a pile of aerial torpedoes stowed in the hangar, he said, 'Scrap the lot or put them away in cotton wool till the next war!' When Buckle asked, 'When will that be, Sir?' Fisher replied, 'In 20 years time!'

Jack knew that he was now on the last lap and that his time in *Furious* was coming to a close. His next letter was dated Sunday, 5 January 1919:

I can say thank you for your letter all right, but I don't know how to go about saying it for the lovely present of a bike and sidecar. I was only looking at one of them in town the other day and wishing all sorts of things. A sidecar will be A* for going shooting or camping out with! I'll not sleep tonight. What with Hunter's, Tony's and the three Jacks' bikes, we should manage to have a pretty hefty time. I don't think I'd mind taking Father down to the docks in the sidecar quite as much as on the carrier! Probably Father would prefer the sidecar! And what about Aunt Eliza – 55 minutes from Portaferry!

Acland is coming on board again on the 28th and as he is staying on I'm going to wangle him as my relief and if that works it shouldn't be too long after till I'm out and in civvies again. I can't find my diary here at all, so I think it must be in my room, either in my black case or in one of the drawers.

He wrote again the next day:

We were out firing this morning and four of us flew off. It was my first flight for most of six weeks, so I was half an hour or so getting into form. This was at about 9.30 am and as I was at 6000 feet for most of two hours with my ordinary clothes on, I was pretty well frozen and did not feel warm again until the evening, after I'd had a very hot bath. There were a great many heavy snow clouds about but I was too cold to go into them, as I'd have liked to. They have been asking for volunteers for a squadron to go to Russia, but I've not done anything about it and I don't think I'll go. I'd like to go in some ways very much, but I'd also like to get home. Regarding demobilisation I've signed umpteen forms since I came back.

It was ten days before he wrote again, explaining that he had been at Turnhouse, which he wrote was an awful place for writing letters. He noted that he had been doing a lot of flying and had got quite keen again. Some fifty years later, in answer to a request in the local newspaper, he wrote to Group Captain BGT Stanbridge, at the Joint Anti-Submarine School, HMS *Sea Eagle*, in Londonderry. He listed the places in which he had served and the aircraft which he had flown all those years ago. Under the heading of Turnhouse he included some types which he had not mentioned in his diaries, the diminutive but very handy Nieuport 11 Bébé scout, the Sopwith Camel, the Sopwith

Triplane and Sopwith Cuckoo and the classic two-seater, the Bristol Fighter. It is not known if he flew the Cuckoo off the deck of *Furious* but at least three of these torpedo bombers are known to have been on the carrier late in 1918. Going back to his letter of January 1919. He continued:

Last Wednesday [8th] I'd a very amusing day. Two of us had an argument with two gamekeepers as to why we were shooting on a certain bit of ground. We managed to out talk them though and got away all right. 1st Spasm.

Then we decided to go to town on the 7.30 pm tender. We got as far as a fairly big turn into the Edinburgh road when we saw another car coming pretty fast – about 30–35 mph, same as ourselves. It was pretty greasy and we swerved well across the road. How we missed that car and a sticky end I don't profess to know, but we did by *inches*. The next thing I knew was an awful crash and I found myself on the floor of the car with a rather painful leg. We hit the kerb with our front left-hand wheel and smashed the axle, then we skidded around on two wheels and hit the opposite back one on the other kerb (the road was as broad as the main Antrim road past Glengormley) [a few miles from Jack's home in Belfast] and smashed both those hubs. We finished up the other way round with a very dilapidated appearance. I was sore for two or three days and can still feel it a bit on my right hip. No one was badly hurt fortunately. Then we managed to get a bus for town – Spasm II!

After dinner we went to see Charlie Chaplin at the pictures. The place was simply packed, people standing everywhere. After we'd watched the show for about half an hour, he suddenly *melted* off the screen. In a few seconds people began to rise and go out, and at the same time smoke began to arrive over the edge of the balcony. I told the chap I was with to sit tight. Then they put on the lights and played the National Anthem to steady people up. By this time everyone was just about choking, but there was no panic fortunately or there might have been a nasty mess up. When we left it was just about impossible within to see or breathe but they kept it under control and no serious damage was done – Spasm III.

I was quite afraid a house would fall on us or something on the way back to the Caledonian!

Having spent the last few years worrying about their son being at war and having read his cheery but sometimes hair-raising letters, one wonders just what conversation might have passed between Mr and Mrs McCleery on reading this.

Jack concluded by referring to the fact that *Furious* had been stripped of her camouflage scheme and looked much better without it. She was now resplendent in Atlantic Fleet Grey.

On 28 January, back in the Orkney Islands for the last time, his letter contained more definite news:

Just a short letter to let you know that my release slip has come through. I'm supposed to wait for a relief, but I am doing my best to get away at once – some time this week. I was put down as 'Proprietor of a flax spinning business' and am not honest enough to disillusion them! We left Turnhouse yesterday morning and rejoined the ship about 10.30 am. We got under way at 3 o'clock and arrived here, Scapa, at 8 pm. It's lovely weather here, but cold. This place looks just the same as ever, no trees; there is snow on the higher islands. The German ships are about three miles from us but plainly visible.

The Battle Cruiser Fleet was at this time responsible for guarding the interned ships. The German destroyers were moored in pairs off Hoy, while the larger vessels anchored around the small island of Cava – on the western side of Scapa Flow. Wireless equipment had been removed from the ships and the guns had been disabled by the removal of their breech blocks. The crews on board were further reduced in size, leaving just sufficient numbers for care and maintenance. They became very demoralised due to isolation, very little to do, lack of hygiene and a monotonous supply of food.

Jack was very much looking forward to coming home:

There is little to do nowadays on board as a great many of the men have gone and most of the time is spent cleaning ship etc. If I can get away from here I shall go to Edinburgh and unless I'm sent off with a draft [of ratings], I should be home at the end of the week, or soon after. The colonel is doing his best for me. I'll wire you if and as I get off and before I cross. I should advise a fairly empty car to meet me – two trunks, kit bag, banjo, gun case and possibly a deck chair.

A few more days elapsed and on 2 February 1919 Jack wrote his last letter from *Furious*, but was there to be a final twist?

We've had the most beautiful bright weather ever since we came here and today is just the same. We've been doing some sailing, but when it comes to that, it's a bit cold. Yesterday (Saturday) two of us went round the Hun fleet in a drifter. The men were evidently getting plenty of exercise as they were using horizontal bars etc and chasing each other up and down the halliards and yardarms. The officers all looked the other way as we came round, naturally enough; it's not their fault that they are there. They are a fine looking and well set up lot of men and though they have to supply their food from Germany, they look far from the starved lot we read of in the papers. Their battle cruisers, *Derrflinger*, *Hindenberg*, *Moltke*, *Seydlitz* and *Von der Tann*, are very fine ships indeed and pretty clean for the most part. Also the light cruisers, some of which are pretty 'hot' ships. Some of the destroyers have started to paint themselves (!) and tidy up but most of them are filthy. I took 14 photos and will wait till I get home to have them developed.

I've done a good deal of revolver shooting up here and have discovered that I'm quite a good shot, even at moving targets. The water here is remarkably clear, and on a calm day one can see to a depth of nearly five fathoms, quite four at any rate.

We are lying just beside where the *Vanguard* went up last time I was here. Today we are at one hour's notice as we are duty or emergency ship in case the Huns start any tricks, which is unlikely as they've no ammunition and most of their guns have their breeches removed.

I'm still waiting for my relief, and at the current rate of

progress may continue to do so! On Tuesday we are going to Lamlash [on the Isle of Arran on the east coast in the Firth of Clyde] for five or six days and then possibly across to Bangor [a well-known and popular resort town on the southern side of Belfast Lough], so I'll see you soon at any rate. Then we may go to Rathmullan [on Lough Swilly on County Donegal] and from there back to dock at Rosyth. I intend to try and get a seaplane if we go to Bangor and fly over Belfast, so if you see one you will know who it is.

In the end Jack, or 'Mac' as he was known to his friends in *Furious*, did not have the opportunity for a spectacular finale of this nature. He may well have had his final flight the following day, when four Camels and two 1½ Strutters were flown off the deck to Smoogroo, being re-embarked later on. *Furious* proceeded to Lamlash with *Vindictive* and *Pegasus* on 4 February, being noted in the log as 'The Flying Squadron'. A railway warrant has been preserved which shows that he travelled from Lamlash to Turnhouse on 6 February and made his way home in the middle of February by the Ardrossan to Belfast ferry. His time flying from *Furious* had come to an end. The ship sailed to Lough Swilly on 14 February but did not call at Belfast either on the way there or back to Rosyth. As for the High Seas Fleet, it was scuttled at Scapa on 21 June 1919. By the end of the month Phillimore, Bell Davies and Acland had all also departed. In July, exercises were carried out with the airship *NS7* landing on deck and being towed astern. *Furious* served in the Atlantic Fleet to the end of the year, including a period in the Baltic Sea assisting the White Russians against the Bolsheviks (from where Jack received a Christmas card and a letter from Acland, who was serving in *Vindictive*) and was then placed in Reserve, pending a decision on her future.

CHAPTER THIRTEEN

What Happened Afterwards

Jack went directly into the family mill and worked more than fifty years for the company, mainly as a director on the sales side. He married Meta in 1922. Their daughter, Barbara, was born in 1923. In 1927, Jack's father suffered a stroke, and was confined to a wheelchair for much of the time. In 1930 his Uncle Hamilton had a heart attack. Meta died on 18 August 1930, not yet twenty-nine years old. Jack's father and his uncle died within two weeks of each other in 1931. Jack and his brother Tony now had full responsibility for the family business and times were tight during the years of the Depression.

Annual reunion dinners were held in London for old shipmates who had served in *Furious*, which had been converted to a fully flush-decked carrier between 1921 and 1925. Jack attended four of these in 1924, 1927, 1931 and 1932. In a letter written by Flight Lieutenant WF Dickson from the RAF Staff College at Andover to his old friend 'Mac', the advertised cost of the dinner in 1927 was, 'not more than 10/6 [52½ p] per head, including two rounds of port but excluding other wines, providing that not less than twenty officers attend.' The souvenir menu cards, which Jack preserved, bear the signatures of Sir Richard Phillimore, Richard Bell Davies, Bernard Smart, Wilfred Acland, Paddy Hayes, William Dickson, Micky Smith and many more. In 1929 Paddy Hayes wrote to 'Mac' and concluded with the following sentiments:

> Please believe me when I assure you that I think of you and the days that have gone – when we were comrades – often and wistfully. God bless old man.

Jack became engaged to Madge Kernahan in January 1934 (and bought a new MG Magnette in February). They married on 25 April 1935 and had their honeymoon in Scotland. Sadly, on 23 October 1937 Jack's wartime companion, Wilfred Acland, now a wing commander, died while trying to rescue passengers from a sinking flying boat off the coast of Greece. Jack and Madge moved from Belfast to Marino (not far from Bangor) where their son John was born in 1938.

During the Second World War Jack was OC Home Guard (anti-aircraft) in nearby Holywood for the duration and would have witnessed the devastation of the Belfast Blitz in 1941. A quarter of the spinning mills in Ulster closed down completely, due to shortage of orders and lack of raw materials. Clonard Mill turned a significant proportion of its workforce over to wartime production of bomb doors and other components for Stirling bombers being built by Short Brothers and Harland in Northern Ireland and also maintained essential yarn supplies spun from scarce raw materials. This included ramie fibre, which had not been processed in Clonard since World War One. It was spun and twisted to make parachute cord. In 1942, Peggy married Jack's good friend Hunter Herriot, who, of course, had also served in the RNAS.

Furious served with distinction throughout the war, hunting U-boats in the Atlantic, escorting convoys to Malta, supporting the Operation *Torch* landings and launching a strike on the battleship *Tirpitz*. She was scrapped in 1948, a sad end for such a historic vessel. Just a year before her first CO, Vice Admiral Wilmot S Nicholson, had died at the age of seventy-five, while Admiral Phillimore passed away in 1940. Jack would have noted with sadness the death in January 1949 of Frederick Rutland by his own hand. Rutland's career had ended in much controversy after he was interned during the war as a suspected spy for the Japanese.

Towards the end of the war Jack and Madge bought an art-deco style bungalow by the shore, as a weekend home, a few miles north of Portaferry, near the village of Kircubbin, and a motor boat named *Old Bill* to go with it. The house was called locally *Queen Mary*, as it was supposed to resemble the liner in some aspects. It had three or four portholes to lend a nautical air, a flat roof and double-bunks in several of the small bedrooms. It soon became the family home and was enlarged and improved. Jack's love of horticulture was given free rein, resulting in a much-admired garden. A lane wound its way down to the shore where a boathouse was built for over-wintering a succession of boats and dinghies. The land down by the shore was mostly rocky and covered with bright yellow whins [gorse], and the small enclosed bay with a jetty for boarding dinghies provided sheltered water for swimming. Family and friends enjoyed hundreds of picnics down at the shore there, and hundreds of races and outings in the various boats. Jack was very happy with his lot, and loved life at Kircubbin (apart from the rabbits which ate his plants and bulbs) – with boating and gardening, and friends and family visiting, and grandchildren.

No doubt he would have been pleased by the success of his friend Dickson who as Sir William attained the rank of Marshal of the Royal Air Force in 1954 and was later the first chief of the defence staff. Air Commodore Harry Busteed passed away in 1965, having served in *Furious* again on her re-commissioning in 1925. Richard Bell Davies died in 1966, having retired many years before in the rank of vice admiral, after a very distinguished career.

Jack continued working at the Mill, taking his turn as managing director, until retirement in 1969. The Mill survived the vicissitudes of a very cyclical trade and was a great boon to the McCleery family during four generations; and provided employment for hundreds of families for over a hundred years. The ownership of the business changed hands in December 1970 and the Mill remained in business until closure in 2006: the last flax spinning mill in Western Europe.

Jack enjoyed pretty good health until his mid-seventies. He died on 1 July 1983, with a cup of tea in his hand, while having his elevenses in the kitchen at home; just as he would have wished. His ashes were scattered by his son and grandsons in the main fairway of Strangford Lough, his favourite playground; on the waters he had so often enjoyed. The wartime sailor and airman of so many years before had returned to the sea.

The Rank Structure of the RN Air Branch/RNAS

Wing Captain	=	Captain RN
Wing Commander	=	Commander RN
Squadron Commander (in command)	=	Lieutenant Commander RN
Squadron Commander (not in command)	=	Lieutenant RN of over four years' seniority (but senior to all Flight Commanders)
Flight Commander	=	Lieutenant RN of over four years' seniority
Flight Lieutenant	=	Lieutenant RN
Flight Sub-Lieutenant	=	Sub-Lieutenant RN
Warrant Officer 1st Grade	=	Commissioned Warrant Officer RN
Warrant Officer 2nd Grade	=	Warrant Officer RN

The flying rank was not necessarily the career officer's substantive rank. As an example, a lieutenant RN could be appointed to flying duties as a flight lieutenant, flight commander, squadron commander or even wing commander. If and when an officer reverted to general service, he could find himself back as a lieutenant. Ranks in the RNAS were denoted by stars over the sleeve lace (one for flight lieutenants and two for squadron commanders) and three stripes in the sleeve lacing for wing commanders. All pilots wore the RNAS eagle badge (otherwise known as the bloody duck) above the loop or executive curl of their left sleeve lace. For an officer transferring in the airship service as it moved from the Royal Engineers to the RFC, RNAS and finally the RAF, the position could become even more complicated, particularly when rapid wartime promotion, temporary and brevet ranks were factored in.

Royal Navy Seaplane and Aircraft Carriers of World War One

HMS *Anne* – Seaplane carrier, gross tonnage 4083. Two seaplanes. Captured German steamer. Commissioned 4 August 1915.

HMS *Argus* – Aircraft carrier, displacement 15,775 tons. Eighteen to twenty landplanes. Requisitioned ocean liner. Commissioned 16 September 1918.

HMS *Ark Royal* – Seaplane carrier, displacement 7450 tons. Five floatplanes and two landplanes. Requisitioned merchant vessel. Commissioned 10 December 1914.

HMS *Ben-my-Chree* – Seaplane carrier, displacement 3880 tons. Four to six seaplanes. Ex-Isle of Man packet. Commissioned 2 January 1915.

HMS *Brocklesby* – Paddle Air Service Scout, gross tonnage 508. Two Sopwith Schneiders or Babies. Ex-Humber ferry boat. Commissioned 27 March 1916.

HMS *Campania* – Seaplane carrier, displacement 18,000 tons. Ten seaplanes but could carry a few Sopwith Pups. Ex-Cunard liner and holder of the Blue Riband 1893–4. Commissioned 17 April 1915.

HMS *City of Oxford* – Seaplane carrier, displacement 7000 tons.

Up to four Short 184s. Ex-merchantman and kite balloon ship. Commissioned August 1917.

HM Submarine *E22* – Gross tonnage 660. Two Sopwith Schneiders. Brief trial in 1916.

HMS *Empress* – Seaplane carrier, displacement 2540 tons. Six seaplanes. Ex-Cross Channel steamer. Commissioned 25 August 1914.

HMS *Engadine* – Seaplane carrier, displacement 1676 tons. Four to six seaplanes. Ex-Cross Channel steamer. Commissioned 11 August 1914.

HMS *Furious* – Aircraft carrier, displacement 22,000 tons. July 1917: three Short 184s and five Sopwith Pups. March 1918: two Sopwith Pups and fourteen Sopwith 1½ Strutters. June 1918: thirteen Sopwith Camels and eleven 1½ Strutters. Ex-light battle cruiser. Commissioned 26 June 1917.

HMS *Golden Eagle* – Paddle Air Service Scout, gross tonnage 800. Two Wight Twins. Ex-Isle of Wight ferry boat. Commissioned July 1916.

HMS *Hermes* – Cruiser, displacement 5600 tons. Two seaplanes. Re-commissioned May 1913.

HMS *Killinghome* – Paddle Air Service Scout, gross tonnage 508. Two Schneiders or Babies. Ex-ferry boat. Commissioned 27 March 1916.

HMS *Manica* – Seaplane carrier, gross tonnage 4120. Kite balloons principally but also Short Seaplanes off East Africa. First hired 11 March 1915.

HMS *Manxman* – Seaplane carrier, displacement 2048 tons. Eight seaplanes. Ex-Isle of Man packet. Commissioned 17 April 1916.

HMS *Nairana* – Seaplane carrier, displacement 3118 tons. Seven seaplanes. Requisitioned Australian steamer. Commissioned 25 August 1917.

HMS *Pegasus* – Seaplane carrier, displacement 3300 tons. Nine seaplanes/landplanes. Requisitioned Great Eastern steamer. Commissioned 14 August 1917.

HMS *Princess Victoria* – Air Service Transport, gross tonnage 1687. One Schneider or Wight seaplane. Requisitioned Larne to Stranraer packet. First hired 1914.

HMS *Raven II* – Seaplane carrier, gross tonnage 4678. Two seaplanes. Ex-German steamer. Commissioned June 1915.

HMS *Riviera* – Seaplane carrier, displacement 1850 tons. Four seaplanes. Ex-Cross Channel steamer. Commissioned 11 August 1914.

HMS *Vindex* – Seaplane carrier, displacement 2950 tons. Up to seven seaplanes. Ex-Isle of Man packet. Commissioned 26 March 1915.

HMS *Vindictive* – Seaplane carrier, displacement 9750 tons. Six seaplanes. Ex-light cruiser. Commissioned 1 October 1918.

Instructions Regarding Precautions to be Taken in the Event of Falling into the Hands of the Enemy

One of the papers which Jack preserved was the following set of instructions for airmen who had fallen into the hands of the enemy.

SECRET – F.S. Publication 34

Not to be Carried in Aircraft

INSTRUCTIONS REGARDING PRECAUTIONS TO BE TAKEN IN THE EVENT OF FALLING INTO THE HANDS OF THE ENEMY.

For the personal information of—

(i) All officers and crews of H.M. airships.
(ii) All pilots and observers of the Royal Air Force.

The enemy will seek to derive information concerning British aircraft from any or all of the following sources:-

(1) From captured material and markings thereon.

(2) From papers found in aircraft

(3) From repeated interrogations of crews carried out by professing sympathy, stimulating professional and technical interest, or by threats.

(4) From note books, personal letters, and personal effects found on aircraft personnel.

(5) From letters written by the personnel of captured aircraft.

(6) From letters written to the personnel of captured aircraft.

(7) From conversations overheard by means of a concealed 'microphone.'

(8) From some form or other of 'confidence trick.'

All that a prisoner of war need give in the way of information, and all that in the interests of his country and comrades he should give, is his <u>name and rank</u>.

The enemy dare not carry their threats into execution, and a prisoner who systematically refuses to give information is respected by his captors.

SECRET

Not to be Carried in Aircraft

These instructions are compiled from reports received from officers and other ranks who have actually been prisoners of war and have experienced one and all of the enemy's various methods of obtaining information. <u>These instructions, therefore, are based on fact.</u>

1.

Don't injure your country or endanger your comrades by being induced or tricked into discussing military or aeronautical matters with **anyone**.

2.

Don't forget that **the only** information which may legitimately be required of a prisoner of war is his name and rank. This is prescribed by the Hague Convention.

3.

Don't assume that anyone is a friend because he wears British or Allied uniform and appears to be a prisoner like yourself, or because he speaks perfect English. He may be an enemy agent.

4.

Don't assume that a nurse or attendant is a friend because she professes to be a neutral and secretly to sympathise with the Allies. She may be an enemy agent.

5.

Don't trust anyone; in the matter of speech, silence on service matters alone is safe.

6.

Don't be deceived by a friendly reception on capture, or by good treatment, which may only be temporary and of set purpose. **Don't** allow wine to unloose your tongue. Expect and guard against these dangers in the period immediately following your capture.

7.

Don't imagine that you are alone with a known brother officer or man because no one else is present. Microphones and similar forms of listening apparatus are probably fitted in the room and enemy ears closely applied to the receivers.

8.

Don't let a map of the front, hung on the wall of your room, betray you into referring to points upon it, or recounting memories suggested by it, even to a known friend. The map is there to provoke you to do so, and enemy ears are listening by means of concealed microphones.

9.

Don't be surprised if you spend a few days in solitary confinement, and that then an apparently lucky chance finds you seemingly alone with a friend. The solitary confinement was designed to make you long for the society of and speech with another, and the accident of the friend's presence was no accident, but designed to give you an opportunity of speech. **But,** the listening apparatus will be in action.

10.

Don't let a subtle suggestion that another officer or man has already talked freely betray you into the indiscretion of thinking that silence is no longer of value. Trivial details ascertained about a man who has not given away anything of consequence may be woven together to create the desired impression in the mind of another. **Don't** under any circumstances discuss another officer or man.

11.

Don't refer under any circumstances to your unit or its position. A careless word may cost old comrades their lives.

12.

Don't carry any paper in aircraft unnecessary for the duty on hand. **Don't** make the slightest mark on a map to indicate a base or station. It might suffice to enable the enemy to fix a position previously unknown to him.

13.

Don't allow your craft to bear any marks of factory origin or identification unless you have express orders to do so. Obliterate all such marks, but the officer in charge should make a written record of them, to be retained at his station, but never to be borne in flight.

14.

Don't carry or permit anyone under your command to carry any papers, official or private, on a flight. An envelope may give away the position of your unit. **Don't** fail to see that all pockets are turned out before undertaking a flight, and **don't** fail to make it a matter of routine to do so, even if you do not expect to cross the enemy lines. Unless it is a matter of strict routine the precaution may be forgotten, and in many cases emergency may carry you over the enemy lines unexpectedly.

15.

Don't allow your kit to bear any tradesmen's tabs or labels bearing any relation to any station or school. Better still, **don't** allow any at all.

16.

Don't be induced by your pride in your technical knowledge or provoked by a suggestion you do not possess it into any discussion whatever upon any question of organisation, disposition, personnel, material, type, morale, duty, performance, speed, endurance, equipment, armament, or any topic whatsoever in relation to your service.

17.

Don't forget to have equally scrupulous care and consideration in matters affecting the sister services.

18.

Don't forget that there are expert interrogators who will obtain information from you if you enter into conversation with them on even seemingly unimportant subjects. Therefore **don't** be interrogated. You need not be. Silence alone is safe.

19.

Don't be afraid to maintain silence except as to your name and rank. The enemy knows this is the full extent of the obligation upon you, imposes the like obligation upon his own officers and men, and will respect you more if he sees that in captivity equally as in action you discharge your duty to your country

20.

Don't forget to destroy, if possible, your machine, maps, &c., by fire if brought down. Instructions in regard to this matter will be issued to you, but **don't** forget the imperative necessity of giving effect to them.

21.

Don't be drawn into any discussion of the American or other Allied aviation programme or its progress. The enemy anxiously desires information on this head.

22.

Don't, if you write a note to say you are safe which is to be dropped over the line, address it to anyone else than **Headquarters, Royal Air Force**. Your letter will be received and your relatives informed by the proper authorities. Never address such a letter to your squadron, wing brigade, or aerodrome, and never indicate the portion of the line on which it is to be dropped.

23.

Don't write to anyone a single word relating to any incident whatsoever preceding your capture except on special occasion the nature of your capture.

24.

Don't address officers or men of your Service in any way indicating their unit or the position of their unit, if you know their home addresses in the United Kingdom, address them there. If you do not know their home addresses, write to them 'care of G.P.O., London' in the case of the Airship Service, and 'care of Air Ministry, London' in case of the Royal Air Force.

25.

Don't flatter yourself that initial affectation of ignorance or initial success in resisting efforts to extract information from you will end the need for watchfulness. There will be renewed efforts, never by direct inquiry, but, perhaps, by casual and seemingly friendly interest. The enemy interrogator is patient and watchful; you must be patient and watchful, too.

26.

Don't believe anything you are told from enemy or possibly enemy sources. Be patient, and, above all, silent.

27.

Don't carry these instructions in your machine, but **don't** fail to carry every word of them in your head; and **don't** fail to give effect to them if you should have the bad luck to become a prisoner of war.

28.

Don't be downhearted if captured. Opportunities for escape will present themselves. Keep your eyes and ears open for any information which you think may be of value should you succeed in escaping.

Extract from 'Mitteilungen aus dem Gabiete des Luftkrieges Nr 38, 29-6-18'

What follows is the contemporary German report on the events of 19 June 1918, when *Furious* was bombed and one of the attacking seaplanes forced down.

On 19 June, 5.30 am FF1692 and 1693 departed List (Island of Sylt) on reconnaissance to the Northwest. Some 100 nautical miles NW a dark wake was seen on the port bow, then a large ship which was recognised as an aircraft carrier with four destroyers. Leading aircraft signalled base by WT then the two seaplanes attacked with bombs and this was met with heavy anti-aircraft fire. Bombs fell alongside the ship. The carrier turned to the Southwest to get into the wind. From the forecastle when running at high speed three land aeroplanes took off. Apart from these another five aeroplanes could be seen arranged on the forecastle. No wakes or wash were seen on the surface of the sea to indicate that any seaplane had taken off. Aeroplanes then lost sight of. Leading seaplane turned East. At a height of about 1000 metres an aeroplane was seen circling, identified as an enemy land single seater. As he saw us he went down in large spirals to 500 metres then turned towards us and performed loops and other aerobatics. He never came nearer than 100 metres and never attacked us. Because of the poor light his exact markings could not be identified but this can only have been one of the aeroplanes from the carrier. Two enemy land single seaters attacked the other seaplane, one from the left and one from the right, while one stuck under the seaplane's tail, the other went down in a steep dive to escape our machine gun fire. The other machine gave up the attack when the seaplane turned towards him. They were using tracer ammunition.

The enemy aircraft attacked us only from astern never from the side; they always dived and flew tight turns to escape our fire. During the second attack the observer's gun jammed, in clearing this he was wounded by a shot in the left hand. The airfight continued until a cruiser and three destroyers were seen. The cruiser signalled with a Morse searchlight and the enemy aircraft broke off their attacks on us. Our own ammunition, despite careful usage, was down to three rounds. The Cruiser was now flown over at a height of 200 metres, it had three masts and three funnels, a bomb fell near to the destroyer. After the bombing attack the seaplane was brought under heavy anti-aircraft fire. Later many Danish sailing boats were seen. Shortly after that we saw an enemy land single seater that did not notice us. The seaplane landed at List on the last of its petrol.

At 11.15, FF1817 and 1796 took off from List. An enemy submarine was attacked with two anti-submarine bombs. No success noted. At 1.20, heading West at high speed the carrier and destroyers were seen. At a height of 700 metres there was heavy anti-aircraft fire from all the ships. The Rotte [two aircraft formation] split up, 1817 flew to the West to look for other enemy naval forces but then turned back again after 20 minutes. The leader's aircraft (1796) attacked the enemy, who were coming from a Northerly direction, with his bombs amidst heavy anti-aircraft fire. The other seaplane (1817) dropped two bombs, when heading Northwest, at the Carrier and the destroyer which was standing off its starboard quarter. It reversed course and again dropped two bombs. This attack was successful and a hit was noticed on the destroyer which was standing to the starboard of the Carrier. The leader's seaplane was lost to sight amidst clouds of anti-aircraft fire and later did not answer its wireless call sign. It was observed that a destroyer pulled out of line and seemed to pick something out of the water but due to the altitude it was not possible to see what this was. Contact with the enemy was maintained until 2.10 during which the action steered different courses. Seaplane (1817) landed back at List at 4.30. Nothing further was seen of the leader's seaplane and it is overdue.

DESCRIPTION OF THE CARRIER
Over 250 metres long with large landing areas fore and aft. Three masted, the bridge is in the front quarter of the ship, two guns seen near the bridge, one funnel after of the 3-legged mast. On the stern in white paint F-U— In the bows stood 6 to 8 aeroplanes apparently ready for flight. The area behind the bridge is apparently used for landings. It is not impossible that the carrier was a new armoured cruiser upon which wooden planks have been laid to make a 'Flugzeugmutterschiff'.

Hints for Flight Sub-Lieutenants

Some extracts from *Hints for Flight Sub-Lieutenants Royal Naval Air Service by Flight Lieutenant* which was published by Forster Groom & Co. Ltd of Charing Cross Road and which Jack purchased in 1916.

A LITTLE FRIENDLY ADVICE

When you receive your first appointment as Probationary Flight Sub-Lieutenant you will become entitled to wear practically the same uniform as a Sub-Lieutenant RN, and you must not forget that in the Navy this takes an immense amount of hard work and some five years to attain.

If you will remember this, and behave accordingly, everything will be made as pleasant as possible for you; but if, on the other hand, you do not, you will be sure to find someone in authority who will do his best to remove that too self-satisfied feeling from you.

Probably you won't like the process, but if it happens you will only have yourself to blame for it.

Remember, also, that until you have proved yourself to be an efficient and useful officer, you are on probation only. You should therefore do all you can to prove your ability and justify your CO in placing confidence in you.

On arriving at your first Air Station, ask for the 1st Lieutenant, or, if he is not available, the Duty Officer, salute him, and say, 'Sub-Lieutenant So-and-So, reporting for duty, Sir.' You will then be told where your quarters are, and will be able to see to the stowing of your kit. Find out as soon as possible what the other Subs are doing, and do the same, if you do not receive any special orders – i.e. if there is flying, go on the Aerodrome and report to the Senior Officer on duty. If there is a lecture, go to that; but don't wait until someone tells you what to do – in the meantime doing nothing. That will he making a bad start, and a good start is half the battle. It is a curious fact that a man who starts badly and gives a bad impression to his Superior Officers in the first three months of his service will have to do altogether exceptionally good work afterwards to remove that impression, so, once more, make a good start.

MESS AND MANNERS

A Mess that is properly run should have the atmosphere of a club, but that does not mean that you can engage anyone in conversation, any more than you would some man very much older than yourself, and whom you do not know very well, at your club. Leave Senior Officers to themselves unless they show they want to talk to you. This is the best rule.

When the Commanding Officer comes into the Mess, always stand up and say 'Good morning' or 'Good evening. Sir,' if you have not seen him before. Don't be late for Mess; but if you should be late for dinner, apologise to the Officer at the head of the table who is acting as Mess President. Never mention a lady's name, and do not use any form of swear word, or tell doubtful stories. If you do you will be fined drinks round by the Acting Mess President, who will call you to order by rapping on the table with his official hammer. When the port is poured out, don't touch your glass until the Mess President says, 'Gentlemen, The King.'

You must then say 'The King' and drink the toast; after that you can do what you like in reason without any fear of being fined or sat upon.

Both the Commanding Officer and 1st Lieutenant should always be addressed as 'Sir.' With regard to the other Officers at the station, who are senior to you, treat them with respect, and call them 'Sir,' too, until you have settled down and found your feet. You must then use your own judgment, being guided by what your brother Subs, who know the ropes, do. A golden rule, however, is, when in doubt, to salute, and pay respect. It won't do any harm, and it will get you the reputation of knowing how to behave, which is no bad asset to have. All the above refers to when off parade. On duty, everyone, even a day senior to you, must be saluted and addressed as 'Sir'.

PARADES

Always try to be as smart as possible on Parade, and when at attention stand at attention; when at ease, stand properly at ease, don't loll about. If you are made to drill with recruits, be the smartest recruit in the squad, and show you know your drill that way – not by claiming to have had previous training, even if you have done your drills before. When you are in charge of a squad yourself, see that they drill properly, and move smartly, and if they don't, after having given them 'as you were' once, stand them at ease, and explain to them what is wrong, You will find the difference afterwards when you put them through the same movement again. Don't forget that men can't drill well if your word of command is bad, so lose no opportunity of improving it by practising in some quiet corner with another Sub. If you make your men move on the last sound of the word of command, you will have no difficulty in getting them smart. It is quite easy to pick up the knack of drilling men, if you will only remember not to run your words of command into one another, and to snap out the final word of the order. That is the secret of making men drill together, and acquiring the alertness that makes them ready for anything.

HOW TO HANDLE THE MEN

The secret of handling men is to be fair with them and to let them see that you will stand no nonsense. If you give, an order, see that it is obeyed smartly, which it will be if you are worth your salt. Only a bad officer has trouble with his men – at least, this is true in ninety-nine cases out of one hundred. Never be sarcastic with them. It is a great mistake. If you have to find fault, do it to the point and don't nag; this is something men won't stand. Always see that any men who are particularly in your charge have all they want or you can get them; this applies more especially on active service. If you come in from a long march or any other tiring duty, see to your men's comfort before your own, and don't go and get food before you know that their dinners are all right. If you have to investigate any complaint made by a man, do it with an open mind and try to see the man's side of the question.

Last, but by no means least, do not ever be seen in uniform with anyone that you would not like to introduce to your own people or your Commanding Officer. Nothing will do the Air Service or yourself more harm than this.

Bibliography

Ship's Logs HMS *Furious* 1917–1919 – files in the ADM53 series held at the National Archive, Kew.

Allen, William J, S.S. *'Borodino'.' M.F.A. No. 6. A Short Account of the Work of the Junior Army and Navy Stores Ltd. With H.M. Grand Fleet. December 1914 – February 1919* (London 1919)

Anon, *The Work and Training of the Royal Naval Air Service* (London 1917)

Barker, Ralph, *The Royal Flying Corps in World War One* (London 1995)

Bell Davies, Vice Admiral Richard VC, *Sailor in the Air* (Barnsley 2008)

Bowyer, Chaz, *Royal Air Force Calshot 1913–1961* (Newcastle upon Tyne 1997)

Brodie, Malcolm. *The Tele – A History of the Belfast Telegraph* (Belfast 1995)

Cheesman, EF, *Fighter Aircraft of the 1914–18 War* (Letchworth 1961)

Churchill, Winston S, *The Great War* (London 1933)

Connon, Peter, *An Aeronautical History of the Cumbria, Dumfries and Galloway Region (Part II)* (Penrith 1984)

Cronin, Dick, *Royal Navy Shipboard Aircraft Developments 1912–1931* (Tonbridge 1990)

Cronin, Dick, 'Tondern – Prelude, Climax and Aftermath' (*Cross & Cockade International Journal* Vol 25 No. 2 1994)

Blundell, WDG, *Royal Navy Battleships 1895–1946* (London 1973)

Brown, Malcolm and Meehan, Patricia, *Scapa Flow* (London 2002)

Bruce, JM, *Short 184* (Berkhamsted 2001)

Bruce, JM, *Sopwith Pup* (Windsor 1965)

Burns, Ian and Nailer, Roger, 'HMS Vindex Mixed Carrier 1915–1919' (*Cross & Cockade International Journal* Vol 17 No. 3 1986)

Ellis, Paul, *Aircraft of the USAF* (London 1980)

Erikson, CT (ed), *Fighter Aircraft of World War 1* (Mitcham 1959)

Fife, Malcolm, *Scottish Aerodromes of the First World War* (Stroud 2007)

Finnis, Bill, *The History of the Fleet Air Arm From Kites to Carriers* (Shrewsbury 2000)

Fitzsimons, Bernard (ed), *Warships of the First World War* (London 1973)

'Flight Lieutenant', *Hints for Flight Sub-Lieutenants* (London 1916)

Friedman, Norman, *British Carrier Aviation* (London 1988)

Gardiner, Ian, *The Flatpack Bombers* (Barnsley 2009)

Graham, Leslie, *Notes on HMS Furious 1917–18* (Unpublished manuscript at the Fleet Air Arm Museum)

Grinnell-Milne, Duncan, *Wind in the Wires* (London 1957)

Haslam, EB, *The History of Royal Air Force Cranwell* (London 1982)

Hayward, Roger, *The Fleet Air Arm in Camera 1912–1996* (Stroud 1998)

Hobbs, David, *A Century of Carrier Aviation* (Barnsley 2009)

Hough, Richard, *The Great War at Sea 1914–18* (Oxford 1983)

Huntford, Roland, *Shackleton* (London 1996)

Jenkins, Commander CA, *HMS Furious/Aircraft Carrier 1917–1948 Part 1* (Windsor 1972)

Kennedy, Paul, *The End of the High Seas Fleet* (London 1973)

Layman, Richard D, *Naval Aviation in the First World War* (London 1996)

Layman, Richard D, 'HMS Ark Royal 1914–1922' (*Cross & Cockade International Journal* Vol 18 No. 4 1987)

Layman, Richard D, Skelton, Marvin L, Wright, Peter, 'Captain Melvin H Rattray RNAS/RAF' (*Cross & Cockade International Journal* Vol 28 No. 2 1997)

Lea, John, *Reggie the Life of AVM RLG Marix CB, DSO* (Bishop Auckland 1994)

Leslie, Stuart, 'Extracts from the Diary kept by Corporal John Tiplady' (*Cross & Cockade International Journal* Vol 23 No. 1 1992)

Lloyd, John, *Aircraft of World War 1* (London 1958)

Logan, Malcolm, *Flying Simply Explained* (London 1943)

Longmore, ACM Sir Arthur, *From Sea to Sky* (London 1946)

Longyard, William H, *Who's Who in Aviation History* (Shrewsbury 1994)

Maguire, WA, *Caught in Time* (Belfast 1986)

Massie, Robert K, *Castles of Steel* (London 2005)

Macintyre, Captain Donald, *Jutland* (London 1960)

Marder, Arthur J, *From Dreadnought to Scapa Flow, Volume 4 1917: Year of Crisis and Volume 5 1918–19: Victory and Aftermath* (London 1969 & 1970)

Moore, Major WG, *Early Bird* (London 1963)

Munson, Kenneth, *Bombers 1914–19* (Poole 1977)

Pitt, Barrie, *Zeebrugge* (Cassell 1958)

Probert, Air Commodore Henry, *High Commanders of the Royal Air Force* (London 1991)

RNAS magazines – *Splash!* (Calshot), *Stunts* (Eastchurch), *The Eagle* (East Fortune), *The Prop* (Isle of Grain)

Rosher, Harold, *In the Royal Naval Air Service* (London 1916)

Saunders, H St G, *Per Ardua the Rise of British Air Power 1911–1939* (London 1944)

Scurrell, Charles E, *Warships of World War 1 No. 6 – Battleships of Other Nations* (London 1963)

Sheffield, Gary, *The Somme* (London 2004)

Sheffield, Gary, *Forgotten Victory* (London 2002)

Sorley, AM Sir Ralph, 'Sorties with Sorley' (*Cross & Cockade International Journal* Vol 37 Nos 2 and 3 2006)

Steel, Nigel & Hart, Peter, *Tumult in the Clouds* (London 1997)

Stephenson, Charles, *Zeppelins: German Airships 1900–40* (Oxford 2004)

Sturtivant, Ray and Page, Gordon, *Royal Navy Aircraft Serials and Units 1911–1919* (Tonbridge 1992)

Thetford, Owen, *British Naval Aircraft since 1912* (London 1971)

Thetford, Owen, *50 Years of British Naval Aviation 1908–1958* (Flight Deck, Autumn 1958)

Thompson, Julian, *The Imperial War Museum Book of the War at Sea 1914–1918* (London 2005)

Till, Geoffrey, *Air Power and the Royal Navy* (London 1979)

Winton, John, *Carrier Glorious* (London 1986)

Wright, Peter, 'Early Days at Eastchurch' (*Cross & Cockade International Journal* Vol 24 No. 2 1993)

Wright, Peter, 'Aspects of the Royal Naval Air Service' (*Cross & Cockade International Journal* Vol 27 No. 4 1996)

Index

PEOPLE

Acland, Captain Wilfred D 99, 110, 117, 120, 137, 144, 146–147, 150–153, 164, 167, 172, 177–179, 184, 187, 190, 192–193, 214, 219, 232–233, 246, 250–251, 258, 262–264
Adam, Lieutenant HW 206–207
Adams, Warrant Officer AF 126–127, 155, 158
Alexander, F/S-L WM 66
Alexander-Sinclair, Rear Admiral ES 140
Allenby, General Sir Edmund 141
Anderson, Arthur (uncle) 7
Anderson, Mary (aunt) 39
Anderson, Sir Robert 3
Andrews, F/S-L E 137
Asquith, Margot 196–197
Babington, Flight Commander John 82
Barnie, Frank 73
Basden, Lieutenant MN 202
Belgium, King & Queen of 207
Beatty, Admiral Sir David 87, 90, 93, 110, 118, 123, 127, 140, 145, 170, 179, 234, 236, 240, 242–244, 250
Begbie, Harold 247–248, 254
Bell Davies VC, Lieutenant Colonel Richard 83, 186, 193, 199, 203, 210, 212, 215, 229, 234, 245, 255, 262–263, 265
Bethmann-Hollweg, Theobald von 86
Bettington, Squadron Commander AF 120
Bickle, Air Mechanic GW 137
Bigglesworth, Major James 22
Bird, F/S-L GA 177
Blériot, Louis 78
Bowater, Captain AW 22 -23, 35
Bowden, Mr 11
Bowhill, Flight Lieutenant FW 80
Bridge, F/S-L BH 120
Brierley, F/S-L 158–159
Briggs, Squadron Commander EF 82
Briggs, Wing Commander ET 76
Brooke, Captain BV 98
Brownrigg, Vice Admiral Sir Douglas 156

Bruce, Jack 94
Buckle, Commander HR 95, 257
Busteed, Wing Commander Harry 19, 109–110, 167–168, 170, 265
Chaplin, Charlie 72, 127, 259
Churchill, Winston 79–80, 86
Clarke Hall, Lieutenant RH 81
Clive, F/S-L RD 137
Cockburn, George 15
Cockey, Captain LH 229
Collet, Lieutenant Charles 82
Collishaw, Flight Commander Raymond 66
Colmore, Lieutenant GC 15
Connaught, Arthur Duke of 238
Cooper, Gladys 185
Cowan, Commodore WH 140
Craig, Hugh 37
Craig, Miss 25, 32, 54, 229
Daglish, TF/S-L GRG 45
Darling, Mr Justice 196–197
Davis, F/S-L NP 177
Dawson, Lieutenant S 214–217, 219
De Villiers, Lieutenant DJJ 206
Dickson, Captain William F 91, 96, 120–121, 127, 144, 151–154, 167, 172–173, 178–179, 214–217, 263, 265
Dolman, F/S-L JW 106
Donald, Flight Commander DG 165
Douglas, S-L Archibald 100, 120
Drew, Sydney 229
Dunning, Squadron Commander EH 69, 71, 90, 101, 103–105, 121–122, 248
Edmonds, Flight Commander CHK 83
Engholm, Frederick W 156
Evans-Freke, Josh C 53
Fisher, Ernest (uncle) 58
Fisher, Jenny (aunt) 58, 70
Fisher, Admiral of the Fleet Lord 89, 257
Flemming, Warrant Officer Dan 108
Flynn, Lieutenant Francis 95
Foch, Marshal of France Ferdinand 240
Fowler, Flight Commander BF 85, 124
French, Percy 159
Gallehawk, Flight Lieutenant Arthur 108,

116, 118, 126, 138, 144, 146, 148, 152, 155, 176, 178–179, 182, 218
Garner, Chief Petty Officer WM 206
Geddes, Sir Eric 132, 179
George V, King 217, 246
Gerrard, Major EL 16, 81
Gibson, Captain LB 195
Gieves, Messrs 17, 24, 28, 30, 35, 48, 97, 184
Gluck, Alma 115
Gooden, Major Frank 218
Goodenough, Commodore WE 98
Grace, Cecil 15
Graham, Assistant Paymaster Leslie 250, 255
Gregory, Lieutenant R 16
Groener, General Wilhelm 239
Grundy, T/PFO HE 60
Haig, Field Marshal Sir Douglas 177
Halsey, Rear Admiral Lionel 128
Hamilton, Admiral Sir Frederick Tower 126
Hamilton, Kathleen 33, 57, 74, 120, 149, 163–164, 166, 255
Hawker VC, Captain Lanoe G 53
Hayes, 2nd Lieutenant Paddy 154, 218, 227, 231, 263–264
Hayward, Mr 30
Haywood, S-L AM 197, 217
Heath, Lieutenant Grahame 202–203, 222
Henning, William J 237
Herriott, F/S-L George 11–13, 18–19, 24–26, 28, 32–37, 44–47, 50–51, 56, 59–61, 63, 65, 68, 70, 75, 91, 93, 102, 109, 118, 136–138, 141–142, 149, 163, 195, 238, 245
Herriott, Flight Commander Hunter 12–13, 28, 54, 60, 65, 113, 160, 163, 245–246, 258, 264
Herriott, Mrs Jane 25, 27, 51, 60, 70, 142, 163, 228, 245
Hipper, Admiral Franz von 181–182, 232–235, 240, 243, 246
Hogg, Alexander 38
Hunter, Mabel (Bunty) 25, 28, 30, 37, 43, 45, 48, 50, 52, 56–57, 99, 109, 126, 149, 163–164, 166, 171, 177, 227
Jackson, Captain WD 64, 71, 172, 176, 178, 185, 207, 214–217, 221
Jellicoe, Admiral Sir John 85, 87, 132, 212
Jock (Jack's dog) 11, 30–31, 45, 142
Jones, Air Mechanic 120
Johns, Captain WE 22
Johnson, Charlie 28
Johnston, Flight Lieutenant PA 24 -25, 34
Kernahan, Madge (wife) 264–265
Keyes, Vice Admiral Roger 175
Kilner, Flight Commander BD 124
Kirk, Rev Mr 157, 160
Knight, TF/S-L RV 47
Langton, F/S-L Joseph 137, 171, 197
Lee, PFO CP 31

L'Estrange Malone, Squadron Commander C 83
Lloyd George, David 179, 244
Longmore, Wing Commander AM 16–17, 34, 81, 91, 102, 104, 132
Long JP & Scott, Maurice 191
Luce, Commodore John 41
Ludendorff, General Erich von 171, 194, 224, 228, 232, 239
Major, Ellen 26
Marix, Flight Lieutenant Reginald 82
Mary, Queen 246
Maud, Queen of Norway 105
Max, Prince of Baden, 228–229
McCann, John 237
McClean, Francis 15
McCleane, Tom 30, 33, 56, 58, 237
McCleery, Amy (aunt) 21, 57, 151, 164
McCleery, Barbara (daughter) 263
McCleery, Fanny (mother) 3, 6, 8, 30, 32–35, 37–38, 43–44, 46–47, 50, 52, 56–57, 59, 64, 68, 70, 75, 93–94, 98, 100, 108–109, 112, 126, 128, 148, 151, 154, 156, 164, 166, 201, 225–226, 228, 249, 260
McCleery, Hamilton (grandfather) 3
McCleery, Hamilton (uncle) 3, 8, 21, 57, 73, 118, 164, 263
McCleery, John (son) 1, 264
McCleery, John Orr (father) 2, 4, 6, 11, 30, 35, 38–39, 43, 45–46, 48, 52, 54, 57, 64, 67- 68, 70, 96, 99, 101, 112, 126, 129, 136, 149, 160, 164, 201, 228, 249, 260, 263
McCleery, Kenneth (brother) 3, 20–21, 33, 47, 52, 57, 99, 123, 125–129, 142, 145, 148, 166, 187, 198
McCleery, Kitty (sister) 3, 20, 25, 37, 43, 47, 57, 120, 125, 142, 147, 149, 154, 197
McCleery, Peggy (sister) 3, 20, 25, 43–44, 47, 57, 76, 120, 125, 132, 147, 149, 154, 264
McCleery, Tony (brother) 3, 20, 27, 29, 36, 47, 50, 52, 57, 91, 96, 112–113, 147, 157, 163–164, 177–178, 200–201, 207, 227, 245, 258, 263
McCullagh, Sir Crawford 5
Mears, Lieutenant HF 183–184
Merriman, Henry Seton 133
Meurer, Rear Admiral Hugo 243–244
Miller, Captain GH 118, 121, 148, 153, 160, 183–184
Milligan, Bessie (aunt) 52
Milligan, John (grandfather) 3
Milligan, John (uncle) 54, 156
Milligan, Willie (uncle) 7, 21
Montgomery, Meta (wife) 58, 64, 66, 70, 72, 75, 91, 93, 98–100, 106–107, 109, 111, 126, 128, 152, 228–229, 263
Moore, Major WG 71, 92, 95, 101, 103, 105, 115, 118, 122, 159, 169, 186, 214

Morrison, Thomas E 237
Napier, Vice Admiral Trevelyan 112, 139, 141, 188
Nash, F/S-L GE 66
Nicholas II, Tsar 47, 185
Nicholson, Captain Wilmot S 90, 105, 119, 130, 166, 203, 248, 264
Noble, Charley 203
Norton, Mr & Mrs 10–11, 22, 33, 39
O'Dowda, Brendan 160
Orr, Eliza (aunt) 4, 20–21, 38, 220, 258
Orr, Jane (aunt) 4
Orr, Jinnie (aunt) 57
Orr, Willy (uncle) 43, 57
Owen, Lieutenant Wilfred 238
Paine, Commodore Godfrey 40–41, 88
Pakenham, Vice Admiral Sir William 110, 139–140
Pemberton-Billing, Noel 196
Penny, PFO DE 24, 31, 33, 64, 65
Pilkington, Barbara 26–28, 32–33, 35, 37, 39, 43–45, 47, 54, 65, 97, 106, 133, 149, 151
Pilkington, Mary 39, 54, 56
Pilkington, Mr 73
Pilkington, Mrs 12, 28, 32, 42, 56, 73, 109
Phillimore, Rear Admiral Richard 109, 119, 123, 127, 166, 171, 179, 213, 215, 255, 262–264
Poland, Lieutenant AL 95, 98, 146
Price, F/S-L 153
Prussia, Henry Prince of 243
Rattray, Lieutenant MH 177, 189, 210
Reardon, Petty Officer TCM 137
Reid, F/S-L EV 66
Reuter, Rear Admiral Ludwig von 246
Richards, Frank 249
Robinson & Cleaver 29, 32
Rodman, Admiral Hugh 209
Ross, Warrant Officer George 122, 189
Russell, Lieutenant Leslie 235
Rutland, Squadron Commander FJ 69, 85, 104, 118–119, 121–123, 138, 155, 169–170, 172–174, 179, 242, 264
Samson, Lieutenant CR 16, 79–81
Sandwell, Flight Commander AH 94
Sayers, WH 71
Scheer, Admiral Reinhard 181, 231–233, 235
Schirra, Flugzeugmaat 203
Scott, Flight Lieutenant 25–26, 35–36, 48–49
Scott-Paine, Hubert 196
Shackleton, Ernest 36
Sharman, F/S-L JE 66
Sharwood, Captain AC 195
Shields, Ella 191
Short, Horace, Eustace and Oswald 15
Sibley, Flight Commander RGD 97, 117
Simms, PFO 64
Sippe, Flight Lieutenant Sidney 82

Smart, Captain BA 110, 118, 120, 124, 214–217, 252, 263
Smiley, F/S-L GF 186
Smith, Doris 57
Smith, 2nd Lieutenant E 203
Smith, Lieutenant Micky 151, 153–155, 157, 159–161, 263
Smith Barry, Major Robert 218
Spencer-Smith, Reverend Arnold 36
Spenser-Grey, Squadron Commander DA 82
Stanbridge, Group Captain BGT 258
Sueter, Captain Murray 78, 81
Swann (Schwann), Commander Oliver 13, 85
Sykes, Lieutenant Colonel Frederick 80
Tate, Harry 58
Templeton, Andrew 237
Tennyson-d'Eyncourt, Sir Eustace 127
Thompson, Alec 54, 237
Thyne, Captain Thomas K 171–172, 190, 195, 207, 214–217, 221
Trendall, F/S-L MHW 188
Trewin, Assistant Paymaster GS 85
Tyrwhitt, Commodore Reginald 82, 180, 188, 244
Vaughan-Lee, Rear Admiral Charles 64
Walker, S-L Philip 102, 120, 134–135
Warneford VC, F/S-L Rex 186
Welsh, Flight Lieutenant WL 83
Wemyss, Admiral Sir Rosslyn 240
Wenke, Leutnant der Reserve 203
White, Commander "Bunny" 56
Wilhelm, Grand Admiral Crown Prince 239, 243
Wilhelm II, Kaiser 224, 228, 239–240, 243
Wilkinson, Norman 169
Williams, Lieutenant NE 214–217
Wilson, President Woodrow 229–231
Wright, Orville and Wilbur 77
Wright, Miss 164
Wemyss, Admiral Sir Rosslyn
Yeulett, Lieutenant WA 214–217
Yorihito, Admiral Prince 238

AIRCRAFT:

AD Admiralty 1000 67
Airco DH4 23, 193
Airco DH9 205–206, 226, 235
Albatros D-III 66, 147
Avro 504B/C/E 34, 37, 41, 43–44, 46, 59, 61, 64, 82, 120, 126
Avro 523 Pike 67
Avro Type D 13
BE2c 25–27, 30, 41, 44, 46, 48, 50–52, 59–60, 65, 122, 126–128, 135, 137, 146, 148, 153, 155, 190, 192, 217–218, 225, 232, 246

BE2e 135, 147, 149–150, 152, 160, 177, 197
Blackburn Triplane 19
Bristol Fighter 259
Bristol M.1C 154, 184
Bristol Scout 18, 38, 46–47, 50, 53–54, 60, 85, 91, 110
Caudron G.II 80
Curtiss BE 52
Curtiss JN.4 19, 27, 36–38, 51, 164
Curtiss H.4 Small America 37
Curtiss H.8/H.12 Large America 37, 63, 156
Eastchurch Kitten 71
Fairey Hamble Baby 137
FBA Type B 64–65
Friedrichshafen FF49c 202–203, 278–280
Gotha G.IV 67–68, 73
Grain Griffin 205–206, 222
Grain Kitten PV7 71–72
Handley Page O/100 61, 156
Maurice Farman S.7 Longhorn 19–22, 30, 36, 38, 42, 50, 58–59, 114, 150
Nieuport 11 Bébé 258
Nieuport 12 46, 54–55
Nieuport Scout 44, 46
Parnall Panther 205
Pemberton-Billing PB25 19
Short Bomber 25, 46, 73–74
Short Gun-Carrying Seaplane 81
Short S.38 13, 79–80
Short S.41 80
Short Type 74 82
Short Type 81 81–82
Short Type 135 82, 90
Short Type 184 83, 85, 93–94, 97–100, 102, 106–108, 110, 112–114, 116–118, 120–121, 125–129, 131, 134 -138, 167, 270
Short 150 hp 74
Short 160 hp 62
Short Type 827 72
Sopwith B.1 205–206
Sopwith Baby 63–64, 67–68, 75, 85, 212, 269–270
Sopwith Camel 97, 113, 133, 158, 188–189, 193, 195, 202–203, 207, 210, 212–213, 215–216, 220, 222, 236, 238, 258, 262, 270
Sopwith 1½ Strutter 46, 53–54, 61, 88, 114, 133, 148, 152–154, 157–158, 160 -161, 165–167, 174, 176, 178–179, 181–186, 189–190, 192, 197–199, 205–207, 212, 217–220, 222, 226–227, 229, 233–236, 238, 251, 262, 270
Sopwith Pup 18, 46, 54–55, 59–60, 68–69, 73, 88, 91, 93, 96, 99, 101–106, 108 -110, 114–115, 117, 119, 121, 123–124, 127–128, 130, 133, 135–136, 152–154, 156, 159, 161, 164, 166, 169–173, 181–182, 184, 187, 190, 192, 234, 269–270

Sopwith Schneider 49, 63, 73, 83, 141, 269–270
Sopwith SS1 Tabloid 82
Sopwith T.1 Cuckoo 127, 132, 259
Sopwith three-seater 82
Sopwith Triplane 19, 24–25, 46, 66, 259
Sopwith Type 807 90
Supermarine PB31E 19
Vickers Gunbus 25

AIRSHIPS:

Coastal Class 49, 79, 159
HMA No 1 78–79
L23 (LZ66) 110, 217
L39 (LZ86) 49
L54 (LZ99) 216
L60 (LZ108) 216
LZ3 78
LZ4 78
LZ25 (ZIX) 82
LZ37 186
North Sea Class 79
NS3 118
NS4 159
NS7 262
R.24 159
R.26 79
SS Class 79
SSZ Class 79
SSZ 59 193

SHORE ESTABLISHMENTS:

Admiralty 6, 132, 208
Calshot 41, 60–69, 72, 120
Cattewater 120
Chingford 41, 64–65
Cranwell 25, 39–56, 59–60, 153, 156, 162
Cromarty 132
Crystal Palace (HMS Victory VI) 7, 9–15, 18, 24, 28
Donibristle 122, 127–128, 151–152, 177, 179, 183, 192–193
Dundee 137, 159
East Fortune 126–127, 144–163, 179, 190, 225–226
Eastbourne 41
Eastchurch 15–39, 41, 71, 74, 91, 110, 120–121, 164, 196
Felixstowe 41
Freiston 41, 57–60, 64–65
Harwich 180
Isle of Grain 69, 71–76, 91, 110, 114, 144, 162, 164–167
Killingholme 41
Londonderry (HMS Sea Eagle) 258

Luxeuil 154
Montrose 148
Redcar 41
Rosyth 91–92, 111–137, 166, 168–227, 229–259, 262
St Pol 16
Scapa Flow 92–111, 260–262
Smoogroo 96, 106, 262
South Shields 137
Turnhouse 162, 186, 189–192, 197–198, 205–206, 212, 214, 217–220, 222, 225 – 226, 229, 232, 235, 241, 246, 250, 258
Vendôme 13
Westgate 137, 156
Windermere 7, 13, 41
Wormwood Scrubs 41

SHIPS

Royal Navy:
HMS *Abdiel* 189
HMS *Aboukir* 203
HMS *Africa* 80
HMS *Agamemnon* 155
HMS *Amphitrite* 188, 201
HMS *Angora* 188, 201
HMS *Anne* 269
HMS *Anson* 139
HMS *Argus* (Conte Rosso) 88, 205, 229, 234, 269
HMS *Ark Royal* 90, 269
HMHS *Asturias* 61
HMS *Aurora* 215
HMS *Ben-my-Chree* 83, 85, 269
HMS *Birmingham* 182
HMS *Britannia* 239–240
HMS *Brocklesby* 269
HMS *Caledon* 140, 215
HMS *Calypso* 140
HMS *Campania* 83–84, 88, 95, 104, 186, 214, 238–239, 269
HMS *Canterbury* 195
HMS *Caradoc* 140
HMS *Cardiff* 99, 139, 247
HMS *Caroline* 221
HMS *Carysfort* 215
HMS *Cassandra* 256
HMS *Ceres* 140
HMS *City of Oxford* 269
HMS *Courageous* 89, 112, 124, 127–128, 139–140, 182
HMS *Cressy* 203
HMS *Dreadnought* 89
HMS *Dublin* 99
HMS *Eagle* 234
HMS *Empress* 82, 155, 270
HMS *Engadine* 82, 85, 88, 212, 270
HMS *Furious* 1, 77, 89–142, 156, 165–191, 193–227, 229–265, 270, 278–280

HMS *Galatea* 140, 202, 215
HMS *Glorious* 89, 112, 121, 124, 128, 139–140, 188, 206, 238–239
HMS *Golden* Eagle 270
HMS *Havock* 32
HMS *Hermes* (pre-WW1) 80–81, 110, 270
HMS *Hermes* (post-WW1) 205, 234
HMS *Hibernia* 80
HMS *Hood* 139
HMS *Hogue* 203
HMS *Inconstant* 140, 215
HMS *Inflexible* 114
HMS *Iron* Duke 89
HMS *Killinghome* 270
HMS *Lion* 109, 111, 113, 135, 140, 182–183, 195, 203
HMS *London* 201
HMS *Lord Nelson* 155
HMS *Malaya* 134
HMS *Manica* 270
HMS *Manxman* 88, 95, 104, 270
HMS *Mary Rose* 128
HMS *Minotaur* 249
HMS *M28* 155
HMS *Nairana* 116, 134, 229, 270
HMS *New Zealand* 114, 140
HMS *Oak* 207, 217
HMS *Pegasus* 113, 116, 118, 125–127, 131, 262, 270
HMS *Penelope* 215
HMS *Phaeton* 187, 215
HMS *Prince* 110
HMS *Princess Margaret* 201
HMS *Princess Royal* 109, 111, 113, 135, 140, 182
HMS *Princess Victoria* 270
HMS *Queen Elizabeth* 89, 236
HMS *Raglan* 155
HMS *Ramilles* 215
HMS *Raven II* 270
HMS *Renown* 109–111, 113, 139, 182
HMS *Repulse* 109–110, 113, 123, 135, 140, 182
HMS *Resolution* 215
HMS *Revenge* 201, 214–215
HMS *Riviera* 82, 271
HMS *Rodney* 139
HMS *Royal Oak* 215, 239
HMS *Royal Sovereign* 215
HMS *Royalist* 140, 215, 219
HMS *Sharpshooter* 195
HMS *Southampton* 98
HMS *Strongbow* 128
HMS *Superb* 107
HMS *Tiger* 109, 113, 135, 140, 182
HMS *Umpire* 227, 235
HMS *Undaunted* 215
HMS *Vanguard* 96, 261
HMS *Valentine* 202
HMS *Valiant* 215
HMS *Verulam* 189

HMS *Viceroy* 215–216
HMS *Vindex* 85, 121, 124, 212, 271
HMS *Vindictive* 249, 262, 271
HMS *Violent* 216
HMS *Wessex* 233
HMS *Wolfhound* 202
HMS *Yarmouth* 105, 109–110
E-Class submarine, E-22 270
K-Class submarine 112–113, 139
Q-boat 139

Royal Australian Navy:
HMAS *Australia* 114, 165
HMAS *Melbourne* 195
HMAS *Sydney* 109, 195

US Navy:
USS *Delaware* 209
USS *Florida* 184, 209
USS *New* York 209
USS *Wyoming* 209

Imperial German Navy:
SMS *Baden* 240
SMS *Bayern* 247
SMS *Bremse* 128
SMS *Breslau* 155
SMS *Brummer* 128
SMS *Derrflinger* 249, 261

SMS *Emden* 109
SMS *Frankfurt* 140
SMS *Frauenlob* 98
SMS *Goeben* 155
SMS *Hindenberg* 261
SMS *Kaiser* 140, 249
SMS *Kaiserin* 140
SMS *Königsberg* 140, 243–244, 246
SMS *Kronprinz Wilhelm* 246, 249
SMS *Markgraf* 249
SMS *Moltke* 249, 261
SMS *Nurnberg* 140
SMS *Pillau* 140
SMS *Prinzregent Luitpold* 249
SMS *Seydlitz* 249, 261
SMS *Von der Tann* 249, 261
U-27 81
UB-50 240
UB-91 230
UB-123 230–231
V-70 247

Merchant Ships:
SS *Borodino* 105–106, 108
SS *Graphic* 8
SS *Hirano Maru* 230
RMS *Leinster* 230
SS *Princess Maud* 143
RMS *Queen Mary* 265